Ignored Racism

Although Latinos are now the largest nonmajority group in the United States, existing research on White attitudes toward Latinos has focused almost exclusively on attitudes toward immigration. This book changes that. It argues that such accounts fundamentally underestimate the political power of Whites' animus toward Latinos and thus miss how conflict extends well beyond immigration to issues such as voting rights, criminal punishment, policing, and which candidates to support. Providing historical and cultural context and drawing on rich survey and experimental evidence, the authors show that Latino racism-ethnicism is a coherent belief system about Latinos that is conceptually and empirically distinct from other forms of out-group hostility and from partisanship and ideology. Moreover, animus toward Latinos has become a powerful force in contemporary American politics, shaping White public opinion in elections and across a number of important issue areas – and resulting in policies that harm Latinos disproportionately.

MARK D. RAMIREZ is Associate Professor in the School of Politics and Global Studies at Arizona State University. His research has been funded by the Ford Foundation. He is the recipient of the 2018 Adaljiza Sosa-Riddell Award from the American Political Science Association.

DAVID A. M. PETERSON is Professor and Whitaker-Lindgren Faculty Fellow in Political Science at Iowa State University. He has coauthored two books: *Mandate Politics* (2007) and *Religious Institutions and Minor Parties in the United States* (1999). He served as the editor of *Political Behavior* from 2015 to 2018. His work has been supported multiple times by the National Science Foundation and the Social Sciences and Humanities Research Council.

Ignored Racism

White Animus toward Latinos

MARK D. RAMIREZ

Arizona State University

DAVID A. M. PETERSON

Iowa State University

CAMBRIDGE
UNIVERSITY PRESS

University Printing House, Cambridge CB2 8BS, United Kingdom

One Liberty Plaza, 20th Floor, New York, NY 10006, USA

477 Williamstown Road, Port Melbourne, VIC 3207, Australia

314–321, 3rd Floor, Plot 3, Splendor Forum, Jasola District Centre,
New Delhi – 110025, India

79 Anson Road, #06–04/06, Singapore 079906

Cambridge University Press is part of the University of Cambridge.

It furthers the University's mission by disseminating knowledge in the pursuit of
education, learning, and research at the highest international levels of excellence.

www.cambridge.org
Information on this title: www.cambridge.org/9781108495325
DOI: 10.1017/9781108861915

© Mark D. Ramirez and David A. M. Peterson 2020

First published 2020

Printed in the United Kingdom by TJ International Ltd, Padstow Cornwall.

A catalogue record for this publication is available from the British Library.

Library of Congress Cataloging-in-Publication Data
NAMES: Ramirez, Mark D., 1977– author. | Peterson, David A. M., 1973– author.
TITLE: Ignored Racism : White Animus Toward Latinos / Mark D. Ramirez and
David A. M. Peterson.
DESCRIPTION: New York : Cambridge University Press, 2020. | Includes
bibliographical references and index.
IDENTIFIERS: LCCN 2019053040 (print) | LCCN 2019053041 (ebook) |
ISBN 9781108495325 (hardback) | ISBN 9781108817943 (paperback) |
ISBN 9781108861915 (epub)
SUBJECTS: LCSH: Hispanic Americans–Social conditions. | Hispanic
Americans–Public opinion. | Whites–United States–Attitudes. |
Racism–United States. | United States–Race relations.
CLASSIFICATION: LCC E184.S75 R34 2020 (print) | LCC E184.S75 (ebook) |
DDC 305.800973–dc23
LC record available at https://lccn.loc.gov/2019053040
LC ebook record available at https://lccn.loc.gov/2019053041

ISBN 978-1-108-49532-5 Hardback
ISBN 978-1-108-81794-3 Paperback

Mark would like to dedicate this book to his family: Kim, Scarlet B., and Albie. They have made sacrifices to support all of his endeavors, but especially this one.
Dave dedicates this book to his mother.

Contents

Figures

Tables

Preface

This research is more timely than we first expected. When we started this project, in 2014, we expected that Whites' animus toward Latinos played an important role in shaping a lot of their opinions about politics and policy. But we expected that most of the findings would suggest that it would be unexplored and important undercurrents of politics. Obviously, the tides have shifted. As we are writing this in July of 2019, a dominant story is President Donald Trump's tweets and comments about "The Squad" – four women of color in the House of Representatives. His tweets suggesting they should go back to their countries and a chant of "send her back" at one of his rallies has once again made race and ethnicity a central piece of the Trump presidency. Alongside this more generalized racism, we are witnessing policies specifically targeting Latino communities. This includes the separation of families at the border, children kept in cages, an increasing number of migrant deaths, a rise in anti-immigrant vigilante groups, and more recently the unlawful incarceration of US citizens of Latina/o heritage by Immigration and Customs Enforcement (ICE). Whites' attitudes about Latinos may have been an undercurrent in 2014, but now they are clearly a tidal force.

We did not anticipate this change. In 2014, the main puzzle we started trying to address was whether certain expressions of anti-Latino or anti-immigrant sentiment were rooted in racial and ethnic animus, and whether this specific type of animus shaped both immigration policy preferences and vote choice. In putting together a module for the 2014 Cooperative Congressional Election Study (CCES), one of us (Ramirez) decided to try a new measure of Whites' animus toward Latinos to test how it would predict immigration attitudes and support for candidates running on anti-immigration platforms. In particular, the goal was to move beyond existing measures and approaches rooted in theories of how Whites perceive Blacks to understanding how Whites perceive Latinos. Much of the extant research, we believed, emphasized social distance and contact, but did not have as much of a focus on the actual content of what Whites thought and felt about Latinos.

Our starting point was to consider the unique legacy of history and culture of Latinos in America and how Whites have racialized Latinos into a distinctive non-White group. What we found was that animus toward Latinos in the past largely mirrors the expression of animus toward Latinos today in a way that mixes animosity toward the group with dislike toward certain ascribed behaviors. In some ways, it is much like how the shift from old-fashioned or biological racism to racial resentment changed the ways in which racism directed toward African Americans is expressed among Whites. What separates it from racial resentment targeted at African Americans is how it is grounded in the historical perceptions of Latinos rather than a shift in norms of equality. Whites' negative attitudes about Latinos are grounded in concerns about language, culture, immigration, criminality, and country of origin. And they always have been. We thought that a new measure of Whites' animus toward Latinos that captured this could help explain some important phenomena in American politics.

Given this intuition, we started trying to develop the measure we use in the rest of this book. We decided to refer to the concept as Latina/o racism-ethnicism (abbreviated as LRE). Conceptually, LRE recognizes that Whites are likely to conflate race and ethnicity with race-neutral behaviors when thinking about Latinos. As such, LRE contains items that refer to the legacy of immigration, linguistic differences, and specific beliefs Whites may hold about Latinos. Out first approach was to use a convenience sample to try to examine the measurement properties of our LRE scale and compare it to several of the competing measures in the literature. The results were clear: LRE is empirically distinct from ethnocentrism, racial resentment, stereotypes of Latinos, cultural preferences, partisanship, and ideology. We were on to something.

The 2014 CCES gave us the opportunity to see how this new measure of LRE predicted two obvious dependent variables: immigration attitudes and vote choice. The specific results are presented in Chapters 4 and 7, respectively. Not to spoil the information provided in those chapters, but LRE helps to explain both Whites' preferences on immigration policy and their vote choice in the 2014 congressional elections. At the time, we expected this to be a single article that introduced the concept of LRE and showed its effects. Because we were both busy with other projects, we did not get around to writing the article. We did decide to replicate some of the measurement results and address some initial concerns with our approach in an additional survey in 2015, but again got sidetracked from writing an article.

Donald Trump's campaign in 2016 jump-started our efforts. Trump's rhetoric and policies made it evident that Whites' attitudes about Latinos was going to be a central concern of the 2016 campaign. We again put a (partial) LRE scale on the 2016 CCES. More importantly, the campaign made it clear that how Whites' animus toward Latinos shaped politics was a bigger question than we initially intended to explore. President Trump tied his rhetoric about Latinos to more than just immigration. He reinforced the existing tropes connecting Latinos with crime and with election fraud. As we were finishing the final details of this manuscript, for instance, he told a group of young conservatives,

And when they're saying all of this stuff, and then those illegals get out and vote, because they vote anyway. Don't kid yourself. Those numbers in California and numerous other states, they're rigged. They've got people voting that shouldn't be voting. They vote many times, not just twice, not just three times. It's like a circle. They come back, they put a new hat on. They come back, they put a new shirt on. And in many cases, they don't even do that. You know what's going on. It's a rigged deal.[1]

These types of cues lead us to conclude that we needed a fuller and richer exploration of how LRE shapes Whites' attitudes about politics.

We set out to do this through a series of experiments. In particular, we focused on how LRE shapes Whites' attitudes about immigration, crime, restrictions on voting, and elections. Overall, the results are clear. LRE plays a foundational role in how Whites think about much of American politics. The differences between Whites who are high in LRE and those who are low in LRE shape how they think about politics and policy. They influence how they respond to information about the world. There is also some evidence that candidates for office respond to these preferences in their campaign appeals.

We do not have the data to test how much of these effects are due to the emergence of Donald Trump as a candidate or the ways in which he

---

[1] Philip Bump, The Selective Socialism of Donald Trump, *Washington Post*, July 23, 2019.

uses race and ethnicity in his rhetoric. We know that his candidacy and presidency have changed how we think and it probably has heightened the role of LRE in public opinion. Unfortunately, it also probably means that race and ethnicity will continue to shape Whites' attitudes for the foreseeable future.

Acknowledgments

This book is the product of many efforts. We utilize concepts, theories, and methodologies that have been constructed across multiple disciplines to document and explain an often ignored form of racism directed toward Latinos. We are foremost grateful to those scholars who have built the foundation for our exploration of this topic.

We are heavily indebted to Rodolfo Espino. The project started with multiple conversations with him about the need to better conceptualize and measure White Animus toward Latinos and the need to move away from strategies that were developed with African Americans in mind. We are grateful for both his friendship and intellectual contribution to this book.

We benefited immensely from Arizona State University and Iowa State University. These institutions provided the space, time, funding, and academic freedom necessary to conduct this research and write this book.

The School of Politics and Global Studies at Arizona State University was gracious enough to host a conference on "Immigration, Ethnicity, and Inclusion" that provided a venue to obtain extensive feedback on an earlier version of this book. We are extremely thankful to the following participants for both helpful and critical feedback on this research: David Becerra, Stanley Feldman, Kim Fridkin, Leonie Huddy, Bradford Jones, Elizabeth Kiehne, Samara Klar, Paul G. Lewis, Jennifer Merolla, Steven Neuberg, and Chris Weber. We are especially indebted to Dan Hopkins for his extensive feedback on the project as well as many of his intellectual contributions to the field that we build on in this book. Funding for this conference was provided by a donation from Arizona State University alumni Brian A. Kopf. We thank the Kopf family for their support in this endeavor as well as their continued support of the School of Politics and Global Studies at Arizona State University. We also owe a debt of gratitude to Cameron Thies for seeing the value of the conference, providing funding for portions of this project when needed including both Congressional Election Study (CCES) modules, and his overall support over the years.

The College of Liberal Arts and Sciences at Iowa State University provided a seed grant that funded the 2018 Qualtrics survey and the conjoint experiment reported in Chapter 6. Additionally, some of the work for this book was supported by the Whitaker-Lindgren Faculty Fellowship in Political Science at Iowa State University. The support of Mary Whitaker-Lindgren and Douglas Lindgren were instrumental in the final stages of this book.

The 2017 Qualtrics survey was collected as part of a larger survey supported by the National Science Foundation Award #1460984.

During the 2018 meeting of the Southern Political Science Association, we received extremely detailed comments on portions of the measurement and immigration chapters of this project from Johanna Dunaway. This feedback was incredibly valuable and helped motivate our examination of the "browning" of crime news. We would also like to thank Eric Gonzalez Juenke and other participants of this meeting for their comments and feedback.

Several people were gracious enough with their time and ability to help us in collecting data for this project. Jillian Courey at Arizona State University helped collect some of the experimental data used in the voting rights chapter. Fabian Neuner provided guidance on designing and implementing the conjoint study. We are thankful for his generosity and intellectual input on this portion of the project. Valerie Hoekstra spearheaded the 2016 CCES module that provided some of the data for this book. She was gracious enough to organize the team survey module. We are thankful for the time she gave to us in this regard.

We also would like to thank Stephen Ansolabehere, Samantha Luks, Brian Schaffner, and Marissa Shih for their work designing and implementing the CCES surveys. This is an invaluable resource and public good. We are thankful for the opportunity to be a small part of it. The 2014 CCES was funded by National Science Foundation Award #1430505. The 2016 CCES was funded by National Science Foundation Award #1559125.

I

Racism Ignored

This book is about how White Americans uniquely express racial-ethnic animus toward Latinos and how this often-ignored form of racial-ethnic hostility shapes their support for policies that adversely impact Latino communities. Its key argument is that the racialization of Latinos has created a belief system among some Whites that mixes attributes of race-ethnicity with race-neutral behaviors. This allows Whites to express animus toward Latinos in a race-neutral manner by blurring the lines between dislike toward the group and dislike toward certain behaviors. This form of racial animus directed at Latinos has been reiterated across time so frequently that these expressions have become a normal and accepted part of American political discourse. This book connects this too-frequently ignored form of animus toward Latinos with a range of political preferences of importance in contemporary politics.

There is little doubt that life for Latino Americans, and people of Latino descent living within the United States, has been replete with difficulty and discrimination. Latinos have been subjected to many of the same forms of social marginalization, segregation, violence, property loss, and violations of civil rights and liberties that other racial and ethnic groups have experienced. These forms of discrimination can be rooted in the same set of ideologies and group dominance orientations regularly used to justify discriminatory behavior (e.g., racism à la in-group favoritism and out-group hostility). But racism toward Latinos takes on an additional unique and more common form exhibited in debates over linguistic preferences, country of origin, American national identity, and immigration. Because it mixes conceptions of race with hostility toward Latino culture, it can be labeled as racism and ethnicism.

This racism-ethnicism toward Latinos, often revealed in statements of failed assimilation and the violation of Anglo-American norms, is the focus of this book.

This form of Latino-specific racism-ethnicism is on display in publications such as *Alien Nation, State of Emergency,* and *Who Are We? The Challenges to America's National Identity.* These writings argue that non-White Latinos who fail to adopt Anglo-American traditions are wreaking havoc on the nation. Economic blight, failing state educational systems, crime, teenage pregnancy rates, the strain on social welfare systems, and poverty are problems all attributed to the arrival of Latino immigrants and Latina/o Americans. In *Who Are We?*, Samuel P. Huntington argues that Latinos are threatening American identity by speaking in their native tongue, engaging in cultural traditions from their country of origin, and maintaining strong ties to family members abroad. Huntington fears that the inability of Latinos to assimilate into Anglo-American society will cause an increase in poverty, violence, and political conflict within the United States. In *State of Emergency*, Pat Buchanan (2006, 28) directly contrasts Latinos in an unfavorable light in relation to White-European immigrant groups stating,

Where the Italians wanted to be part of our family, millions of Mexicans are determined to retain their language and loyalty to Mexico. They prefer to remain outsiders. They do not wish to assimilate, and the nation no longer demands that they do so ... We are in the midst of a savage culture war in which traditionalist values have been losing ground for two generations.

In the book jacket of *Alien Nation*, Peter Brimelow writes that Latinos within the United States

are less educated, less skilled, more prone to trouble with the law, less inclined to share American culture and values, and altogether less likely to become Americans in name or spirit.

Sometimes these statements of failed assimilation are interwoven with arguments about the racial superiority of Americans with White-European ancestry, a need for White nationalism, and a desire for racial segregation. Few would doubt that within this context, statements of failed Latino assimilation and adherence to Anglo-American norms represent part of a racial ideology of old-fashioned racial bigotry rooted in a belief in the superiority of the White race.

1.1 IS IT RACISM?

At the same time, similar language is used by many Americans who do not formally endorse racial bigotry or associate themselves with White supremacist ideologies, White nationalism, or racial segregation. Such comments frequently appear in interpersonal debates, among media pundits, and during online public discussions. For instance, a citizen at a town hall in Colorado asked "Why is it that the Irish, Italians and Eastern Europeans were able to assimilate and Latinos, to some extent, still have not?"[1] White Americans often seem at ease expressing this particular view because it gives the appearance that they dislike certain behaviors rather than Latinos as a group. In fact, many citizens endorse the idea that Latinos fail to adhere with Anglo-American norms while proclaiming racial neutrality (e.g., "I am not a racist").

In speaking about Latinos, one blogger wrote, "I just want better educated, safer, and cleaner people living around me ... I'm not racist at all."[2] A citizen on another popular website posed the question,

> Why do Mexicans refuse to assimilate into the US culture? A LOT of them refuse to learn English, start gangs, stare at us like we don't belong here, and speak Spanish fluently in public ... The Irish, Germans, Japanese, etc, have ALL learned English and are now functioning members of US society ... Do NOT call me a racist, because I know there are a lot of brain-washed idiots out there who will play the race card with me as soon as they read this. It doesn't make me a racist to want my country to be able to be UNITED.[3]

These comments often cross the line between claims of racial-neutrality and outright bigotry toward Latinos. One such case is a blogger who commented on a message board that,

> This is an american english seaking country and was once nice until all of them came along and polluted it with their diseases and prehistoric, unintelligent culture ... Also, no I'm not racist, it's just that things have gone out of control with all of these illegal mexicans in our country and their rude, ignorant behavior on top of it and they are the ones who are racist because they figure since they are all heavily populated out here like roaches, they want to be the only race around and run things the way they want it.[4]

Perhaps the most notable example of how people that potentially harbor racism-ethnicism toward Latinos express their beliefs in statements

---

[1] David Conde, "The Assimilation of Latinos," *La Voz*, April 12, 2017, available at www.lavozcolorado.com/detail.php?id=9084.

[2] http://mexicans-go-home.com/whats-worse-the-blacks-or-these-filthy-mexicans/comment-page-2/.

[3] Yahoo!Answers, "Why Do Mexicans Refuse to Assimilate to US Culture?" answersyahoo.com (2009), available at https://answers.yahoo.com/question/index?qid=20091101171443AAAMExO.

[4] http://mexicans-go-home.com/whats-worse-the-blacks-or-these-filthy-mexicans/comment-page-2/.

about failed Latino assimilation, and still deny overt racism, is a pair of statements by President Donald Trump. While campaigning for president, Trump frequently made comments about the inability of Latinos to assimilate, questioning their character and desire to adhere to Anglo-American norms. His most infamous quote is,

[W]hen Mexico sends its people, they're not sending their best. They're not sending you. They're not sending you. They're sending people that have lots of problems, and they're bringing those problems with us. They're bringing drugs. They're bringing crime. They're rapists. And some, I assume, are good people.[5]

Although many people view these comments as a direct expression of Trump's racist belief system, Trump asserted in an interview with Howard Kurtz on Fox News "I don't have a racist bone in my body ... I love the Mexican people."[6] Subsequently, it appears that while people are quick to deny they believe in the racist ideologies of the past, they are free to express their displeasure with how Latinos have assimilated in the United States as well as a sense that Latinos fail to adhere to traditional Anglo-American norms of behavior.

The use of this type of language and imagery is not all or nothing. Sometimes speakers will pick and chose which aspects of the racism-ethnicism they highlight, denying some aspects to illustrate the "real" problem that underlies the anti-Latino affect. Then-White House Chief of Staff John Kelly, in an interview with National Public Radio, used this type of an appeal to justify harsh immigration policies stating,

[T]he vast majority of the people that move illegally into the United States are not bad people. They're not criminals. They're not MS-13. Some of them are not. But they're also not people that would easily assimilate into the United States into our modern society. They're overwhelmingly rural people in the countries they come from fourth, fifth, sixth grade educations are kind of the norm. They don't speak English, obviously that's a big thing. They don't speak English. They don't integrate well, they don't have skills. They're not bad people.[7]

5 Phillips, Amber. "'They're Rapists.' President Trump's Campaign Launch Speech Two Years Later, Annotated." *Washington Post*. June 16, 2017, available at www .washingtonpost.com/news/the-fix/wp/2017/06/16/theyre-rapists-presidents-trump-campaign-launch-speech-two-years-later-annotated/.

6 Robert King, "Trump: I'm Not a Racist," *Washington Examiner*, July 5, 2015, available at www.washingtonexaminer.com/trump-im-not-racist/article/2567627.

7 "Transcript: White House Chief of Staff John Kelly's Interview with NPR," National Public Radio, May 11, 2018, available at www.npr.org/2018/05/11/610116389/ transcript-white-house-chief-of-staff-john-kellys-interview-with-npr.

Kelly's comments tap into the perception of Latinos as violent criminals, although it explicitly rejects the breadth of the applicability. At the same time, it highlights the lack of assimilation due to language, education, and more generally cultural differences between Latino immigrants and the, presumably, Anglo-American culture. This rhetorical technique adds legitimacy to the second set of statements by rejecting an explicit racial motivation.

How much do these statements represent anti-Latino affect hidden in the language of failed assimilation and norm violation? How does the endorsement of these statements relate to support for policies that adversely affect the Latino community? How do beliefs about failed Latino assimilation and norm violation relate to favoring political candidates that voice similar concerns over America's growing Latino population? In this book, we examine the ingredients of these views and the consequences that they have on contemporary politics. We argue that these beliefs represent a unique form of Latino-specific racism-ethnicism distinct from explicit racial and ethnic animus and the endorsement of traditional stereotypes. As we will show, these less-overt expressions of racial and ethnic animus toward Latinos influence not only the debate over immigration, but also supposedly race-neutral policies and the public's electoral choices.

1.2 THE ARGUMENT OF THIS BOOK

We argue that beliefs about the inability of Latinos to assimilate and adhere to Anglo-American norms are a complex expression of anti-Latino sentiment and a preference for traditional patterns of Anglo-American family and social organization. These beliefs developed through a process of "racializing" Latinos to be a phylogenetically and culturally (e.g., behaviorally) distinct group from Whites – a process that began in the early colonial period as White Europeans created a set of economic and political institutions to subjugate the early mestizo population. This historical racialization process has resulted in a common set of beliefs that persist today regarding Latina/o assimilation, agency, cultural inferiority, and criminality. Thus, many of the modern criticisms of Latinos stem from discriminatory institutions of the past.

This form of racism-ethnicism, masked in criticism of Latina/o behavior and culture, is particularly common today given that many White Americans prefer to avoid more direct forms of racism and ethnicism. Just as norms of equality and a desire to not appear racist constrained the willingness of White Americans to express overt bigotry toward African Americans (Kinder and Sanders, 1996; Kinder and Sears, 1981; Sears et al., 2000a), many people are unwilling to explicitly state their dislike toward Latinos or are unaware that they hold such beliefs (Pérez, 2010; Weyant, 2005). Subsequently, studies that rely on measures of traditional forms of racism can attenuate the role played by racism-ethnicism toward Latinos in people's political preferences and behavior. Instead, Americans who harbor Latino-specific racism-ethnicism feel more comfortable expressing these sentiments using arguments about how Latinos violate Anglo-American cultural norms. This allows people the comfort of harboring animus toward Latinos, while, at least in their own minds, appearing to support norms of equality and racial neutrality. Our primary argument is that these beliefs, what we refer to as Latina/o racism-ethnicism (LRE), are consequential to a range of salient political choices.

1.3 A LOOK AHEAD

In the chapters that follow we provide a detailed look at how the racialization of Latinos into a distinct non-White group shapes the way racism-ethnicism is expressed toward Latinos, as well as the effect of this form of racism-ethnicism on people's political preferences.

Chapter 2 contains the theoretical discussion detailing how the historical racialization of Latinos resulted in a distinct form of anti-Latina/o attitudes we refer to as LRE. Starting as early as the Spanish colonial caste system, the ancestors of modern Latinos faced discrimination that led Whites to view them as a non-White racial group. The discrimination Latinos faced resulting from the caste system limited their social mobility, helping to create a belief that Latinos were incapable of assimilating into colonial society. Other types of formal and informal practices of discrimination against Latinos (e.g., the *California Land Act*, Operation Wetback, the Zoot Suit Riots) had a similar effect, reinforcing beliefs about the inability of Latinos to assimilate as well as creating an impression that Latinos fail to adhere to Anglo-American norms. Thus, various historical institutions are partly responsible for shaping how Whites perceive Latina/o identity and ultimately shape the way that animus is expressed toward Latinos today. We refer to this animus as LRE because it conflates beliefs about Latinos as a non-White racial group with prejudice toward Latino culture. The chapter then describes why contemporary White Americans feel comfortable expressing this type of animus toward

Latinos and why it should connect to a wide range of political choices in contemporary American politics.

In Chapter 3, we explain our approach to measuring LRE. Evidence is presented showing that White Americans are more inclined to express animus toward Latinos in the language of LRE rooted in the historical racialization of Latinos rather than in more common forms of racial animus. We provide evidence that LRE is a coherent belief system distinct from other beliefs, such as ideology, ethnocentrism, and old-fashioned racial stereotypes. We then establish that responses to our measure of LRE are indeed capturing concerns about race. The chapter concludes by discussing some potential criticism to our approach.

Chapter 4 examines the most contentious debate directly involving Latinos – immigration. We explore common explanations for White opposition to open immigration policies and show how LRE is associated with both general opposition to immigration and a range of specific immigration-related policies.

Chapters 5 discusses how LRE relates to supposedly race-neutral policies – crime control and policing. Although neither policy should trigger beliefs about race or ethnicity (i.e., all citizens are equal before the eyes of the law), we show that this is far from the case. We suggest that news reporting of crime has increased the connection between Latinos and criminal behavior. This reporting is shown to increase the relationship between LRE and support for punitive crime control policies. Moreover, LRE is related to opposition to the policy of body cameras – especially in environments where the Latina/o crime narrative is accentuated. The connection between LRE and these policies illustrates the permeating role of this belief in shaping supposedly race-neutral policies.

Chapter 6 extends this analysis by examining the role of LRE in supporting laws related to voting registration and identification. We describe the debate over laws aimed at preventing voter fraud and how these laws potentially impact Latinos. We then show evidence that Whites harboring LRE are more likely to support laws that increase the barriers to voting than do Whites who feel amicable toward Latinos. Moreover, our evidence suggests that support for more-restrictive voting laws is related to LRE rather than specific threats posed by the growing Latina/o population.

Chapter 7 documents the role of LRE in contemporary elections. We argue that the rise of Latina/o political candidates, as well as the increased anti-Latina/o immigration rhetoric of the last several decades, has created an environment where LRE plays an important role in how White

Americans vote. We examine the role of LRE in the US House, Senate, and gubernatorial elections in both midterm and presidential election years. The evidence shows a consistent relationship between LRE and voting for Latina/o congressional candidates as well as Senate and state gubernatorial candidates that take a hardline immigration stance. Our evidence also points to LRE having played a significant role in the election of President Donald Trump – providing a more accurate predictor of voting for Trump than traditional explanations focusing on authoritarianism and ethnocentrism.

Chapter 8 discusses how our findings speak to the future of Latinos living in the United States. We suggest that LRE will most likely be a persistent presence in US politics, but can be muted when policy agendas shift and the electoral benefits of campaigning toward those who harbor LRE subside.

2

The Racialization of Latinos

Modern racism-ethnicism derives from a "racialization" process where race and ethnicity are constructed over time. Whereas biological accounts of race and ethnicity viewed these identities as concrete and static (Park, 1928; Stoddard, 1920), contemporary conceptualizations of race and ethnicity demonstrate their fluidity in response to social, economic, and political environments (Omi and Winant, 1994). The history of each racial and ethnic group results in distinct racialization narratives that shape how people view each group as well as how people perceive their own racial and ethnic identities. The construction of a minority group into a racial category takes place in contrast to the framing of the dominant racial group as economically, linguistically, culturally, and socially superior. Within the United States, Latinos have been constructed into their own racial category that is "not-White" rather than integrated into the same racial category as Whites (Feagin, 2013). Instead, Whites have regulated Latinos into an inferior pan-racial and ethnic identity.[1]

This racialization process is responsible for the cognitive associations between race/ethnicity and beliefs about the group: the group's characteristics, culture, adherence to norms, attitudes, and behaviors. These associations become how people view race and ethnicity in the world – what some have referred to as people's racial or ethnic "common sense" (Omi and Winant, 2007; Whitehead, 2009). Since the expression of racial and

---

[1] Various groups associated with the Latina/o label have undergone their own racialization process. However, Whites have also lumped these groups into the broader category of Latino, failing to recognize the distinctions between these group members. In this research, we focus on the similarities of the racialization process of these various Latino groups.

ethnic animus is the result of these cognitive and affective associations, we expect this racialization process also shapes the language people use to justify their racism-ethnicism toward racial and ethnic groups.

Although the history and experiences of racial and ethnic groups are interwoven, such connectivity does not preclude distinct narratives that attempt to construct the identities, characteristics, culture, and other attributes of group members. For instance, drug use has been used to characterize various minority groups within the United States. Yet, these drug narratives are quite distinct. Drug abuse among African Americans was connected to heroin and jazz music during the Depression era and crack cocaine in the 1980s. The latter linked African Americans to violence, robbery, and negligent parenting (Ortiz and Briggs, 2003; Welch, 2007). Mexicans, on the other hand, were constructed as lazy marijuana smokers by immigration opponents as part of an effort to reduce demand for Mexican labor (Meier, 1994). Similar attempts to limit Chinese immigration in California during the 1860s resulted in a narrative portraying Chinese as black-market traders addicted to opium and limiting Indian immigration in the early 1900s (Musto, 1991). All of these characterizations continue today in some form despite being forged decades ago. Even the recent attention paid to opioids among Whites illustrates the racialization of the drug narrative. Instead of being seen as criminal activity to be denigrated, much of the recent discussion of opioid addiction and abuse among Whites has focused on the problem as a medical issue, requiring more treatment-based solutions and not the incarceration of users.

We suspect there is a strong path dependency where past constructions of racial and ethnic groups are reinforced across time, although we do not rule out that contemporaneous events can diminish, alter, or accentuate past constructions of a group. However, the narratives that shaped the public's understanding of racial and ethnic groups in the past are likely to continue to drive perceptions of those group members today. These narratives are passed on to each new generation at an early age, ensuring the continuation of how people perceive racial and ethnic differences as well as shaping awareness of individual racial and ethnic identities. For instance, the experiments by Clark and Clark (1950) demonstrate that children as young as three years old have developed conceptions of racial differences and associations of "good" or "bad" with various racial skin tones. Other research demonstrates how these racial and ethnic narratives can impact childhood development (Bergner, 2009), how children adapt to cultural barriers (Ford, 1994), and the early development of individual cultural identities (Phinney, 1989). These racial narratives then become stored in memory and form a baseline set of knowledge about group members, which becomes automatically triggered in the presence of racial and ethnic cues (Devine, 1989; Dovidio et al., 1997; Jonas and Sassenberg, 2006).

Information counter to these racialized narratives can minimize the use of beliefs about racial and ethnic groups in specific situations, but does not have a long-term effect on beliefs about the group as a whole (Blair et al., 2001; Holt, 2013; Peffley et al., 1997; Power et al., 1996; Sinclair and Kunda, 1999). Television shows and films often portray racial and ethnic minorities in positive ways, countering existing narratives as part of the racialization process. However, most of these countering effects have been limited to short-term evaluations of specific group members rather than the entire group. When encountering information about a group member who does not fit the common racialization narrative, people usually will not view that specific group member as representative of the group, which means their beliefs about the group do not change (Rothbart and John, 1985). This suggests that the long-term negation of prevailing racial and ethnic narratives takes more than short-term exposure to counter information regarding the dominant perception of racial and ethnic groups (Gawronski et al., 2008). Instead, racialization narratives should be viewed as the default option of how most people view racial and ethnic group members. Unless a person actively inhibits the common characterization of racial or ethnic group members, the application of the dominant narrative will likely occur (Bodenhausen et al., 1999; Moreno and Bodenhausen, 1999).

Yet, race and ethnicity are fluid constructs that can be updated to reflect changes in the sociopolitical environment. These sociopolitical changes might reduce the transmission of previous characterizations of racial and ethnic groups as well as alter those characterizations (Blanchard et al., 1994). For example, the condemnation of racism amidst norms of equality coupled with the long-term economic inequality that African-Americans have faced since the Civil War resulted in several changes in how White Americans expressed racial animus toward African Americans. These broader contextual changes led to the characterization of African Americans as lacking individualistic values and a strong work ethic that changed the manner in which animus was expressed toward African Americans (Kinder and Sanders, 1996). The historic forms of animus toward African Americans built from earlier racialization processes persisted among a minority, while a much larger portion of the public felt comfortable expressing animus toward African Americans in the newfound language of value deficiency.

Understanding the racialization of Latinos is necessary to understanding the current expression of anti-Latino sentiment and White support for policies that directly or indirectly impact Latinos. Without knowing how Latinos have been constructed in the past and present, it becomes difficult to determine how racism-ethnicism is expressed toward Latinos and the degree that Latino-specific racism-ethnicism shapes people's political choices. Instead, we end up with the fallacy of assuming that a single form of animus applies equally to all groups, which potentially attenuates the role that racism-ethnicism plays in contemporary American politics.

2.1 THE HISTORICAL ROOTS OF LATINA/O RACISM-ETHNICISM

We argue that examining the history of Latinos provides insight into how racism-ethnicism is held and expressed in contemporary society. A historical approach also reveals that many of the beliefs about modern Latinos are not new – they are not the result of a newly empowered segment of angry Whites who are now willing to explicitly discuss their animus toward Latinos – but instead represent how some Whites have historically depicted Latinos and their forbears. Indeed, our analysis shows that many of these beliefs stem from institutions designed by Whites (and the earlier Spanish colonizers) that intentionally or unintentionally shaped how Latinos were integrated into US society and were perceived by Whites.

Specifically, we describe how the common racialization of Latinos as a non-White racial and ethnic group generated the following four beliefs: (1) Latinos fail to succeed because of personal shortcomings rather than institutional discrimination, (2) Latina/o culture is inferior to Anglo-American culture, (3) Latina/o migration is distinct from past immigrant groups as Latinos do not want to assimilate into US society, and (4) Latinos are inherently criminal.

2.1.1 The Racialization of the Mestizo People in the Colonial Period

The racialization of Latinos emerged as White Europeans began to settle into the Americas. Spanish settlers, who were predominately men, engaged in interracial relationships with people indigenous to the area. This Spanish colonization and cohabitation with indigenous people led to a significant "mestizo" population that mixed both Spanish and indigenous culture and identities. Racial-ethnic animus and discrimination toward the mestizo population was immediate and driven by past events in Spain. Prior to the discovery of the Americas, Spain experienced a wave of nationalism, resulting in the Reconquista – a retaking of the Iberian Peninsula from Islamic and other non-Christian settlers. This resulted in *limpieza de sangre* or "cleanliness/purity of blood" laws. The *limpieza de sangre* laws required Spanish Christians to demonstrate that their ancestry was free of Jewish and Muslim origin in order to obtain upward mobility and access to the new colonies. The practice evolved in Spain's American colonies, where upward mobility and positions of authority could only be obtained by demonstrating racial purity from indigenous bloodlines. Purity of blood laws resulted in a caste system within the Spanish colonies. The mestizo people were prohibited from holding private and public positions of power, treated as unequal socially, and did not have the same legal protections that "pure-blood" Spaniards enjoyed. The Spanish also deemed many mestizo traditions stemming from their native ancestry as crimes – sometimes punishable by death (Kalunta-Crumpton, 2012; Terraciano, 1998). Subsequently, the early mestizo people were viewed as "alien" outsiders with inferior, sometimes immoral, traditions and subjugated to menial positions in society.

The relationship between the early mestizo people and non-Spanish White-European settlers resulted in a similar caste. Although the roots of mestizo people often predate those of White-European or Anglo-American settlers in the United States, the English and other immigrant groups viewed people of mestizo origin as outsiders who were unable to assimilate into Anglo-American culture. Some of the hostility between early Anglo-American settlers and the mestizo people derived from conflict between Spain and England in the sixteenth century (Moore and Pachon, 1985, 4–5). The English were not only competitors in trade and colonization with the Spanish but were also opposed to Spain's alignment with Roman Catholicism, which was adopted by many mestizo people. Spanish- and native-language use among mestizo people also reinforced separation between the mestizo population and Anglo-Americans. As Anglo-American expansion into areas previously under Spanish control increased (e.g., Florida, Texas, New Mexico, Arizona, and California), Anglo-Americans developed a worldview that their colonization of mestizo people was "liberating" these groups from Spanish rule and the less-desirable Spanish and native cultures (Hero, 1992, 32). This "liberation" was often nothing more than the forced taking of land, property, and life (Delgado, 2009; Foley, 2014; Villanueva, 2017). This belief in the superiority of Anglo-American culture helped to justify the movement of Anglo-Americans into new territories in the South and Southwest (Moore and Pachon, 1985, 6).

Thus, even in the colonial period we see the emergence of a set of beliefs that still plays an important role in how Whites express Latino racism-ethnicism today: the belief in the mestizo people as culturally inferior; the belief that sanctions were an appropriate response to challenge mestizo customs and norms that differed from the Spanish and other White-European settlers; the belief that the mestizo people were not part of Anglo-American society; and the failure to recognize the institutional barriers facing the mestizo people (or at least a lack of desire to address them).

2.1.2 Institutional Discrimination and the Racialization of Latino Identity

The history of Latinos in the United States resembles the treatment of their mestizo ancestors in the colonial period. Latinos often faced institutional barriers to assimilating into Anglo-American culture, advancing in social and political positions of power, and maintaining their livelihood. The continued discrimination against Latinos created barriers that resulted in Latinos, and their culture, being viewed in a derogatory fashion. In most cases, this institutional discrimination has been ignored as a hinderance to Latina/o advancement and assimilation with Whites. Instead, blame is attributed toward Latina/o agency (i.e., deficiencies in Latina/o culture and behavior).

The aftermath of the Treaty of Guadalupe Hidalgo provides an example of how hardships facing Latinos became attributed to Latina/o culture rather than to discriminatory institutions. The 1848 Treaty of Guadalupe Hidalgo, ending the Mexican–American War following the annexation of the Independent Republic of Texas from Mexico, had a provision granting Mexican nationals living in areas conceded by Mexico to the United States the choice of citizenship in either country. The provision provided these new Mexican American citizens with the same civil rights and legal protections as all Americans and specifically stated that they would be able to maintain their existing property rights in the conceded territories.

In practice, the treaty was rarely implemented as written. Various institutions were created by Whites that led to the violation of the civil and property rights of many Mexican American citizens (Del Castillo, 1992). *The California Land Act*, for instance, altered the terms of the Treaty of Guadalupe Hidalgo by creating a Public Land Commission where Mexican Americans were given a two-year period to submit land claims for their existing property. This eliminated due process rights within the court system, which were more favorable toward landowners. Legal precedent set in *Plume* v. *Seward* had a burden of proof that favored the rights of initial ownership over the rights of squatters, whereas the Public Land Commission placed the burden of proof on landowners (Chanbonpin, 2005). Plaintiffs had to pay for land surveys, extensive paperwork fees, and various litigation costs to keep their property, which was outside the reach of many rural landowners – particularly since the rancheros in the West mostly favored a feudal-style agricultural economy relying on honor and trade rather than on money.

As the Gold Rush motivated land speculators to move West, a large number of White-European squatters challenged the property rights of Mexican American citizens. Many Mexican Americans were unable to submit claims and lost their land, which was their dominant source of livelihood. Even those who submitted claims and retained their land eventually lost their property due to debts incurred while trying to prove initial ownership (Del Castillo, 1998). As Latinos were pushed out of their land, and subsequently their livelihood as rancheros and vaqueros, they were ill-prepared to assimilate into Anglo-American society. Their traditional lifestyles did not translate well with the faster-paced Anglo-American work style, which was viewed by many Whites as a sign that Latinos were lazy, deficient in intelligence, and lacking useful skills.

This made Latinos a frequent scapegoat for whatever turmoil White settlers experienced. For instance, Harrison Gray Otis, president of the Times-Mirror Company (publisher of *The Los Angeles Times*) wrote an editorial in the *Santa Barbara Journalist* "blaming the lazy ways of the natives" for an economic recession in Southern California in the late 1800s (Camarillo, 1975, 49). The problems facing Latinos, and the ills of the nation, were rarely blamed on institutional discrimination, but rather on the character and agency of Latinos as a group.

Cubans, Dominicans, and Puerto Ricans living in the American South (e.g., Florida, Alabama, and Georgia) faced similar, although less formal, forms of institutional discrimination related to the belief that Latina/o tastes and preferences were less sophisticated than those of Anglo-Americans. For instance, Whites often justified the taking of land from these Latino groups through a philosophy of "good use" of land (Earle, 2012). This philosophy was rooted in Anglo-Protestant traditions that argued that God designated man as the steward of the environment, responsible for ensuring its "proper use" (Guth et al., 1993). Whites viewed the cultivation of some native crops (e.g., corn, common beans, and squash) as less desirable than cultivation of crops native to Europe. This meant that Whites were able to take some of the best land from Latinos, rendering the Latina/o population into lower-class jobs and poverty.

De León (2010) further documents this view with a historical analysis of Anglo-American attitudes toward Latinos during this era. He provides evidence of an informal moral code among Whites that depicted Latinos as culturally "defective," which was used as justification for the subjugation of Latino populations. Whites often spoke of Latino "docility, ignorance, decadence, mediocrity, antagonism toward work, submission to vice, and hedonistic proclivities" (De León, 2010, 24). According to his analysis, cultural inferiority made up a significant portion of White Animus toward Latinos,

Where whites were energetic, Mexicans seemed backward; where whites were ambitious and aggressive, Mexicans seemed apathetic and complacent; where whites considered themselves inventive, Mexicans seemed anachronistic; and where whites knew their direction, Mexicans appeared to be going nowhere.

In the West, these perceptions extended beyond Mexicans to those with Central and South American heritage. For instance, many Chileans migrated to Northern California to participate in the Gold Rush. Although Chileans identified as racially "White," the White-European settlers labeled them as non-White Latinos, creating a new pan-ethnic identity for Chileans that connected them to the Mexican Americans already living in the area (Purcell, 2016). Along with this label came the existing negative characterization of Chilean culture, language, and traditions. Similarly, Puerto Ricans, Dominicans, and Cubans in the Northeast faced a similar sustained attack on their culture, language, morality, and education (Duany, 1998, 2016; Grosfoguel and Georas, 2000; Perez, 2016). This was likely part of a larger effort to keep them in subordinate positions of political, social, and economic power, creating a cheap working class of Latina/o laborers, but also preventing Latinos from fully assimilating into Anglo-American society.

2.1.3 The Continued Push to Marginalize Latinos

As Latinos were pushed out of their traditional lifestyles, they were often ill-prepared for work in the urban economy of the progressive era. Many Latinos took jobs as manual laborers working on municipal transit systems, in mines, and in low-paying agricultural jobs in the newly formed agrocapitalist industry that emerged in the wake of the loss of the smaller farms and rancheros. Cubans in the South were able to find work in American-owned sugar factories, and some continued their native trade as tobacco farmers and cigar traders. Yet, most other Latina/o groups did not fare so well. Many Latinos remained unemployed, as Whites deemed them "undesirable" due to their culture and Spanish-language use (Camarillo, 1975). The popular news presses of this era would often describe these unemployed and vagrant Latinos as "degenerates," "culturally inferior," and "lazy" (Meeks, 2010). Afro-Cubans particularly had a difficult time finding employment given that many Whites viewed them as Blacks – fueling the notion among most Whites that all Cubans (as well as Dominicans and Puerto Ricans) were a non-White lower class (Perez, 2016).

Subsequently, Latinos were viewed as distinct from other immigrant groups. In particular, a narrative formed that Latinos were unable or unwilling to assimilate into Anglo-American culture. Although concerns about assimilation (along with the associated labels of being called "un-American" or "alien") were part of the immigrant experience for most immigrant groups, this posed a special challenge for Latinos because most Whites do not view Latinos as a White racial group (Feagin, 2013; Feagin and Dirks, 2004). Whereas White-European immigrants were eventually integrated into Anglo-American society, Latinos continue to face concerns about their "differentness" due to their skin tone (see Feagin and Cobas, 2008). This made it difficult for Latinos to overcome the stigma associated with being racially different – a barrier that White-European immigrant groups did not have to overcome.

The economic hardships and international wars following the early progressive era amplified this "differentness" between Latinos and citizens/immigrants of White-European ancestry. In the 1920s, the declining economy carried nationalistic tensions into the workplace and various racial and ethnic groups competed for a scarce number of jobs. Subsequently, the American labor unions spearheaded efforts to depict Latina/o immigrants as un-American and undeserving of employment. The American Federation of Labor and the National Club of America created a national campaign that suggested that Latinos were taking jobs from "real Americans" (Balderrama and Rodriguez, 2006; Hoffman, 1974). Secretary of Labor William N. Doak responded by organizing the mass deportation of thousands of Latina/os, including a substantial portion of US citizens of Latina/o descent. Doak was able to utilize

the US Border Patrol, formed in 1924, to conduct the raids, as well
as overlook illegal deportation of US citizens by local officials. These
deportations were implemented with little to no regard for the civil or
human rights of the deportees. Historian R. Reynolds McKay (1982, 560)
notes that,

> These violations included illegally imprisoning immigrants, deporting US born
> children, not permitting returnees to dispose of their property or to collect their
> wages, deporting many not legally subject to deportation because of their length
> of Texas residence, separating families, and deporting the infirm.

Many women, children, and the ill died en route to the border due to heat
exhaustion and a lack of water. Once arriving across the US–Mexican
border, these deportees often had nowhere to go and no resources to
survive. Although the economic downturn led to conflict within the labor
unions among various racial and ethnic groups, Latinos were the only
group that faced mass deportations of this magnitude.

Similar deportations occurred on a local scale. For instance, the Phelps
Dodge Corporation encouraged local sheriff Harry Wheeler and a citizen
posse to illegally deport hundreds of mine workers, a majority of whom
were Latina/o, after a labor strike at the Copper Queen Mine in Bisbee,
Arizona. Although striking workers of various immigrant groups were
rounded up, the posse also kidnapped local Latinos who did not work
in the mines (including US citizens of Latino descent and their families).
The kidnapped victims were held at gunpoint by a mob of White citizens
and forced onto railroad cars. They were then shipped across the desert
to Tres Hermanas, New Mexico, without food or water, which led to
several deaths. When questioned by the Arizona attorney general about
the kidnappings and deportations, Wheeler suggested that Latina/os were
not Americans, stating, "Perhaps everything that I did wasn't legal ... it
became a question of 'Are you American, or are you not?'" (Capozzola,
2008).

The Great Depression led to further mass deportations of Latinos,
including US citizens of Latino ancestry. During this period, labeled the
Mexican Repatriation, an estimated 400,000–2,000,000 Latinos were
deported to Mexico. Many of these deportees had no ties to Mexico and
many were not Mexican. Some were tricked or coerced into deportation
after being recruited into the United States decades earlier. Thus, the ease
with which Latinos could be deported (typically by train) to Mexico
most likely reinforced the view that they were un-American. It also made
it difficult for those remaining in the country to assimilate, as Latinos
fearing deportation remained reclusive.

2.1.4 Historical Segregation, Modern Hate

During the civil rights era, Latinos faced many of the same forms of institutional discrimination as did African Americans. Latinos were segregated from Whites in movie theaters, restaurants, barbershops, swimming pools, churches, dance halls, country clubs, hotels, parks, hospitals, and government facilities (Meeks, 2010; Perales, 1974). In California, Latinos were forced to attend "Mexican" schools. Latinos in these schools were treated as second-class citizens: taught by the lowest paid teachers, forced into classrooms deemed unsuitable for White children, and assigned books discarded by White public schools (Strum, 2016). Latina/o children were required to attend these segregated schools, with the hopes of keeping Latina/o culture and behaviors away from White children (Behnken, 2011). Such segregation created a barrier to Latina/o education, which reinforced the belief that Latinos were unintelligent and culturally incapable of progressing in Anglo-American society.

Demeaning of Latina/o culture persists today, with criticism of their language, food, family structure, music, morals, and personalities common justifications for discriminating against Latinos as a racial-ethnic group (Buriel and Vasquez, 1982; De Garine, 2001). Indeed, mid-twentieth–century sociologists viewed Latinos as illiterate, superstitious, and wedded to a detestable language (Davis and Senior, 1949). Unfortunately, these depictions of Latinos have also served as the basis of physical attacks against Latinos, such as the 2008 hate crime against Luis Ramirez in Shenandoah, Pennsylvania, and the assault of a consulate employee in San Diego for speaking Spanish.[2] Similar hate crimes have recently occurred against Marcelo Lucera, who was murdered in 2008, Domingo López Vargas and other day laborers in Georgia, who were targeted and beaten amid a flurry of anti-immigrant sentiment by teenagers, José Osvaldo Sucuzhañay, who was beaten to death with a bat while leaving a church event after being taunted with racial slurs, and Iván Ponce De León-Najera, who was assaulted outside a gas station after being accused of "stealing our jobs."

---

[2] Office of Public Affairs, US Department of Justice, "Two Shenandoah, PA, Men Convicted of Hate Crime in the Fatal Beating of Luis Ramirez" Justice.gov (2010), available at www.justice.gov/opa/pr/two-shenandoah-pa-men-convicted-hate-crime-fatal-beating-luis-ramirez. Regina Ruis, "Mexican Consulate Employee Beat Up for Speaking Spanish," NBC San Diego, May 20, 2016, available at www.nbcsandiego.com/news/local/Mexican-Consulate-Employee-Beat-Up-For-Speaking-Spanish-380333741.html.

2.1.5 The Depiction of Latinos as Criminals

Assaults on Latina/o culture, particularly defining Latinos as immoral, have contributed to the Latina/o criminality narrative. The Latina/o criminality narrative came to particular prominence in the postwar era as the burgeoning civil rights movement limited the ability of Whites to subjugate minorities through formal segregation and Jim Crow laws. Instead, Whites turned to crime control as a means to keep Latinos in an economic, political, and socially subservient position – much like they did with African Americans (Alexander, 2010). Part of this was the accentuation of the Latina/o crime narrative – the linkage between Latina/o identity and criminal behavior.

Latina/o criminality was not new. The Spanish outlawed many mestizo traditions and behavior in the colonial period, thus starting the linkage between modern-day Latina/o identity and criminality. This narrative was continued in the postcolonial period as simply being "Latina/o" became a crime. Latinos were lynched for a variety of reasons associated with their race and ethnicity, such as for speaking Spanish, competing for jobs with Whites, looking at White women, acting "uppity," being "too Mexican," or rejecting the advances of White men (Delgado, 2009). In fact, some estimates suggest that Latinos in the Southwest were lynched at a rate roughly equal to the lynching of African Americans (Carrigan and Webb, 2003, 414).

The Latina/o criminality narrative, however, made national headlines during the Zoot Suit Riots of 1943. White servicemen on leave during World War II systematically attacked Latina/o Americans and immigrants in the Los Angeles area for dressing in distinctive Latino clothing known as "zoot suits." The zoot suits typically had pants that were high-waisted with baggy legs, and the jackets had wide lapels and starkly padded shoulders. The style required much more fabric than was allowed due to war rationing and was offensive to servicemen and other Whites. However, the attacks extended beyond those wearing zoot suits. Latinos were attacked for any identifying racial or ethnic trait such as having slicked-back hair or speaking Spanish. Latinos were beaten, robbed, and sometimes forcibly undressed in public. The riots spawned similar attacks against Latinos in Chicago, Detroit, San Diego, Oakland, Philadelphia, Texas, and New York (Novas, 2007).

The Zoot Suit Riots contributed to the portrayal of Latinos as criminals. For many Whites throughout the nation, the coverage of the Zoot

Suit Riots was an introduction to a particular subculture of Latinos. Adding to this cultural shock, the portrayal of the Latina/o victims in the riots as the perpetrators of the riots helped bring the Latina/o crime narrative to mainstream America. It did not help that White police officers frequently arrested Latina/o victims and let the White criminal offenders go. In addition, much of the early conflict was with US servicemen, leading to the view that Latinos were unpatriotic. This bolstered the idea that Latinos as an immigrant group were failing to assimilate into Anglo-American society.

After the riots, Latina/o youth were targeted by police more frequently and portrayed in the tabloid media as juvenile delinquents. Rodriguez (1997) documents a sharp increase in the portrayal of Latina/o youth as criminal delinquents in films starting in the 1960s. This narrative continued into the 1980s, where popular film, television, and music disproportionately focused on Latina/o youth as gang bangers and drug lords (Berg, 2002; Romero, 2001; Simonett, 2006; Valdez and Halley, 1999).

Recently, the racialization process connecting Latina/o identity to crime has been supplemented with arguments that (1) all undocumented immigrants, whom are mostly Latina/o, are criminals by the mere circumstance of entering the country without the means to obtain legal documentation and (2) Latinos are more prone to engage in criminal behavior due to a cultural and moral defect. As argued by Chavez (2013, 3), Whites perceive Latinos as "the quintessential illegal aliens," and thus "their social identity has been plagued by the mark of illegality, which in much public discourse means that they are criminals and thus illegitimate members of society." Anti-immigration advocates frequently use the term "illegal" to discuss undocumented immigrants, arguing "The direct and honest word is "illegal" because it is actually illegal to cross the border of any country without proper documents" (Rubio, 2011). This term, however, dehumanizes Latinos as a group and aids in the construction of Latinos as criminals unable to adhere to Anglo-American legal norms.

Adding to this narrative is a return to arguments depicting Latinos as prone to violent criminal behavior. Such arguments were popularized by conservative talk show hosts such as Glenn Beck and Lou Dobbs. Glenn Beck, for instance, introduced the topic of immigration on his November 8, 2007 show with "America's border crisis. Rape, drugs, kidnapping, even murder. It is beginning to look a lot more like a border war."

Conservative talk show host Bill O'Reilly frequently depicted Latinos as violent due to their culture, such as in his statement during a January 4, 2007 broadcast, arguing, "Number one, the illegal aliens shouldn't be here. And number two, the culture from which they come is a lot more violent than the USA." Similar claims are made by US politicians. In a May 5, 2006 posting on his website, Congressmen Steve King (R-Iowa) wrote, "The lives of 12 US citizens would be saved who otherwise would die a violent death at the hands of murderous illegal aliens each day. Another thirteen Americans would survive who are otherwise killed each day by uninsured drunk driving illegals." Although some Latinos (immigrant or otherwise) do engage in unlawful behavior, as do US-born non-Latino citizens, the scholarly consensus indicates that Latinos *do not* increase crime and may be associated with lower levels of criminal behavior (Karmen, 2000; Lee and Martinez Jr., 2009; Longazel, 2013; Martinez Jr., 2014; Sampson et al., 2005). Yet, the criminality narrative continues, with Latinos, like African Americans, being overrepresented as criminals in television news (Dixon and Linz, 2000a). This leads to the perception among the Whites that Latinos are more likely to be physically violent and engage in criminal behavior (Jackson, 1995; Varela, 2013).

2.1.6 The Stigma of Being Latina/o

This racialization process has limited the ability of Latinos to be fully integrated into US social, economic, and political institutions. A study by Feagin and Dirks (2004) shows that between 86 and 100 percent of Whites classify Irish Americans, English Americans, and Italian Americans as "White," but tend to classify Mexican Americans, Puerto Ricans, or Cuban Americans as "non-White" (see Feagin, 2010; Gonzalez, 2015; Lacayo, 2016). Whereas the Irish, Italians, Germans, and Jews were eventually recognized as "White," facilitating their assimilation into Anglo-American society, the racialization of Latinos as a non-White group means it is unlikely they will become integrated at all in the same way as these past immigrant groups have been. Instead, centuries old narratives of Latinos as unable to assimilate, being culturally inferior, deficient in positive Anglo-American traits, and inclined to criminal behavior continue to contribute to how White Americans think and feel about Latinos. We suspect these themes in the racialization narrative of Latinos provide the basis for how White Americans commonly express animus toward Latinos – a topic we explore in the next chapter.

2.2 THE IMPORTANCE OF UNDERSTANDING LATINA/O RACISM-ETHNICISM

The failure to understand how Latinos have been racialized results in under-estimating the extent that race matters in how Americans think about politics and policies that impact the Latina/o community. Relying on old-fashioned racism or expressions of racism toward African Americans misses the more acceptable and ingrained ways that animus and race-ethnicity are discussed regarding Latinos. Scholars have documented the overall decline in claims of biological or genetic racism coinciding with increases in support for egalitarian values (Bobo et al., 1997; Schuman et al., 1997; Sears et al., 2000a). This does not mean that some Americans do not endorse genetic and biological differences in racial and ethnic groups. Sniderman and Piazza (1993, 45) show that roughly 50 percent of White Americans in 1991 were willing to rate African Americans as violent – a traditional measure of overt racism. Moreover, the recent rise of Donald Trump has coincided with an increase in overt expressions of hate and a potential increase in public acceptance of explicit racial appeals (Crandall et al., 2018; Valentino et al., 2018). In Chapter 3, we show that around 20 percent of White Americans are willing to express overt, old-fashioned forms of racism toward Latinos, but this underestimates the number of White Americans that hold the specific form of Latina/o racism-ethnicism (LRE) illustrated here.

2.2.1 Are People Still Hiding Their Racial Beliefs?

This apparent decline in the need to hide ones racial beliefs still does not eliminate the possibility that some people will shy away from expressing such views because they fear social sanctions, want to avoid cognitive dissonance with beliefs related to equality, or they are unaware of their own implicit biases.[3] People who express the form of LRE, as described in the introductory chapter, often make claims denying overt racial beliefs. Even White supremacy groups attempt to steer away from being labeled as bigots, racists, Nazis, and White supremacists. Instead, these groups, including the Ku Klux Klan, have adopted labels intended to cloak their connection to these past overt forms of racism such as White

---

[3] The evidence supporting the return of explicit racial appeals is also consistent with the argument that implicit racial appeals are now explicit and known for what they actually are, rather than the decline in effectiveness of implicit appeals.

nationalists, alt-right, or Identitarian. Even those who express opinions that are deemed racist by the most racially woke members of society often state that they are not racist.

Such behavior can be explained by modern racism theories. Racial resentment and symbolic racism theories suggest that White Americans feel social pressure to avoid overt expressions of racial animus toward African Americans (Kinder and Sears, 1981). Instead, they cloak their animus and prejudices in the language that African Americans fail to conform to American values of individualism and self-reliance (Kinder and Sanders, 1996). Racial resentment theory, in regard to Latinos, suggests that White opposition to many policies that appear to benefit Latinos might derive from racial animus cloaked in the language that Latinos fail to assimilate into Anglo-American society, adhere to inferior cultural norms, lack agency, and engage in criminal behavior. This difference arises because the prejudices and discrimination faced by Latinos in America are distinct from those faced by African Americans (Sanchez, 1997). Thus, we expect that racism-ethnicism toward Latinos maintains some distinction from resentment toward African Americans or other racial groups. Operationally, the distinction may be slight, but substantively we find it to be important.

Consistent with modern racism theories, people engage in a variety of dissonance-reduction mechanisms to square their expression of LRE with a desire to not be a racist. Thus, LRE allows racial animus to be expressed without the internal guilt – often because many ordinary White Americans do not have the knowledge that their beliefs have racist origins – rooted in historical and contemporary discriminatory institutions.

Unlike racial resentment or symbolic racism theories, we do not argue that the current expression of LRE is new or is a response to changing norms. Instead, it is the result of a historic process that continues to shape how people understand Latinos as a racial and ethnic category today. We have shown in this chapter that LRE has been a common form of racial antipathy toward Latinos since at least the Spanish colonial period.

Furthermore, we make no claims about LRE being a covert or overt form of animus. That, we believe, is in the eye of the beholder. Many of us will view expressions of LRE as overt forms of animus toward Latinos: attacks on their language, culture, and appearance. Others may view expressions of LRE as a covert form of animus that is distinct from blatant expressions of hatred toward Latinos simple because they are Latinos. Still others may fail to see how expressions of LRE can be considered racial or ethnic animus at all. Whether or not LRE *is* a form of animus, however, is a question we take up in the next chapter.

2.2.2 LRE and Whites' Policy Preferences

We believe that LRE has important political consequences – shaping the political opinions of White Americans. A growing number of scholars have suggested that racial prejudice cloaked in arguments that Latinos violate Anglo-American culture are responsible for White support for policies that negatively impact Latinos. Piatt (1990) and Tatalovich (1995) both describe how the English as the official language of the United States movement arose from White supremacy groups. These groups employed strategies to avoid specific statements framing the issue in terms of White supremacy. Instead, they coded their arguments in the language of protecting Anglo-American culture and the benefits of a "common" Anglo-American language. Román (2013, 23) argues that subtle forms of racism toward Latinos are responsible for anti-immigration sentiment, stating that supporters of restrictionist policies are "jingoistic at best and racist at worst." Sobczak (2010, 130) also concludes that these expressions represent a "subtle racism" that potentially "sustains a prominent role in shaping American's views on immigration." Other scholars have documented the myriad ways that Latinos face subtle forms of racism in the workplace where Whites remain in privileged positions of power. This subtle racism takes the form of racist jokes, tokenism, subtle putdowns, and social exclusion (Feagin and Sikes, 1994; Jiménez, 2010; Vallejo, 2015; Vasquez, 2011). The content of these workplace forms of subtle racism appear to mirror the racialization narrative of Latinos focusing on language, cultural differences, and criminality.

Our argument in the remainder of the book is simple: When Latinos are made a visible and accessible racial-ethnic group regarding a political choice, LRE is likely to be an important belief associated with that choice. As we show, this extends to issues such as immigration, where the impact of policy choices directly and clearly affects the Latina/o community, but also to supposedly race-neutral issues such as crime and voting rights where it is less clear that there is a racial-ethnic dimension to why people might support or oppose such a policy.

2.3 CONCLUSION

Although a majority of Whites do not appear to subscribe to ideologies explicitly supporting White supremacy, they are socialized to the common racialization narrative that places Latinos as a subservient race and ethnicity relative to Whites, (i.e., they still do not view Latinos as part of their racial and ethnic in-group). Instead, the racialization process normalizes

certain depictions of group members making, it socially acceptable to
reiterate those particular group attributes of popular racial and ethnic
narratives. This is partly because these narratives mix attributes of race
and ethnicity with race-neutral behaviors. This allows people to disapprove of the racial and ethnic group while appearing only to disapprove
of the behavior tied into the group. Hearing opinion leaders reiterate these
concerns over time increases the social acceptability of repeating these
points. In the next chapter, we explore whether this racialization narrative
has influenced the manner in which contemporary White Americans think
and speak about Latinos and whether or not such beliefs are a form of
racial animus.

3

The Measurement of Latina/o Racism-Ethnicism

In this chapter, we describe the development of the Latina/o racism-ethnicism (LRE) scale that we use throughout the book. First, we briefly review the concept of LRE in order to detail its main attributes. We explore the meaning and form of LRE through a meta-analysis of focus group data pinpointing the main ways that White Americans express their opinions toward Latinos. Second, we use the latter information to develop and describe a set of survey questions we use to measure LRE. Third, we demonstrate the scale's internal consistency and its ability to measure a single coherent latent belief system. Fourth, we provide evidence related to the construct validity of the scale. Specifically, we attempt to distinguish the measurement of LRE from similar concepts such as old-fashioned or traditional forms of racism, ethnocentrism, and partisan principles. Finally, we provide evidence consistent with the argument that our measure of LRE is race-laden. The chapter concludes with an assessment of the strengths and weaknesses of the scale and a recommendation about when the scale should be employed.

3.1 CONCEPTUALIZING LRE

The racialization of Latinos that we described in the previous chapter has resulted in a unique expression of how White Americans describe Latinos. Latinos are often described as "alien" outsiders who are incapable of or unwilling to assimilate in the way past immigrant groups have done. Implicit in this description, sometimes explicit, is that Latina/o culture, traditions, and behaviors are inferior or less desirable than those of Anglo-Americans. There is also a tendency to explain the problems of

Latinos as resulting from individual shortcomings and ignore the institutional discrimination that has characterized the lives of Latinos within the United States. One particular individual-level attribute that White Americans associate with Latinos is a failure to adhere to norms of civil obedience. Latinos are commonly viewed as criminal deviants ranging from undocumented to drug dealers, rapists, and murderers. The racialization process has made these beliefs part of a "common sense" view among Whites – a standard set of beliefs that Whites cull from memory when thinking about Latina/o group members or Latina/o immigrants. It also has become the common and acceptable manner in which to express animus and resentment toward Latinos.

3.1.1 Focus Groups as a Validation of LRE

The argument we laid out in the previous chapter is that the unique history of Latinos in America has resulted in a particular set of attributes that White Americans ascribe to Latinos. Testing the accuracy of this claim requires us to examine how White Americans think about, talk about, and perceive Latinos. There is no single way of doing this and our approach is to use multiple avenues of analysis to validate the importance of LRE. The simplest first step is to see how White Americans talk about Latinos when asked. How much of their language matches our expectation about how they will describe Latinos? Are Whites likely, without prompting, to depict Latino culture as less desirable than Anglo-American culture? Do Whites see the difficulties Latinos face as resulting more from their failings or from institutional limitations?

In order to validate whether this conceptualization of LRE represents a common belief, we examine data from a series of focus groups. Obtrusive and unobtrusive interview techniques that are commonly employed to understand Whites' racial attitudes are less capable of providing a complete and in-depth view of the nature of LRE. Focus groups allow citizens to interact with other citizens in a setting that is more comfortable than a survey or experimental study. The interaction is guided by a moderator who facilitates a conversation among citizens that is more consistent with how people discuss issues of race at home or with friends (Walsh, 2003). This technique provides a more detailed and precise look at how people think without the time constraints and close-ended characteristics of more commonly used interview techniques.

Focus groups do have limitations. First, the samples are rarely generalizable to the population, making population-based surveys a valuable means to gauge more generalized opinions. Second, focus groups have been criticized as being a bit too intrusive. As Polsby (1993, 84) states, "a really skilled moderator ought to be able in two short hours to get a focus group of 'approximately 12 people' to say nearly anything." In other words, the focus group moderator might steer the content of the conversation in a manner that supports the goals of the researcher rather than allowing citizens to discuss the issue freely.

Our approach to minimize these concerns is to conduct a meta-analysis of existing focus group data from the past twenty years. Meta-analyses are common ways to summarize the results from multiple preexisting studies. They are more commonly used in quantitative studies, but our approach here mirrors that work. All of these focus groups were collected for purposes divergent from our research. This approach increases the odds that we obtain focus group data from a wider range of citizens (locations, time periods, age groups, demographic backgrounds) and ensures that we have no influence on how the moderator discussed the issue of race with focus group subjects. Of course, this approach does not completely eliminate these concerns, but it does provide an improvement relative to conducting a single set of focus groups.

To obtain our sample of focus group data, we searched *Google Scholar* for "focus group" studies conducted since 2000 where White Americans were interviewed on any topic relating to their relationship with Latinos. Using *Google Scholar* limits our results to studies published in academic journals and books. However, this limitation has the benefit of ensuring better quality data, since each of these studies underwent the scientific peer-review process. The search resulted in eight published studies on topics unrelated to how White Americans express racism-ethnicity toward Latinos. Instead, these studies focused on how White Americans understood the impact of Latinos in the development of their communities, within the workplace, and on local educational systems. All of these studies relied on nonrepresentative samples of White Americans using a variety of nonprobability sampling techniques, typically self-selective sampling via advertisements or snowball sampling through community organizations. Some of the focus groups relied on students or community leaders, while others selected participants based on their socioeconomic status (i.e., working class, middle class).

The details of these focus groups are shown in Table 3.1. The result is 25 unique focus groups consisting of more than 200 White Americans from a diverse set of backgrounds. The focus groups were conducted in both urban areas with large populations (i.e., Los Angeles or Minneapolis)

TABLE 3.1 *Focus group studies of Whites' beliefs about Latinos*

Study	Purpose	Location	Size	Participants	Themes
Millard and Chapa (2004)	Understand Latina/o incorporation in schools and new communities	Fox and Mapleville, MI	2 groups (n = 9, n = 12)	White citizens and White students (Latina/o focus group not used)	C_1, I
Culver (2004)	Investigate the rapid influx of Latinos on policing	Sedalia, Knob Noster, and Warrensburg, MO	Sedalia (n = 11); Warrensburg (n = 10); Knob Noster (n = 8)	City officials, community and church leaders	A, C_1, C_2
Paxton and Mughan (2006)	Examine beliefs about immigrants	Columbus, OH and Los Angeles	4 groups (n = 9–13)	White, fourth-generation Americans	A, C_1, C_2
Spanierman et al. (2008)	Probe Whites views toward race in schools	University of Illinois at Urbana-Champaign	n = 11	White college students	I
Fennelly (2008)	Attitudes toward Latinos in the workplace and community	Rural Minnesota community of 20,000	3 focus groups (n = 7, n = 9, n = 5)	Community leaders, working-class and middle-class Whites	A, C_1, I, C_2
Fennelly and Orfield (2008)	Investigate attitudes toward immigration	Saint Paul and Minneapolis	6 focus groups	White citizens	C_1, I
Younes and Killip (2010)	Investigate the perception of new Latina/o residents	Rural town	2 groups (n = 5, n = 6)	White citizens	A, C_1, I, C_2
Leitner (2012)	Review understanding of community	Rural Minnesota	3 groups (n = 5–10)	White citizens	A, C_1, I, C_2

Notes: Theme abbreviations: A = assimilation, C_1 = prefer Anglo-American culture, I = ignore institutional discrimination, C_2 = criminal behavior.

to small Midwestern rural communities and college towns. Some of these locations had large historic Latina/o populations. Other focus group sites had small recent influxes of Latina/o citizens or immigrants enter their communities, while others were towns with no significant Latina/o population. This provides a broad range of citizens with potentially different views and experiences with Latinos. We rely on the original authors' choices about the appropriate and representative quotes from these groups and the quotes we provide illustrate the evidence the original authors relied on in making their claims.

3.1.2 How People Express LRE

In none of the focus groups did participants express overt forms of hostility toward Latinos as a group or toward individual group members. Racism in terms of genetic inferiority or overt expressions of White supremacy did not appear in any of the focus groups, although the presence of such forms of racism was mentioned as being present in several of the communities. For instance, a woman from Michigan said:

there are prejudice people here, a shocking number that I ran across a few years ago when they were going to auction off all the Ku Klux Klan stuff. I was just shocked that you could sell hate things for profit. (Millard and Chapa, 2004, 106)

A student from Illinois expressed a similar shock at the prevalence of racism in their community, stating:

I didn't realize the things [racists incidents] were still happening today ... and my cousin ... tells me some stories and it's appalling. (Spanierman et al., 2008, 853)

Yet, a woman in college from Michigan suggested racism has become more subtle in its expression, saying, "we're not racist like our parents" (Millard and Chapa, 2004, 102). But this statement was countered by another college-age woman who believed racism was still present in her community:

most of us – will allow the Mexicans to live here and, you know, pretty much do whatever they want, just like a normal person, but I think there are some racists in our school. (Millard and Chapa, 2004, 102)

Disparaging remarks toward Latinos more often reflected their inability to assimilate and a preference for Anglo-American culture, language, and behavior. The inability of Latinos to assimilate like other immigrant groups have done was a theme in five of the eight studies. This sentiment was expressed by a man in the Minnesota Twin Cities area who said:

There's no assimilation; like our forefather – they came here to be Americans. (Fennelly and Orfield, 2008, 16)

A man in rural Minnesota made a similar statement:

My folks both came from Holland years ago, and they came through the same thing we are talking about here. When my older brothers and sisters were close to going to school, they were still talking Dutch at home. And my mother and dad decided, hey, we gotta stop this because when the kids get to school they're gonna have to talk English. Well they realized that on their own. (Leitner, 2012, 839–840)

However, another man in this focus group recognized the higher standard that is often applied to Latinos:

If you're White, you're prejudiced against the colored. Automatically. 'Cuz you're born and raised, you can't deny it … Now there's two Irish people in town, immigrants that I got to know pretty well. No problem at all. They're White. But now if they were black, or yellow or something else … I think there'd be uh, reservation there. (Leitner, 2012, 836)

A participant in a rural Midwestern focus group also made a positive comparison between today's Latino immigrants and previous immigrant groups suggesting:

they probably suffered a lot of the things that our ancestors suffered entering Ellis Island. (Younes and Killip, 2010, 18)

The inability of Latinos to assimilate was overshadowed in almost all of the focus groups by a preference for Anglo-American culture, language, and behaviors. This was discussed in seven of the eight focus groups, with almost all of the groups mentioning a strong preference for English- over Spanish-language use. For instance, a woman from the rural Midwest expressed her dislike of the Spanish language explicitly:

I mean you go into Wal-Mart and behind you is probably five, six, I don't care if it's Mexicans … they're all jibbering and jabbering and you know very well they're talkin' about ya. I mean, it sure makes you feel like it, or whatever. And it's, you know, I mean I just think it's really rude. (Leitner, 2012, 839)

Yet, in some instances, Spanish-language use was seen more as an impediment for Whites to get to know Latinos in their community. When asked what is keeping Whites and Latinos from integrating more socially, focus groups participants in Michigan blamed Spanish-language use:

[woman] If somebody's speaking Spanish ... and we don't know it, we can't, you know, if they're sitting down to coffee and conversing in Spanish.

[man] You're being mutually excluded, yup.

[woman] You're not gonna join in. So they're kind of creating their own isolation. (Fennelly, 2008, 164)

However, beyond language use there was a clear preference for Anglo-American culture and behavior. When asked what besides learning English would help Latinos, a man in Minnesota replied:

Culture, our culture. Blending with us, I think. You know, getting away from their culture more or less, what they've had. (Fennelly, 2008, 164)

Focus group participants were not shy about expressing a preference for Anglo-American culture and did not see multiculturalism as a desirable goal. A woman in Los Angeles thought that Latinos need to "adapt or change to fit our society" (Paxton and Mughan, 2006, 552). A man in Columbus, Ohio echoed the view that Latinos need to "learn our customs," while a man in Los Angeles stated that Latinos need to "accept our values if not our opinions" (Paxton and Mughan, 2006, 552).

Many of these comments seem to put the blame on Latina/o community members for failing to assimilate into US society. People view Latinos as personally responsible for their lot in America, and the negative backlash against them, rather than a result of any institutional barriers. Comments reflecting the presence or, more often the lack, of institutional racism were reflected in six of the eight studies. The denial of institutional racism or discrimination was more often expressed by the failings of Latina/o community members, but sometimes were expressed through the explicit denial of racism. A college student in Illinois represented this view with the statement:

I think the further we get away from the fifties [1950s], the more we get into the society that's grown up with a racially integrated and equal society, I think the less we'll see racism as a problem. (Spanierman et al., 2008, 15)

Moreover, many focus group participants see Latina/o community members as receiving special benefits that give them an advantage, rather than being the victim of institutional forms of racism and discrimination. A common comment across many of the focus groups was that Latinos receive special treatment and benefits. An exchange between focus group participants in Minnesota, for instance, implied that Latina/o immigrants were getting tax breaks:

[woman 1] They do get a tax break.

[man] That's another thing. They don't pay taxes for, what? Five to seven years?

[women 2] I think they changed it now. Three to five. (Fennelly, 2008, 169)

Another woman expressed a similar concern regarding social service benefits:

I think the government's going overboard with 'em. I mean, they should treat 'em all the same, whether they're Mexican or whatever ... they shouldn't be treated better than we are. (Leitner, 2012, 835)

Latinos were also viewed as having an easier time with law enforcement – a belief contrary to the decades of institutional injustice facing minorities in the United States. A government official in Missouri believed officers were more likely to let a Latino motorist off the hook during a traffic stop because officers do not want the hassle of communicating with non-English speakers:

You wonder how much is being done to use discretion to drop the situation because the officers can't understand the language so they go 'uh, okay, well here's your driver's license back, just slow down' ... they can't deal with it. (Culver, 2004, 336)

An unidentified focus group member in rural America took this view further saying "if you put on your sombrero you can get away with anything" (Younes and Killip, 2010, 15).

Focus group participants were also cynical about the ability of Latinos to obey Anglo-American norms of civil obedience. This theme appeared in five of the eight studies, although it was one of the more prominent themes in the focus group discussions in which it did appear. Latinos were often described as lawbreakers, drug dealers, and aggressive. Statements of Latino criminality were also conjoined with the belief that most Latinos are undocumented and subsequently engaged in criminal behavior. White Americans asked to express what they think when they see a hypothetical Latina/o frequently responded with comments such as "I wonder where he's from and if he's legal" to "is he here legally?" to "are they legal or not?" (Younes and Killip, 2010). Other focus groups indicated that the undocumented nature of some Latinos made it more likely for them to commit other crimes. For instance, a Missouri man claimed:

I think officers think that when they pull over Hispanics, they are going to be using different [fake] I.D.'s. (Culver, 2004, 338)

Similarly, a Minnesota woman portrayed Latinos as inherently criminal:

And when you think of Mexican, I'm sorry but I think of drug dealers. I don't want my kids around them. Something might go wrong. (Leitner, 2012, 837)

Many other focus group participants made specific claims about feeling unsafe in Latina/o neighborhoods. Although crime had officially declined in one rural Minnesota community, focus group members in this town felt crime had gotten worse over time. They also associated this perceived increase in crime with the Latina/o population:

[woman] I usually walk the south end of town, the southwest end of town, and one time we did walk up this way and came back through Shadduck and down the trail that way and we walked really fast down Main Street, just simply because of the different nationalities, the Hispanics, I'm sure and, uh, we just didn't feel safe like we do when we walk, even though it's well lit, there was just this weird feeling, I guess, because of it.

[man 1] And so you see this, what look like very moral people, just like I see 'em here in town, and yet everybody's carrying a knife? Or something like that? ... Well in the last five-ten years, it's very common that somebody gets stabbed or maybe two or three of 'em in one fight.

[man 2] There's more trouble in town too. Well, you look in the paper, you can see it in the paper. A lot of driving violations. A lot of fights and stuff like that. In other words you kind of wonder about walking downtown at night. (Fennelly, 2008, 163)

Thus, the perception that Latina/o members of the community disobey legal norms appears to be an important part of the Latina/o narrative – how White Americans understand Latina/o group members. Moreover, it is something that White Americans feel comfortable discussing in the presence of other Whites and when unprompted by researchers. These are the ideas that appear to be the most accessible in the minds of the focus group participants. Overall, these focus groups confirm many of the claims in the racialization narrative of Latinos. White Americans are open in expressing their resentment toward Latinos in the language of failed assimilation and the violation of Anglo-American norms. Although traditional forms of racism were seen mostly as a characteristic of a bygone era, disparaging comments toward Latinos were common in these focus group sessions. Even though most of these participants were likely unaware of the cultural history that got them to this place, they readily used the language steeped in the historical legacy of discrimination against Latinos. These expressions are not merely ethnocentrism or rejection of some other, but are specific to perceptions of Latinos.[1]

While the data from these focus groups provide evidence of how these Whites refer to Latinos in more or less unscripted sessions, there are clear limits to our ability to make more general claims about the attitudes White Americans hold about Latinos. The data are not representative and it is difficult to test hypotheses about how these attitudes shape other attitudes and behaviors. To test these hypotheses we need more-structured questionnaires and more-representative samples. In other words, we need surveys. The focus groups provide us with the general ideas about what we should measure to tap White Americans' LRE and we lean on these results in developing our original measure of this core concept. Therefore, we now turn toward a more systematic set of measures of LRE.

3.2 THE MEASUREMENT OF LRE

Focus groups allow scholars to see the unstructured language Whites use. In contrast, surveys allow researchers to conduct stronger tests about the structures of the underlying attitudes, make generalizable claims about the LRE and its relationship to other features of American politics, and develop experimental tests of the effects of LRE. The essential first step in conducting this type of survey research, particularly with a new concept like this, is to develop a measurement scheme grounded in the understanding of the concept, which the focus group meta-analysis allows us to do. While testing the validity of our measurement approach is vital, there is not necessarily a single definitive approach. Instead, we go at this from several angles, relying on multiple different data sources to demonstrate the validity of our measurement approach. First, we compare the patterns of responses to our measure to measures in the existing academic literature. Next, we show that LRE is a coherent belief, one that is unique from other dominant measures of anti-Latino sentiment. Following this, we demonstrate that it is not merely a measure of partisanship or cultural preferences. Finally, we show that the concept and the measures are specifically about race and ethnicity through an experimental design.

We measure LRE by constructing a multi-item scale from four survey questions that mirrors the themes of the Latina/o racialization narrative

---

[1] We also found that focus group participants spoke about economic-/job-related concerns and Latinos burdening social welfare services. However, these comments were restricted to only a few of the focus group sessions and were less frequent in those discussions than were the topics we have outlined here.

and are validated in the focus group analysis. Since LRE is a less-explicit, or more socially acceptable, form of racial and ethnic animus, we rely on the question wording strategy of the racial resentment toward African Americans scale developed by Kinder and Sanders (1996). However, each question was reworded, when appropriate, to fit the historic racialization and focus group discussions of Latinos.

These items were included on a convenience sample of college students, the 2014 and 2016 Cooperative Congressional Election Study (CCES), and several opt-in Internet panels using Survey Sampling International's (SSI) and Qualtrics' online polling platforms. Details of each sample are provided in Appendix A. The specific question wording can be found in Appendix B.

Survey respondents were asked to indicate whether they agree or disagree, and how strongly they did so, with the following statements:

. *The Irish, Italians, Jews and many other ethnic groups immigrated to the United States legally. Latinos and Hispanics should do the same without any special favors.*

. *Anti-immigration sentiment and racism have created conditions that make it difficult for Latinos and Hispanics to succeed in America.*

. *Latinos and Hispanics would be more welcome in the United States if they would try harder to learn English and adopt US customs like past immigrant groups have done.*

. *Critics of immigration and the media have overblown the number of crimes committed by Latinos and Hispanics within the United States.*

Response options range from "strongly agree," "somewhat agree," "neither agree or disagree," "somewhat disagree," or "strongly disagree."[2] The LRE scale is constructed by combining responses to these four statements into a single additive scale.[3]

These questions are a bit more subtle in their approach relative to existing measures of racism or ethnocentrism (Kinder and Sanders, 1996, 106). They do not require Whites to rate how much they dislike Latinos,

---

[2] Statements 3 and 4 are reverse coded, where more agreement indicates lower levels of LRE.

[3] The 2016 CCES included a two-item version of the index using statements 1 and 2.

declare their opposition to a Latino neighbor or in-law, or endorse biological forms of racism by stating Latinos are lazy, untrustworthy, or unintelligent. Instead, the questions differentiate between respondents who endorse the more common forms of racism-ethnicism toward Latinos from those who are more sympathetic toward Latinos in a way that reflects both the historical circumstances outlined in the previous chapter and the language prominent in the meta-analysis of the earlier focus groups. The questions resemble other forms of subtle, symbolic, or modern racial resentment toward African Americans (Henry and Sears, 2002; Kinder and Sanders, 1996; McConahay, 1986; Sears, 1988), but are more consistent with the ideas and language Whites use when making disparaging remarks toward Latinos.[4]

How does this measure differ from other available measures of Whites' negative attitudes about Latinos? The American National Election Study (ANES) is a large, national survey that is conducted, generally, every two years. Since 1980, the ANES has included "feeling thermometers" about groups and individuals, including Latinos. These questions ask respondents to rate Latinos on a 0–100 scale, where higher values are warmer assessments of Latinos. In general, anything below 50 is seen as a "cold" response. Since 1994, the ANES has asked respondents about their acceptance of various stereotypes of Latinos, including whether they are lazy, untrustworthy, and unintelligent. The General Social Survey (GSS) is a similar national survey designed to explore a large number of social attitudes of Americans. Starting in 1990, the GSS asked respondents if they would be supportive of a relative marrying a Hispanic. Each of these questions has been used to test general sentiment toward Latinos. Figure 3.1 presents the percentage of White respondents who express a negative attitude for each of the measures.[5]

It appears that White Americans are more willing to provide a negative response to the LRE questions than to other commonly used questions

---

[4] Although the LRE and racial resentment questions appear similar, the slight differences in content are important. For instance, whereas White Americans criticize African Americans for failing to work hard to earn their lot in life in the way past immigrant groups have done, White Americans comment that Latinos fail to assimilate in the way that past immigrant groups have done.

[5] For the feeling thermometer, we coded any response below the midpoint of the scale (50) as feeling "cold" toward Latinos. For the stereotype measures, we code any endorsement that Latinos are lazy, unintelligent, or untrustworthy regardless of the strength of that belief as negative. For the marriage question, any opposition is coded as a negative response regardless of the strength of that belief.

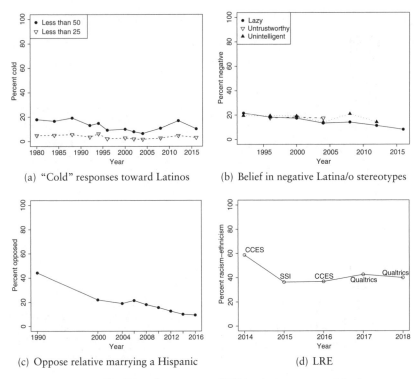

(a) "Cold" responses toward Latinos

(b) Belief in negative Latina/o stereotypes

(c) Oppose relative marrying a Hispanic

(d) LRE

FIGURE 3.1 Traditional measures of White Animus toward Latinos

aimed at measuring racism toward Latinos. As Figure 3.1 shows, fewer than 20 percent of White Americans are willing to provide a "cold" response when asked how they feel toward Hispanics and Latinos in the ANES. We see a similar pattern in the percentage of White Americans willing to provide a negative response to the ANES group stereotype measures typically used as an indicator of old-fashioned racism. Negative responses to these questions also show a decline over time, which is most evident in the GSS question about a relative marrying a Hispanic. Whereas more than 40 percent of White Americans were opposed to a relative marrying a Hispanic in 1990, less than 20 percent of White Americans say they are opposed to this in the more recent administrations of the survey.

Overall, few White Americans explicitly endorse these explicit and better-recognized forms of racism toward Latinos. For each of the surveys, approximately 20 percent endorse the negative, racist belief. Moreover, openly negative beliefs regarding Latinos has declined over time. In contrast, between 37 percent (2016 CCES) and 58 percent (2014 CCES) of

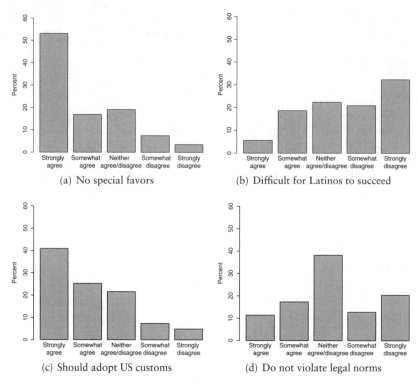

(a) No special favors

(b) Difficult for Latinos to succeed

(c) Should adopt US customs

(d) Do not violate legal norms

FIGURE 3.2 Whites' racism-ethnicism toward Latinos, 2014 CCES

White Americans demonstrate having some LRE (on average agreeing with statements that are part of the Latina/o racialization narrative). This is consistent with the argument that White Americans are more comfortable expressing these views regarding Latinos.

Figure 3.2 shows the distribution of responses to the LRE questions among respondents in the 2014 CCES. We examine this sample because it is well-matched to the US population and it contains all four questions. A majority of respondents endorse the statement that other immigrant groups have succeeded without special favors and that Latinos should do the same. A similar number of respondents supported the statement that Latinos should try harder to learn English and adopt US customs. Almost half of the respondents disagree that racism has made it difficult for Latinos to succeed in America and more White Americans disagree than agree with the statement that Latina/o criminality has been overblown.

3.2.1 Is LRE a Coherent Belief?

It would be possible for people to answer the LRE questions as individual complaints – agreeing with some statements and disagreeing with others in a haphazard manner. For example, people who respond that Latinos should not receive any special favors could be expressing their support for self-determination and equality. Failing to endorse the statement that Latina/o criminality is overblown could reflect a high need for security and safety. In this scenario, responses to each statement would reflect a unique belief that does not correspond to the concept we define as LRE. In other words, the questions would not belong together as a group. In contrast, if the racialization of Latinos has led to these statements being a common form of LRE, then we should observe that responses to these questions reflect a single underlying construct where responses to each questions coalesce around a single coherent belief that we call LRE.

We first test for internal consistency by examining Spearman's rank correlation coefficient, ρ. Spearman's rank correlation coefficient, ρ, is a nonparametric measure of rank correlation that assesses the association between responses to each of the LRE statements. Spearman's ρ ranges from -1 to 1. A value of -1 indicates a perfect negative monotonic relationship, 0 indicates no monotonic relationship, and 1 indicates a perfect positive monotonic relationship. The Spearman ρ coefficients indicate a modest to strong relationship among responses to the LRE statements. The highest correlations appear in the 2015 SSI sample, ranging from 0.48 (statements 1 and 2) to 0.70 (statements 1 and 4). The lowest correlations appear in the 2018 Qualtrics study, where the ρ correlation ranges from 0.23 (statements 1 and 2) to 0.55 (statements 1 and 3).

Cronbach's α provides an alternative approach to assess the internal consistency of responses to the LRE scale. This statistic is often reported as a measure of a scale's reliability and ranges from 0 to 1. Values of the statistic around 0.70 or higher are usually heralded as an indicator of an internally consistent scale. The scale shows a modest to strong degree of internal consistency in each of the samples, with α ranging from 0.56 in the two-item version contained in the 2016 CCES to 0.83 in the SSI study. In the 2014 CCES, our most representative sample, Cronbach's $\alpha = 0.78$.

Table 3.2 provides further evidence that responses to the LRE statements measure a single latent belief about race and ethnicity rather than representing discrete beliefs about undesirable behaviors. If responses to the statements reflected displeasure at various behaviors (e.g., not speaking English, a concern over crime, valuing equality), then we would likely observe responses to these statements representing multiple beliefs, that

TABLE 3.2 *LRE scale metrics*

	Student 2014	CCES 2014	SSI 2015	CCES 2016	Qualtrics 1 2017	Qualtrics 2 2018
Descriptive						
Mean	2.78	3.66	2.92	3.51	3.38	3.22
Standard deviation	(0.86)	(0.94)	(1.13)	(1.04)	(0.85)	(0.80)
Principal components analysis						
Eigenvalue	2.17	2.67	2.98	1.48	2.10	2.13
(% variance explained)	54	67	72	74	52	53
Confirmatory factor analysis						
CFI	1.00	0.99	1.00	1.00	1.00	1.00
TLI	1.02	0.98	0.98	1.00	1.00	1.01
SRMR	0.01	0.01	0.00	0.00	0.01	0.00
RMSE	0.00	0.05	0.02	0.00	0.00	0.00
N	141	735	333	724	812	1,041

The LRE scale ranges from 1 to 5, with higher values indicating greater resentment toward Latinos. The principal components analysis uses the polychoric correlation matrix due to the ordinal nature of the response options for each item. The confirmatory factor analysis tests the hypothesis that the scale measures a single latent belief. White respondents only.

is, multiple latent factors. However, if we observe a single latent factor, then it is likely that responses to these statements represent a single belief rooted in the common racial-ethnic component across statements – LRE. A principal components analysis reveals a single common element to these questions, which is consistent with the argument that responses to these statements capture a single belief relating to LRE. Finally, we subjected the LRE scale to a confirmatory factor analysis to test the hypothesis that responses to these statements represent a single belief. In each of the samples, all of the model-fit statistics indicate that responses to the statements are a good fit for our model.[6] White Americans appear to be responding to these LRE statements as if they are part of a single, coherent belief system.

3.2.2 Is It a Unique Form of Racism-Ethnicism?

Although we have established that the LRE scale measures a single belief, we still have not confirmed that this belief is a unique form of

---

[6] In general, a comparative fit index (CFI) above 0.9, a Tucker–Lewis index (TLI) above 0.95, a root-mean-square error (RMSE) below 0.08, and a standardized root-mean-square residual (SRMR) less than 0.08 indicate a well-fitting model.

racism-ethnicism targeting Latinos that is distinct from other forms of anti-Latino sentiment. In particular, there are two other beliefs that are prominent in the academic literature on the topic. The first is what we refer to as old-fashioned racism. Old-fashioned racism connects to the belief of qualitative differences between races and ethnicities, often tied to supposed biological differences. The belief in these differences manifests as endorsement of negative stereotypes of non-Anglo groups. For LRE to be a meaningful concept, it cannot simply be a manifestation of these more general old-fashioned racist notions of Latinos. If Whites' LRE is a reflection of the same belief system that structures these older, more well-known forms of racial animus, then the traditional measures used in the sources like the ANES and GSS capture the important concept and our measure provides no additional power in explaining modern American politics.

The second belief that is widely used in the academic literature to measure negative attitudes about racial and ethnic groups is ethnocentrism. This is defined as a generalized hostility toward out-groups (Kinder and Kam, 2010). Ethnocentrism has powerful effects on opinions about a wide array of policies, including responses to terrorism, immigration, welfare, and gay marriage (Kinder and Kam, 2010). It is different from both old-fashioned racism and our concept of LRE in that it is not targeted at specific groups. It is a more general attitude about "others." It is plausible that our measure of LRE is simply a downstream consequence of this general attitude about other groups. We need to demonstrate that our concept and measure, grounded in and specific to the cultural identity of Latinos in America, are distinct from this more general attitude.

An exploratory factor analysis is one way to test whether responses to the LRE statements are related to the same beliefs typically labeled as old-fashioned racism and ethnocentrism. We compare responses to the LRE statements to traditional measures of Latina/o stereotypes because the stereotype measures are the most commonly used indicators of old-fashioned racism toward Latinos (Branton et al., 2011; Burns and Gimpel, 2000). These same items have been used to construct measures of ethnocentrism by combing beliefs about multiple out-groups relative to beliefs about Whites (Kinder and Kam, 2010; Valentino et al., 2013). If the LRE scale represents the same belief system as either old-fashioned racial stereotypes (OFRSs) or ethnocentrism, then the exploratory factor analysis should uncover a single latent factor, that is, questions regarding LRE would be related to the same latent belief as questions regarding OFRSs. If the LRE scale represents a belief system that differs from these more traditional forms of racism and ethnic hostility, then the exploratory factor analysis should uncover multiple latent factors, that is, the factor loadings for the LRE statements would relate to a separate latent belief than the stereotype or ethnocentrism questions.

We have two data sources that contain the necessary questions for this analysis. Our student sample has the advantage of being flexible and cheap. We can add as many questions as we want without worrying about the costs. It is useful for exploratory work, but does not generalize to the national population. The 2016 CCES, in contrast, is matched to the US population and does allow for these generalizations to that population. The trade-off is with the number of questions. The student sample contained measures asking if Hispanic Americans (as well as White Americans, Black Americans, Asian Americans, and Muslim Americans) are hardworking, intelligent, and trustworthy. The 2016 CCES asked respondents if Hispanic Americans, White Americans, and Muslim Americans are intelligent and trustworthy.

Table 3.3 shows an exploratory factor analysis of the LRE items and OFRS questions. The factor analysis implements an oblique rotation

TABLE 3.3 *Factor analysis of LRE, OFRSs, and ethnocentrism*

	Student sample		2016 CCES	
	OFRS	LRE	OFRS	LRE
LRE				
Should immigrate legally, no special favors	0.11	0.72	0.03	0.88
Difficult for Latinos to succeed	−0.06	0.76	−0.04	0.83
Should adopt US customs	0.09	0.71	–	–
Do not violate legal norms	−0.10	0.74	–	–
OFRSs				
Latinos untrustworthy	0.87	−0.02	0.88	−0.08
Latinos unintelligent	0.92	−0.09	0.92	0.05
Latinos lazy	0.86	0.00	–	–
Ethnocentrism				
Out-groups untrustworthy	0.89	0.06	0.93	−0.14
Out-groups unintelligent	0.92	−0.03	0.85	0.12
Out-groups lazy	0.89	−0.07	–	–
Eigenvalue	4.84	2.20	3.33	1.72

Columns are factor loadings from an exploratory factor analysis using an oblique rotation and the polychoric correlation matrix for ordinal response items. N = 141 in the student sample. N = 687 in the 2016 CCES. White respondents only.

since LRE is likely to be correlated with old-fashioned racism and ethnocentrism. In both samples, responses to the LRE statements relate to a separate factor than the measures of OFRS and the measures of ethnocentrism. The OFRS measures and the combined measures of negative beliefs toward out-groups relate to the first factor that we label as OFRS. Responses to the LRE statements relate to the second factor that we label as LRE. The correlation among factors in the student sample (0.05) and 2016 CCES (0.21) is surprisingly small and inconsistent in direction. The evidence here points to LRE representing a separate belief system than what is commonly referred to as old-fashioned racism or ethnocentrism.[7]

3.2.3 Is LRE a Measure of Partisan Principles or Cultural Preferences?

It is also possible that LRE is not a distinct belief system, but instead is a proxy for partisan principles or cultural preferences. Partisan identification and ideology, for instance, have traditionally been used to explain racial policy preferences and have been argued to be a better explanation for racial attitudes than modern and symbolic forms of racism (Sniderman and Carmines, 1997; Sniderman and Tetlock, 1986; Sniderman et al., 2000).

What we are defining as LRE may also merely be a reflection of people's preference for Anglo-American culture and values. Indeed, support for statements about adopting English and American culture or assimilating into American society may reflect preferences about culture and behaviors rather than concerns about race, that is, a preference representing in-group favoritism rather than out-group hostility.

In order to test these concerns, we rely on a series of confirmatory factor analysis models (see Tarman and Sears, 2005). These models test whether the data provide a better fit to the partisan principles or cultural preferences models relative to the LRE model. This method also provides an additional means to test whether the LRE model is a better fit to the data relative to an old-fashioned racism model.

---

[7] There is another possible concept that might be connected to Whites' animus toward Latinos. System justification theory holds that Whites' concerns about Latinos may be rooted in a desire to maintain the status quo. Similarly, if Whites hold the belief that the existing system is a meritocracy, then animus toward Latinos may stem from the perception that Latinos are not suffering from discrimination, but are not succeeding despite the meritocratic system. Unfortunately, none of our data has a direct measure of belief in system justification theory.

The LRE model asserts that LRE represents a distinct latent belief system from old-fashioned racism, partisan principles, and cultural preferences. This model is tested by specifying four different beliefs represented by four separate factors in the model (i.e., LRE, OFRS, partisan principles, and cultural preferences).

The common racism model tests the assertion that LRE reflects the same belief system as OFRSs. This model is tested by specifying a three-factor model (i.e., OFRS, partisan principles, and cultural preferences) where OFRS and responses to the LRE statements are related to a common belief system or factor.

The partisan principles model tests the argument that LRE is an expression of partisan identity and ideological conservatism.[8] According to this model, LRE can be explained by these partisan principles rather than representing a distinct belief about race. This model is tested using a three-factor model (i.e., partisan principles, old-fashioned racism, and cultural preferences) where partisanship and ideology are related to the same belief or factor as responses to the LRE statements. In other words, it removes partisan principles as a separate belief system from LRE.

The cultural preferences model tests if LRE is an expression of cultural preferences that favor Anglo-American traditions.[9] According to this model, people are not expressing racism when responding to the LRE statements. Instead, they are expressing their preferences toward preferred behaviors. This model is tested using a three-factor model (i.e., partisan principles, old-fashioned racism, and cultural preferences) where cultural preferences are related to the same belief as responses to the LRE statements.

For each of the models, we restrict the number of observed indicators of each latent belief system to an equal number in order to avoid biasing the analysis in favor of any single model. The model fit-statistics for each of these models is shown in Table 3.4. The only model to clearly pass the thresholds of acceptability (see fn 4) is the four-factor LRE model. The partisan principles model comes close, passing acceptability on two of the four indicators of a well-fitting model. However, all of the model-fit

---

[8] For this analysis, we operationalize these concepts using the seven-point partisan identification and ideological self-placement scales found in ANES.

[9] We specifically ask respondents whether they agree or disagree with several statements, asking (1) if Anglo-American values are preferable to those of other countries and (2) if people from other countries would be better off if they followed Anglo-American culture and traditions.

TABLE 3.4 *Comparison of LRE, principled conservatism, OFRSs, and a preference for Anglo-American culture*

Model tested	χ^2	CFI	TLI	SRMR	RMSE
LRE	40.42*	0.98	0.96	0.03	0.05
Partisan principles	98.91*	0.94	0.91	0.05	0.08
OFRSs	379.22*	0.76	0.61	0.11	0.18
Cultural preferences	308.21*	0.84	0.75	0.08	0.14

*$p < 0.05$. Test statistics from confirmatory factor analysis. All variances of latent factors are constrained to 1. Data from 2016 CCES. White respondents only.

statistics indicate that the LRE model is a better fit to the data than is the partisan principles model. The model-fit indicators also suggest that the LRE model is a better fit to the data than are the cultural preferences or OFRS models. Neither of the latter models comes close to passing the conventional thresholds of acceptable model fit. Figure 3.3 presents a graphical representation of the four-factor LRE model, which is the model that best fits the data.

Since there is likely to be variability across samples, we tested the partisan principles model within the four samples that included measures of partisan principles. These results are shown in Table 3.5. Without the inclusion of the cultural preference and OFRS latent factors (these variables were not included in all of the surveys), the partisan principles model performs poorly, passing only the SRMR threshold for acceptable fit.

3.2.4 Is LRE about Race-Ethnicity?

The analysis points to LRE as representing a distinct and internally coherent belief system, but it still has not firmly established that responses to the LRE statements reflect anti-Latina/o animus. We employed a survey experiment within the 2015 SSI study in order to tease out the role that anti-Latina/o animus plays in how LRM relates to racial policy preferences. The experimental design exposed respondents to a hypothetical Mexican or Irish immigrant who has either assimilated into Anglo-American culture and norms or continues to adhere to the culture and norms of their country of origin. This resulted in four treatment conditions that allow us to tease out the role of race from desired or undesired behaviors mentioned in the LRE statements: Mexican assimilated, Mexican unassimilated, Irish assimilated, and Irish unassimilated. Respondents were asked,

TABLE 3.5 *Multiple tests of the partisan principles model*

Data tested	χ^2	CFI	TLI	SRMR	RMSE
2018 Qualtrics	242.80*	0.80	0.67	0.07	0.16
2017 Qualtrics	151.24*	0.86	0.76	0.07	0.14
2015 SSI	684.82*	0.72	0.64	0.09	0.17
2014 CCES	206.41*	0.85	0.75	0.06	0.19

*$p < 0.05$. Test statistics from confirmatory factor analysis. All variances of latent factors are constrained to 1. White respondents only.

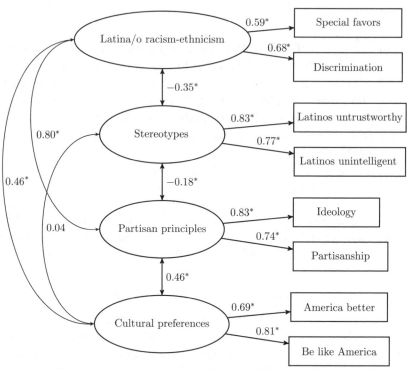

FIGURE 3.3 Four-factor model of LRE, negative Latina/o stereotypes, partisan principles, and cultural preferences, 2016 CCES

[Jack Murphy/Jose Garcia] recently immigrated to the United States from [Ireland/Mexico]. He mostly speaks [English/(Gaelic/Spanish)], lives in a [suburban/(Irish/Mexican)] neighborhood, and works in a small market that sells [American/(European/Hispanic)] products. Some people have praised him for adapting to the US way of life, but he says he is just proud [to become a US citizen/(of his Irish heritage/of his Mexican heritage)]. To what extent do you think immigrants like [Jack/Jose] should be allowed to live and work in the United States?

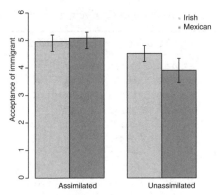

FIGURE 3.4 Acceptance of Irish or Mexican immigrants by assimilation level

Response options on the outcome variable were "strongly in favor," "favor," "slightly favor," "slightly oppose," "oppose," and "strongly oppose."

Figure 3.4 displays the means in each condition. Respondents were supportive of both the Irish and Mexican immigrant in the assimilation conditions and less supportive of the immigrants in the low-assimilation conditions. Specifically, a one-way analysis of variance shows that there is no difference in support for the assimilated Irish immigrant (mean = 4.9) and the assimilated Mexican immigrant (mean = 5.0), $F_{df=(1,175)} = 0.31, p < 0.58$. However, there is a difference between the assimilated immigrant versus the unassimilated immigrant for both races. Support is higher for the assimilated Irish immigrant than the low-assimilated Irish immigrant, $F_{df=(1,168)} = 4.47, p < 0.03$. Support is also higher for the assimilated Mexican immigrant than for the low-assimilated Mexican immigrant, $F_{df=(1,152)} = 10.14, p < 0.01$. Finally, race and assimilation have a compounding effect on support for the immigrant. Respondents were more supportive of the low-assimilated Irish immigrant (mean = 4.5) than for the low-assimilated Mexican immigrant (mean = 3.9), $F_{df=(1,147)} = 5.78, p < 0.01$. Thus, Mexican immigrants are penalized more for failing to assimilate than is a White-European Irish immigrant. These findings are also consistent with a similar experiment showing that race-ethnicity, rather than cultural behaviors, are related to Whites' opposition to immigration (Hartman et al., 2014).

Next, we estimated a series of models on support for the specific immigrant to test whether LRE has a differential effect on the treatments

TABLE 3.6 *Disentangling principles from prejudice*

	Model 1		Model 2		Model 3	
LRE	−0.12	(0.11)	−0.41*	(0.10)	−0.14	(0.13)
Race (Mexican = 1)	1.08*	(0.38)	−0.34*	(0.15)	1.07*	(0.39)
Assimilation	−0.63*	(0.15)	−0.85*	(0.42)	−0.74	(0.42)
Liberal	0.52*	(0.24)	0.57*	(0.23)	0.52*	(0.24)
Conservative	−0.38	(0.25)	−0.51*	(0.25)	−0.38	(0.25)
Partisanship	0.12	(0.17)	0.18	(0.17)	0.12	(0.17)
Moral traditionalism	−0.20*	(0.10)	−0.21*	(0.10)	−0.20*	(0.10)
Sex	−0.07	(0.14)	−0.09	(0.14)	−0.07	(0.14)
Age	−0.05	(0.08)	−0.01	(0.09)	−0.05	(0.08)
Education	0.12	(0.07)	0.12	(0.08)	0.12	(0.08)
Race × LRE	−0.48*	(0.13)			−0.48*	(0.14)
Assimilation × LRE			0.08	(0.15)	0.04	(0.14)
Constant	5.51*	(0.54)	6.20*	(0.53)	5.56*	(0.54)
R^2	0.35		0.32		0.35	
N	322		322		322	

*$p < 0.05$. Coefficients are regression estimates with robust standard errors in parentheses. Dependent variable is support for the immigrant among White Americans. *Source:* Data from 2015 SSI study.

using ordinary least squares regression. If partisan principles or cultural preferences explain the role that LRE has on racial policy preferences, then the race of the immigrant should not matter in how LRE impacts support for the immigrant. However, if LRE has a stronger relationship with support for the immigrant when the immigrant is Mexican relative to when the immigrant is Irish, then there is evidence that LRE is race-laden.

Model 1 in Table 3.6 tests these expectations with an interaction between the LRE scale and a race dummy variable indicating if the immigrant was Irish (0) or Mexican (1). The coefficient on the interaction is negative and statistically significant, indicating that support for the immigrant declined for the Mexican immigrant among respondents exhibiting higher levels of racism-ethnicity toward Latinos. In contrast, the LRE coefficient represents the effect of LRE on support for the immigrant when the immigrant is Irish. The coefficient is statistically indistinguishable from zero, indicating that LRE has no discernable effect on support for the Irish immigrant. These findings provide evidence that LRE is race-laden and specific to Latinos. It has no effect on the Irish immigrant, but decreases support for the Mexican immigrant.

If LRE was primarily capturing people's opposition to failed assimilation, rather than race, we would expect that the effect of LRE on opposition toward the immigrant would increase when the immigrant in the vignette fails to assimilate. We test this expectation with an interaction between the LRE scale and an assimilation variable (0 = high assimilation, 1 = low assimilation). This is shown in model 2. The interaction is statistically insignificant, suggesting that support for the statements regarding failed Latina/o assimilation and norm violation represent opposition to Latina/o race and ethnicity more so than opposition to concerns about assimilation. This does not mean that White Americans are not concerned about assimilation and preserving traditional Anglo-American values. The coefficient on the assimilation variable represents the effect of the assimilation treatment when LRE is zero. It shows that even among people with no racism-ethnicism toward Latinos, an immigrant who fails to assimilate will be less supported than an immigrant who does assimilate. White Americans care about assimilation, but that is not reflected in their support of statements on the LRE scale. Model 3 shows that these results are robust when both interaction terms are included in the same model. Again, we find that assimilation has no effect on the relationship between LRE and support for the immigrant. Instead, the LRE scale is shown to be race-laden.

In order to illustrate these relationships, we reestimated model 1 in Table 3.6 using an ordered logistic regression. We then used those estimates to graph the predicted probability of opposing each immigrant. These predicted probability estimates are shown in Figure 3.5. At low levels of LRE, opposition to each immigrant is low. As LRE increases, opposition for the Irish immigrant, regardless of the level assimilation, remains steady. In contrast, as LRE increases, opposition for the Mexican immigrant increases. This is for both the assimilated and unassimilated Mexican immigrant, with the most opposition for the unassimilated Mexican immigrant among respondents high on the LRE scale.

3.3 CONCLUSION

This chapter began by outlining the idea of a concept we labeled LRE. We started with little evidence beyond a theory that there existed a unique expression in how White Americans routinely express antipathy toward Latinos. A meta-analysis of focus group participants allowed us to dive deeper into how White Americans think and feel about Latinos in a setting that is more aligned with everyday social interactions among friends, family, and community members. The focus groups provided a glimpse of LRE that simply could not be captured with the superficiality of survey

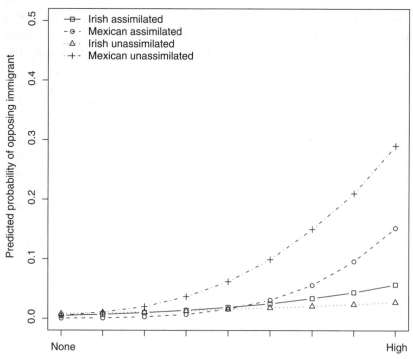

FIGURE 3.5 Opposition to Irish or Mexican immigrants across levels of LRE

and experimental designs. The analysis showed important heterogeneity in how citizens discuss Latinos. For instance, some of the participants believe Latinos were getting ahead with special favors, while others were able to recognize how institutional forms of discrimination made it diffi-cult for Latinos to obtain the success that past White immigrant groups have achieved. In other instances, focus group participants chastised Lati-nos for not wanting to assimilate into Anglo-American culture, while oth-ers were aware that assimilation did not come quick for past immigrant groups either.

The focus groups were important in showing how specific beliefs about Latinos fit together to structure a coherent belief system regarding the inability of Latinos to assimilate and abide by Anglo-American norms. A common theme among focus group participants centered around Latino agency. Among participants we suspect harbor LRE, Latinos were blamed for failing to assimilate as quickly as past immigrant groups have done. These focus group participants also placed responsibility for this fail-ure on Latinos rather than any institutional or discriminatory factors, that is, Latinos themselves do not want to assimilate even if given the opportunity. This individual-level blame was extended toward their use of the Spanish language, which was deemed "rude" and a key factor keeping Latinos from being accepted into Anglo-American society. Latinos were also blamed for their lot in life and viewed as receiving special benefits. Surprisingly, Latinos were argued to be more privileged in the United States than White Americans. Finally, the agency argument also extended into Latino criminality. Latinos were labeled as troublemakers – a trait attributed to their culture and upbringing rather than something constructed by the media or politicians.

The end result of the focus group analysis was a rich and meaningful portrait of how White Americans express animus toward Latinos in the language of failed assimilation and failure to adhere to Anglo-American norms. Just as important is what focus group participants did not say. They did not express resentment toward Latinos in the same way they express animus toward African Americans. The failure of Latinos to become model citizens is a result of their desire to remain "Mexicans" or citizens of another country rather than a lack of work ethic. Focus group participants did not express resentment toward Latinos in the language of "individualism" and "self-reliance," as White Americans commonly do when thinking about African Americans (Kinder and Sanders, 1996). When focus group participants did talk about Latinos in the workforce, Latinos were more often described as "hardworking" (Fennelly and Orfield, 2008; Leitner, 2012). This is in direct contrast to the complaints some White Americans have levied against African Americans as being lazy and unwilling to work (Gilens, 2000). Another difference appears in how Whites discuss Latina/o criminality. Latina/o criminality is discussed more in terms of Latinos disobeying laws rather than being biologically predisposed to being physically aggressive and violent in the same manner as African Americans are often described (Entman and Rojecki, 2000; Peffley et al., 1997). Overall, the focus groups corroborate the historic racialization of Latinos and provide a way forward into further investigations of how LRE is expressed as well as its political consequences.

We were able to leverage the insight of the focus groups to create an LRE scale that mirrors the main themes of how citizens express antipathy toward Latinos. The scale exhibits an adequate degree of internal consistency and responses to each statement are related to a single latent belief system rather than representing ad hoc responses to individual behaviors. The statements representing LRE exhibit various distributive properties of a valid scale. Finding that LRE relates to opposition of a Hispanic but not a White immigrant provides an important piece of construct validity for our measure. We further were able to demonstrate that this latent belief system we have defined as LRE is distinct from alternative forms of racism, partisan principles, and preferences about culture. This does not mean that LRE is not related to these other beliefs. We found a strong correlation between LRE and partisan principles despite these being distinct sets of beliefs. But we did not find evidence that responses to the LRE statements are merely a proxy for conservative ideology.

We recognize that some scholars will prefer a more direct and simple measure of LRE that is not diluted by any mention of undesirable behaviors, ideological preferences, and avoids any indication that respondents might make an inferential leap about public policy when answering the LRE questions.[10] Certain research questions might require such refined and specific measures and we certainly do not discourage their use. However, such attempts would likely fail to capture the complexity of how White Americans express their racism-ethnicism toward Latinos and attenuate the extent of LRE. Attempting to understand how LRE shapes people's political preferences requires examining the various ways this belief is expressed that many of the current measures of related concepts fail to capture. We believe that we can move forward in a manner that illustrates a more complete picture of the role of LRE in American politics.

Our approach provides an alternative to the more common methodology of asking direct questions about how White Americans "feel" toward Latinos, view Latina/o work ethic, or would feel comfortable with a Latina/o in-law. The latter approaches capture some people's dislike toward Latinos – but only if (1) respondents are willing to express a view likely to be construed as racist and (2) these questions capture the way White Americans think about Latina/o race and ethnicity. We have provided evidence in this chapter that should lead readers to have some reservations that either of these propositions are true.

Much like the modern racism, symbolic racism, and racial resentment scales, our measure of LRE provides a way to measure how Whites commonly discuss their animus toward Latinos. The value added by the LRE

---

[10] We conducted multiple discriminant validity tests that indicate the LRE scale does not relate to theoretically unrelated constructs (abortion, gay marriage, the Medicare Accountability and Cost Reform Act, requiring fuel-efficient cars, and the Congressional Education Reform Act). This provides additional evidence that LRE is not simply a proxy for ideology or a similar set of guiding principles.

scale to previous work on modern racism, symbolic racism, and racial resentment is that it explicitly takes into consideration how White Americans think about Latinos and express antipathy toward Latinos in a way that is distinct from African Americans and other minority groups from which the social distance and stereotype measures derive. We also differ in that we do not believe this is a necessarily covert means of expressing animus. Instead, it is simply a more socially acceptable means to discuss it.

The conceptualization and measurement of racial and ethnic attitudes is difficult and controversial (Feldman and Huddy, 2005; Sears et al., 2000b; Sniderman and Tetlock, 1986; Wilson and Davis, 2011). We suspect that many of these controversies will follow us in this endeavor to create a measure of LRE. However, the need to document this distinct form of racism-ethnicism and its political consequences requires moving forward. Fortunately, past scholarship provides an important map to navigate through many of the criticisms levied on existing measures of racism and ethnicism. We used this critical literature as a guide to engage with the most visible threats to the scale's validity and show that the scale holds up fairly well to the most common critiques. Perhaps the most important finding from this chapter is that responses to the LRE scale are indeed race-laden. People respond to the LRE questions in a manner consistent with their beliefs about race more so than their beliefs about desired behaviors or partisan principles. Given this key finding, we move ahead to the next chapter and began to examine the predictive validity of the LRE measure.

4

Why White America Opposes Immigration

[C]itizenship is not limited by birth or background. America, at its best, is a welcoming society. We welcome not only immigrants themselves but the many gifts they bring and the values they live by ... Immigration is not a problem to be solved. It is a sign of a confident and successful nation. And people who seek to make America their home should be met in that spirit by representatives of our government. New arrivals should be greeted not with suspicion and resentment but with openness and courtesy.
President George W. Bush, Remarks at Ellis Island, July 10, 2001

As he campaigned for the presidency, George W. Bush often spoke of forging closer ties to Mexico and, as the opening quote demonstrates, the importance of reforming US immigration policy in a manner more welcoming to people who desire to become US citizens. On September 4, 2001, President Bush held an historic summit in Washington, DC with the president of Mexico, Vicente Fox. Presidents Bush and Fox had agreed to form a Joint Border Development Planning Commission to patrol and manage the 2,000-mile border between Mexico and the United States. They were also working on proposals to expand free-trade agreements, which included allowing Mexican trucks unlimited access on US roadways. At the forefront of this summit was a reformation of US immigration laws. Both leaders desired an expansion of temporary guest worker programs and appeared amenable to granting citizenship to undocumented Mexicans already living within the United States.

The attacks on September 11, 2001 altered the course of the country's immigration debate. The revelation that several of the hijackers were living within the United States after their visas expired refocused immigration reform on a more coordinated effort among federal agencies to review and monitor visa applicants and immigrants living within the country. Immigration became viewed as a national security concern, with efforts to enact more restrictions on immigration framed in terms of preventing future terrorist attacks against the United States. The result was the Homeland Security Act of 2002 that integrated Immigration and Customs Enforcement, US Customs and Border Patrol, the US Citizenship and Immigration Services, the US Coast Guard, and the US Secret Service into a single federal agency. The post-9/11 reaction also led to significant changes in the implementation of immigration policy. Resources were poured into securing the US borders. Local law enforcement agencies became surrogate immigration enforcement officers through programs such as Secure Communities. These changes coincided with an increase in the deportation of undocumented immigrants (particularly criminal deportations). The projected growth in immigration enforcement also led private prison companies to expand their business into operating for-profit immigration detention centers, providing a corporate sponsor to more restrictive immigration laws and enforcement.

This context provided an environment for anti-immigrant rhetoric that was decisively anti-Latina/o. Lou Dobbs, Glenn Beck, Bill O'Reilly, Brit Hume, and Sean Hannity fed cable news viewers with stories of an immigrant invasion from Mexico and other Latin American countries. As noted by the media watchdog group, Media Matters for America, these commentators promoted a "series of myths" that spread "resentment and fear, seemingly geared toward creating anti-immigrant hysteria" (Waldman et al., 2008). Latinos became a stigmatized group associated with undocumented immigration, which shifted the immigration debate away from national security concerns and toward the traditional racialization of Latinos' narrative. Immigration news became a debate over Latina/o assimilation, agency, criminality, and the degeneration of Latina/o culture (Branton and Dunaway, 2008, 2009a; Haynes et al., 2016).

State and federal elections in 2004 saw the rise of candidates for public offices opposed to immigration. For instance, Jim Gilchrist, cofounder of the anti-immigrant vigilante group the Minuteman Project, ran for California's 48th Congressional District. Kris Kobach, a lawyer for the anti-immigrant Federation for American Immigration Reform ran for Kansas's 3rd Congressional District. Not all of these candidates were successful, but they managed to increase the salience of immigration and put pressure on other political candidates to alter their public position on the issue. Whereas President Bush had previously considered a pathway to citizenship for undocumented citizens living within the United States as part of his partnership with Mexico, he openly rejected such proposals during the 2004 election. He also began to support hardline immigration policies, such as ending the long-standing policy to "catch and release" undocumented immigrants. President Bush's public positions on immigration, like many other public officials, began to toughen as anti-immigrant sentiment heightened among the public.

On December 16, 2005, the US House of Representatives passed the Border Protection, Antiterrorism, and Illegal Immigration Control Act (H.R.4437). The bill required new border fencing, required local law enforcement to take custody of undocumented immigrants, imposed legal and financial penalties on undocumented immigrants and people who help undocumented immigrants, and set up a Fraudulent Document Center within the Department of Homeland Security. The Senate, more insulated from the whims of the public's newfound hysteria over immigration, favored a more balanced solution to immigration that included tougher border security, along with reforms that would allow immigrants to live and work within the United States. Since the House of Representatives' version of the bill did not address many of the work visa reforms favored by the Senate, H.R.4437 eventually failed to pass a Senate vote. Although H.R.4437 was never enacted into law, its passage in the House sparked large organized protest marches across forty-three states, with major protest events in Los Angles, Phoenix, Houston, Dallas, and Chicago. The protests energized both sides of the debate, making additional efforts at reform difficult.

Other efforts at immigration reform faced similar outcomes. On May 25, 2006, the Senate passed the Comprehensive Immigration Reform Act of 2006 (S.2611). The bill established a new guest worker program and a path to citizenship, while increasing border security and tougher oversight of employers who attempted to hire undocumented workers. However, the House of Representatives was unable to reconcile S.2611 with its version of the bill that favored tougher restrictions on immigration and no pathway to citizenship. These differences led to the failure of both bills at the end of the legislative session.

State governments began to enact their own immigration reform legislation, most notably Arizona's SB1070 (Support Our Law Enforcement and Safe Neighborhoods Act) and Alabama's HB56 (Beason-Hammon Alabama Taxpayer and Citizen Protection Act). Both of these bills allowed local law enforcement to check the immigration status of anyone in their custody suspected of being an undocumented immigrant. This led to an increase in racial profiling of Latinos and an increase in state legislation targeting Latina/o populations (Campbell, 2011) These bills were eventually challenged in the court system, with the major provisions of the Arizona bill, and similar legislation, upheld as constitutional.

The US Senate continued working to pass bipartisan legislation that increased border security, while adding visas and work permits. The most notable legislation was the 2013 Border Security, Economic Opportunity, and Immigration Modernization Act (S.744). The centerpiece of the legislation created a pathway to citizenship for undocumented immigrants and included key provisions of the failed 2007 Development, Relief, and Education for Alien Minors (DREAM) Act. The DREAM Act would have granted legal status to undocumented immigrants brought into the United States as children. The Republican-controlled House of Representatives opposed these parts of the bill, labeling them as amnesty for criminals. Thus, the impasse on immigration reform continued.

Legislative gridlock led President Obama to unilaterally address several key immigration issues. On June 15, 2012, President Barack Obama announced the Deferred Action for Childhood Arrivals (DACA) policy, allowing children who were brought into the United States without documentation a deferment from deportation and the ability to obtain a work permit. President Obama also ordered the protection from being deported of undocumented immigrants who had been in the country for more than five years. Ultimately, these policies were terminated by the Department of Homeland Security under the administration of President Donald Trump in 2017. Subsequently, immigration policy remains a divisive issue in contemporary American politics, with little agreement on how the nation's immigration system should work or what to do with the undocumented immigrants already living within the country.

Our goal in this chapter is to illustrate the role that Latina/o racism-ethnicism (LRE) plays in shaping public opinion toward immigration policy. Given that the national debate on immigration focuses on Latina/o immigration, making the prototypical immigrants in the minds of most Americans Latina/os (Valentino et al., 2013), we expect immigration policy preferences to be strongly connected to people's beliefs about Latinos. Concerns over failed Latina/o assimilation, and the violation of Anglo-American norms by Latinos, are likely to be associated with a desire to enact policies that have a negative impact on Latina/o communities such as restrictive immigration laws.

4.1 AMERICAN PUBLIC OPINION TOWARD IMMIGRATION POLICY

American public opinion contributes to the indecisiveness and discord in the country's immigration debate. Polls over the last twenty years reveal that Americans are divided over specific policy proposals to reform immigration and also possess opinions that are not entirely in favor or against immigration (Muste, 2013; Segovia and Defever, 2010). A vocal minority of Americans consistently oppose most forms of immigration (e.g., pathways to citizenship, workplace visas, family reunification, DACA), while a similar number of Americans consistently support more welcoming immigration policies. But there are some Americans who favor policies that ease the ability of immigrants to become US citizens, while also favoring tougher enforcement of existing immigration laws. These citizens often change their opinion toward immigration policy reforms in response to small changes in the framing or wording of a policy proposal (Brader et al., 2008; Haynes et al., 2016; Masuoka and Junn, 2013). Subsequently, what the public wants in terms of comprehensive immigration reform depends on who you ask, when you ask, and how you ask it. We suspect that taking into consideration the degree White Americans feel comfortable expressing LRE can explain some of this heterogeneity in opinions.

We begin by analyzing the 2014 and 2016 Cooperative Congressional Election Studies (CCESs). Both surveys are well-suited for our purposes. First, each survey is matched to the US adult population. Each survey also contains numerous questions related to specific immigration reform policy proposals being debated at that time. Respondents in the 2014 CCES were interviewed during a midterm election where Republicans attempted to define the election as a referendum on the Affordable Care Act. The lack of immigration reform in the years prior to the 2014 midterm election meant immigration was still brewing as a political problem, but the spotlight of the election was focused on attacking Democrats over health care. Respondents in the 2016 election, in contrast, were interviewed during a presidential election, with immigration playing a central role in Donald Trump's campaign. There was an increased emphasis on border security (i.e., building a wall) and frequent disparaging comments directed at Latina/o immigrants. Together, the 2014 and 2016 CCESs provide two different glimpses of American public opinion toward immigration policy on a range of specific proposals that have divided Americans for almost two decades.

Respondents in the 2014 CCES were asked five questions about immigration that reflect some of the most contentious policy proposals debated during the various attempts to reform the nation's immigration system. Specifically, respondents were asked, "What do you think the government should do about immigration? Select all that apply ..."

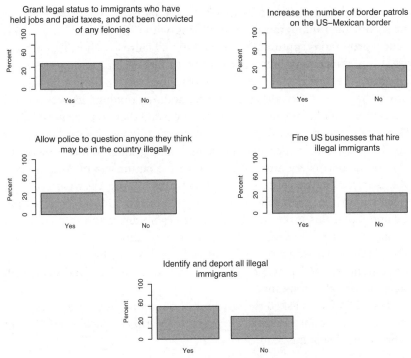

FIGURE 4.1 American public opinion toward immigration policy, 2014 CCES

. *Grant legal status to all illegal immigrants who have held jobs and paid taxes for at least 3 years, and not been convicted of any felony crimes.*

. *Increase Border Patrols along the US–Mexico border.*

. *Fine US businesses that hire illegal immigrants.*

. *Allow police to question anyone they think may be in the country illegally.*

. *Identify and deport illegal immigrants.*

Response options were either "yes" or "no" for each item. For this analysis, we examine White respondents only.

The percentage of White respondents agreeing or disagreeing with each policy proposal is displayed in Figure 4.1. One of the most controversial policies debated at the federal level is a pathway to citizenship for undocumented immigrants already living within the United States. This policy proposal is captured by the first item. Figure 4.1 shows 46 percent of White Americans favor a pathway to citizenship, with 54 percent opposing the policy. A slightly less controversial set of policy proposals are strengthening security along the border and sanctioning business owners that employ undocumented immigrants. We find that 60 percent of White Americans favor increasing border patrols, while 64 percent favor fines for businesses that hire undocumented immigrants. White Americans do not support every attempt to enforce the nation's immigration laws. An estimated 61 percent of White Americans oppose allowing police to question anyone they believe to be undocumented. However, it should be noted that this proposal provides even more discretion to police than do laws such as Arizona's SB1070 that only allow police to question the immigration status of people already in custody. Finally, a majority of respondents (60 percent) say it is okay to round up and deport all undocumented immigrants.

The 2016 CCES asked the same set of questions, but replaced the fine businesses and policy authority items with questions regarding DACA and work visas. The items read,

. *Grant legal status to people who were brought to the US illegally as children, but who have graduated from a US high school.*

. *Increase the number of visas for overseas workers to work in the US*

The percentage of White respondents who agree or disagree with each policy proposal is displayed in Figure 4.2. We find a slight majority of respondents (52 percent) approve of a pathway to citizenship for undocumented immigrants who have held jobs, pay taxes, and lack a criminal record. A slight majority of respondents (52 percent) also favor increasing patrols along the border. We find that 55 percent of respondents disapprove of President Obama's DACA policy and 84 percent of respondents oppose increasing the number of work visas for immigrants. Respondents are also split between those who want to deport all undocumented immigrants (46 percent) and those who do not (54 percent).

We do not find evidence that most White Americans are ambivalent or inconsistent in their immigration policy preferences – although this is likely the case for some respondents. Instead, we observe a strong degree of consistency in respondents' immigration policy preferences. This is

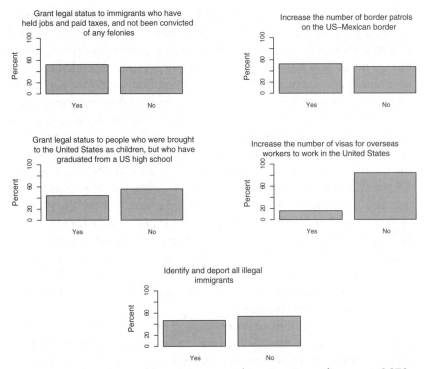

FIGURE 4.2 American public opinion toward immigration policy, 2016 CCES

particularly true among opponents of immigration.[1] For the 2014 CCES, the Spearman ρ correlation coefficient ranges from a weak -0.11 (grant legal status and fine businesses questions) to strong 0.47 association (the increase border patrols and allow police to question anyone questions). The average of all item correlations is 0.32. For the 2016 CCES, the Spearman ρ correlation coefficient ranges from a weak 0.14 (work visa and grant legal status questions) to a strong 0.67 association (the grant legal status and DACA questions). The average of all item correlations for the 2016 CCES is 0.36. Overall, these findings show a consistent pattern of Americans favoring tougher security and being divided on whether to welcome those who wish to work in the United States or become citizens.

[1] For instance, among those who favor deporting undocumented immigrants in the 2016 CCES, 78 percent oppose DACA, 76 percent oppose a pathway to citizenship, 76 percent favor increasing border patrols, and 93 percent oppose increasing the number of work visas. Among respondents who oppose deporting all undocumented immigrants, 64 percent favor DACA, 77 percent favor a pathway to citizenship, and 32 percent oppose increasing border patrols.

We suspect that LRE can explain why some people support welcoming immigration policies, while others oppose them. LRE should be connected to immigration policy preferences because most people perceive the modal immigrant to be a Latina/o. There is ample evidence that public debate over immigration, along with the anti-immigration rhetoric of public officials and television personalities, has focused on defining immigration as a problem concerning Latina/o immigrants (Branton and Dunaway, 2008, 2009a; Haynes et al., 2016; Valentino et al., 2013). Valentino et al. (2013), for instance, examine the frequency of immigration stories in the *New York Times, Houston Chronicle, Seattle Times, San Francisco Chronicle, Charlotte Observer, Chicago Tribune,* and *Washington Post* between 1985 and 2009. These stories were searched for the mention of "Hispanics" or "Latinos," "Asians," "Africans," and "Muslims." They find that in the post-9/11 era, Latinos were by far the most common group mentioned in stories about immigration. Further, their analysis shows that as Latinos become more connected to immigration in the media, attitudes toward Latinos became more strongly connected to the public's immigration policy preferences.

Given the information environment and the reality that Latinos comprise the majority of the US immigrant population, it is likely that the typical image of an immigrant in a person's mind is someone of Latina/o origin. Supporting this notion is the reality that debates over border security more often focus on the border between the United States and Mexico, suggesting that opposition to immigration is nothing more than opposition to Latina/o immigration. Moreover, some restrictive immigration policies would adversely affect Latina/o communities. For example, laws that allow police to question anyone in their custody they suspect might be undocumented have been shown to lead to the profiling of Latina/o citizens.[2] Thus, we expect that those harboring any type of racial or ethnic animus toward Latinos to be more supportive of such policies.

Previous studies highlight the role that more traditional forms of Latina/o racial stereotypes have on people's immigration policy preferences (Ayers et al., 2009; Branton et al., 2011; Burns and Gimpel, 2000; Valentino et al., 2013), but likely attenuate the role that race and ethnicity play in these attitudes. As noted in Chapter 3, these other concepts related to old-fashioned racism are distinct from, and not as

---

[2] Although such laws could be applied broadly to any immigrant group, their implementation has focused exclusively on citizens and immigrants of Latina/o origin (see *Ortega Melendres, et al. V. Arpaio, et al.*, 13-16285 9th Cir. 2015; *Arizona v. United States,* 567 US 2012).

widely held as, LRE. The more narrowly held beliefs cannot adequately explain the more widespread support for restrictive immigration policies. We expand upon these studies by examining the role that LRE plays in how White Americans think about immigration policy. We argue that since LRE is the more common form of animus toward Latinos, it should be associated with White Americans' immigration policy preferences.

4.1.1 Current Explanations of Public Opinion toward Immigration Policy

The relationship between LRE and immigration policy preferences should be tested taking into account alternative explanations of why people support restrictions on immigration. Taking these alternatives into consideration will allow us to be as certain as possible that any relationship we discover between LRE and people's immigration policy preferences is genuine. Fortunately, there has been a growth in studies concerning why people support restrictive immigration policies that provide a clear direction about what are these other potential explanations of people's immigration policy preferences (Hainmueller and Hopkins, 2014).

Realistic group conflict theory: Some of the earliest studies on why people oppose immigration relate to realistic group conflict theory – a theory that explains how groups react when threatened by new groups. According to this view, real or perceived competition between groups leads to intergroup conflict and support for policies that advantage one group over the other. The theory predicts that Whites who experience or perceive competition with Latinos (e.g., competition for jobs, educational services, social benefits) will be more likely to support restrictions on immigration as a means of reducing that competition. Realistic group conflict theory has been used to explain public opinion toward various policies that adversely impact Latina/o communities. Huddy and Sears (1995) show that, among White Americans, perceived conflict with Latinos is associated with support for English-only language educational programs. Other studies have shown that White Americans living in Latina/o neighborhoods are more likely to favor restrictions on immigration (Hood and Morris, 2000). Rapid increases in the Latina/o population within previous White neighborhoods has also been shown to be associated with support for tough-on-immigration policies (Newman, 2013; Rocha and Espino, 2009).

Labor market competition has also been explored as a reason why many people oppose immigration (Scheve and Slaughter, 2001). According to this view, people who are in direct competition with immigrants for jobs or economic benefits should be more likely to favor restrictions on immigration as a means to enhance their own economic self-interest. Low-skilled domestic workers, as well as those facing unemployment or economic hardships, are expected to oppose immigration due to competition with low-skilled immigrant labor. High-skilled workers in direct competition with high-skilled immigrant labor are also expected to oppose immigration. Various tests of the labor market competition hypotheses, however, have failed to bear out these predictions (Citrin et al., 1997; Hainmueller and Hiscox, 2007; Hainmueller et al., 2015). Instead, factors associated with low-skilled labor (i.e., less education) are associated with favoring restrictions on immigration regardless of competition with immigrant labor (Espenshade and Calhoun, 1993; Hainmueller and Hiscox, 2010). High-skilled domestic workers, in contrast, are more likely to support welcoming immigration policies, even if they are in direct competition with high-skilled immigrant workers. Subsequently, scholars have argued that education, unemployment, and economic hardships are related to favoring restrictions on immigration due to their mutual association with cultural preferences and racial attitudes (Hainmueller and Hiscox, 2010; Tingley, 2013).

Economic optimism: The economic optimism theory argues that opinions toward immigration policies are guided by concerns about the national economy rather than a person's individual financial circumstances. In other words, when people think about immigration they are more likely to consider the impact new immigrants will have on the nation's economy rather than its impact on them personally. Citrin et al. (1997) examine the 1992 and 1994 American National Election Studies (ANESs) and find that optimism about the national economy is related to support for more welcoming immigration policies. Pessimism about one's personal economic situation had no discernible relationship with immigration policy preferences. They suggest that a person's opinion toward immigration policy is closely related to their belief about the impact that immigration will have on the national economy, with people who perceive the nation's economy as able to withstand new immigrants more likely to support welcoming immigration policies.

Cultural preferences: A preference for Anglo-American culture should also be related to support for policies that restrict immigration. Various scholars have outlined how the immigration debate primes nationalist tendencies and identities, which strengthens the connection between a preference for Anglo-American culture and immigration policy preferences (Branton et al., 2011). These nationalists beliefs relate to a narrow conception of what it means to be an American (Li and Brewer, 2004), which triggers hostility toward out-groups – in this case Latina/o immigrants who are seen as lacking these Anglo-American cultural values. Branton et al. (2011) examine White respondents to the 2000 and 2004 ANESs and find that White Americans who prefer Anglo-American moral traditions are more likely to favor decreases in immigration relative to White Americans who are less supportive of Anglo-American moral traditions. Perceived membership in a national Anglo-American community has also been shown to relate to support for more restrictive immigration policies (Schildkraut, 2005).

Racism and out-group hostility: Public approval of anti-immigrant policies is also argued to be related to racial animus directed toward Latinos as well as ethnocentrism. Various studies have shown that people who endorse old-fashioned forms of explicit racism are more likely to oppose opening immigration policies. Specifically, studies have demonstrated an association between rating Latinos coldly on a thermometer scale, wanting to avoid socializing with Latinos, or belief in old-fashioned racial Latina/o stereotypes and opposition to welcoming immigration policies (Ayers et al., 2009; Branton et al., 2011; Pérez, 2010; Valentino et al., 2013).

Predispositions and personality traits associated with a reverence for in-group loyalty and a disdain for out-groups have also been theorized to explain anti-immigration sentiment (Banks, 2016; Hetherington and Weiler, 2009; Kinder and Kam, 2010). For instance, Kinder and Kam (2010, 125–150) show that ethnocentrism, a preference toward in-groups relative to out-groups, is associated with support for restrictions on immigration, a belief that immigrants take away American jobs, and a feeling that immigrants threaten American cultural identity. Authoritarianism, a tendency to favor strict obedience to those in power, has also been shown to relate to support for more-restrictionist immigration policies (Hetherington and Weiler, 2009). Subsequently, this line of research suggests that it is not prejudice toward any single group that is responsible for White opposition to immigration, but more generalized beliefs toward out-groups and authority that apply broadly to all potential immigration groups.

Partisan principles: The partisan principles theory predicts that citizens will rely on partisan cues and ideological beliefs when forming their preferences toward immigration policy. Partisan and ideological cues guide people's decisions on many public policy issues. However, Hainmueller and Hopkins (2014, 244) note that research on the public's immigration-related attitudes has been "divorced from research on political partisanship and ideology." This is because partisan public officials and activists do not provide a clear division on the issue of immigration. Left-leaning minority rights activists have sided with right-leaning big business organizations and free-market conservatives in favoring more welcoming immigration policies. Working-class Democrats, in contrast, have aligned with far-right nationalism (White supremacy) in opposing immigration. Thus, partisanship and ideology have crisscrossed the usual political cleavages, making it difficult for citizens to align these identities with their immigration policy preferences.

4.2 THE ROLE OF LRE

We begin an initial examination of the relationship between LRE and immigration policy preferences using the 2014 CCES. The CCES contains measures related to each of the theories that might alternatively, or in conjunction with LRE, explain people's immigration policy preferences. Partisanship and ideology are measured using the ANES seven-point self-identification scale. Economic optimism is measured by asking respondents whether the nation's economy has gotten better or worse over the past year. Cultural preference is measured by asking respondents how much they agree that American culture and values are superior to the culture and values of other countries. Racism and out-group hostility is measured with two questions from the racial resentment scale that measures subtle racism toward African Americans. Realistic group conflict theory is controlled for by including a measure of the county-level percentage change in the Latina/o population. Direct measures of labor market competition are not available in the CCES. However, we do control for economic vulnerability using each respondent's education and perceived change in household income.

Since respondents' immigration policy preferences are measured by a "yes" or "no" binary choice, we model each outcome using a logistic regression estimated with maximum likelihood. The results, summarized in Table 4.1, show that opinions toward immigration policy are related to several factors: age, ideology, economic optimism, cultural preferences, and LRE. LRE is associated with White Americans' favoring laws that restrict immigration: that undocumented immigrants who have jobs and pay taxes without a criminal record should not have a pathway to citizenship; that the US government should identify and deport all undocumented immigrants; that border patrols along the US–Mexican

TABLE 4.1 *Logistic regression estimates of immigration policy preferences on LRE, 2014 CCES*

	Grant legal status		Deport illegals		Increase border patrols		Fine businesses		Police profiling	
LRE	-0.92*	(0.22)	0.86*	(0.23)	0.89*	(0.20)	0.78*	(0.19)	0.63*	(0.23)
Sex	0.28	(0.24)	-0.34	(0.26)	-0.23	(0.25)	-0.17	(0.24)	-0.22	(0.24)
Age	0.22*	(0.08)	-0.15	(0.08)	-0.03	(0.08)	0.15*	(0.07)	0.06	(0.08)
Education	0.02	(0.08)	-0.12	(0.09)	0.09	(0.08)	0.01	(0.08)	-0.03	(0.09)
Economic optimism	-0.16	(0.15)	-0.30	(0.22)	-0.13	(0.14)	-0.13	(0.16)	-0.33*	(0.15)
Δ Household income	0.09	(0.14)	0.05	(0.15)	0.14	(0.12)	0.11	(0.12)	0.14	(0.15)
Unemployment	0.32	(0.48)	-0.44	(0.51)	-0.35	(0.60)	0.24	(0.56)	-0.63	(0.55)
Partisanship	-0.01	(0.08)	0.02	(0.09)	0.13	(0.09)	0.09	(0.08)	-0.01	(0.08)
Ideology	-0.19	(0.10)	0.24*	(0.11)	0.01	(0.09)	-0.10	(0.10)	0.21*	(0.10)
Cultural preference	-0.01*	(0.00)	0.01	(0.00)	0.01*	(0.00)	-0.00	(0.00)	0.02*	(0.00)
Racial resentment	-0.34*	(0.17)	0.26	(0.16)	-0.03	(0.16)	-0.19	(0.14)	0.21	(0.17)
% Hispanic change	0.00	(0.00)	0.00	(0.00)	0.00	(0.00)	0.00	(0.00)	-0.00	(0.00)
Constant	4.90*	(1.17)	-2.41	(1.47)	-3.44*	(1.04)	-1.31	(1.20)	-4.19*	(1.26)

*$p < 0.05$. $N = 580$. Coefficients represent logit estimates with standard errors in parentheses. White respondents only. We find no evidence of multicollinearity with the mean variance inflation factor for the model = 1.65.

border need to be increased; that businesses employing undocumented immigrants receive financial penalties; and that police should be able to stop and question anyone who they believe is an undocumented immigrant. The relationship between LRE is statistically significant for each policy, meaning that this relationship is unlikely to be observed by chance. Moreover, the relationship appears substantively important – larger than the relationship between any of the other factors and people's immigration policy preferences.

We do find that, controlling for LRE, all of the measures associated with realistic group conflict theory (change in the Hispanic population, being unemployed, and experiencing a long-term decline in household income) are not related to the public's immigration policy preference. Moreover, racial resentment toward African Americans does not show a relationship to immigration policy preferences in four of the five models. The latter finding is consistent with the argument that opposition to immigration is specifically targeted toward Latinos and shows the distinctiveness of the LRE scale, despite its similarity to the traditional racial resentment toward African Americans scale.[3]

We visualize the relationship between LRE and people's immigration policy preferences in Figure 4.3. The figure plots the predicted probability of supporting a policy that restricts or limits immigration for all five policy proposals. For instance, the relationship between LRE is negative in the case of granting legal status to undocumented immigrants and substantively large. A person who does not harbor any racism-ethnicism toward Latinos (a 1 on the LRE) would have a 90 percent probability of supporting a pathway to citizenship for undocumented immigrants who have jobs, pay taxes, and do not have a criminal record. If that same person were to possess the maximum amount of racism-ethnicism toward Latinos (a 5 on the LRE), the probability that they would support a pathway to citizenship would drop to around 20 percent. The figure shows that the relationship between LRE is positive and substantively large for

---

[3] We also reestimated the models using a measure of the importance that respondents place on national security since the origins of the contemporary conflict over immigration in the post-9/11 world framed undocumented immigration as a national security concern. We found no evidence that respondents rating national security as an important goal were consistently more likely to endorse immigration restrictions. National security concerns were only relevant on opinions toward police profiling of immigrants, with people valuing national security less likely to support police stop-and-question laws ($\beta_{ml} = -0.21$ $t = -2.01$). This suggests that national security concerns are not the driving factor in the immigration policy debate.

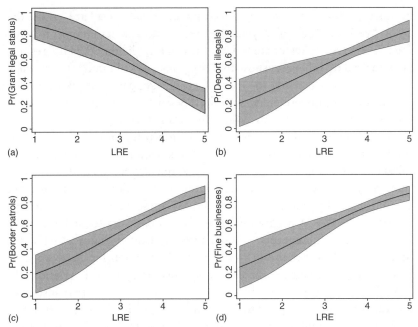

FIGURE 4.3 Effect of LRE on immigration policy preferences, 2014.
Pr = probability

each of the other policy proposals. For instance, across the range of LRE found among White Americans today (from 1 to 5 on the LRE), the probability of supporting the deportation of all undocumented immigrants increases from about 20 percent to just over 80 percent. Similar effect sizes are shown between LRE and increasing border patrols as well as between LRE and sanctioning businesses that hire undocumented workers.

We test the robustness of these findings using the 2016 CCES. The 2016 CCES includes many of the same measures used in the 2014 CCES, but also measures of group-specific stereotypes described earlier. We use these in-group versus out-group stereotypes to create a measure of ethnocentrism similar to Kinder and Kam (2010), which takes the difference between favorable beliefs about in-group members (White Americans) and out-group members (Hispanic Americans and Muslim Americans). The 2016 CCES also contained questions on child-rearing practices that measure authoritarianism (Hetherington and Weiler, 2009). Thus, we are able to test whether LRE provides any leverage in explaining immigration policy opinions beyond what can be explained by existing measures of old-fashioned racial stereotypes and ethnocentrism.

Since respondents' immigration policy preferences are measured by a "yes" or "no" binary choice, we model each outcome using a logistic regression estimated with maximum likelihood. The results, summarized in Table 4.2, show that opinions toward immigration policy are related inconsistently to several factors: age, partisanship, economic optimism, cultural preferences, and ethnocentrism. In contrast, LRE is consistently associated with White Americans favoring laws that restrict immigration: opposing a pathway to citizenship for undocumented immigrants who have jobs and pay taxes without a criminal record; allowing the US government to identify and deport all undocumented immigrants; allowing an increase in border patrols along the US–Mexican border; fines for businesses that employ undocumented immigrants; opposing the DACA program that provides a pathway to citizenship for undocumented immigrants brought into the United States as children; and opposing an increase in work visas. The relationship between LRE is statistically significant for each case, meaning that this relationship is unlikely to be observed by chance. Moreover, in the two instances where ethnocentrism relates to immigration policy preferences (deporting undocumented immigrants and opposing the DACA program), LRE shows an equal or larger substantive effect.

We visualize the relationship between LRE and people's immigration policy preferences in Figure 4.4. The figure plots the predicted probability of supporting a policy that restricts or limits immigration for all five policy proposals. The effect sizes are somewhat smaller than those found in the 2014 CCES, which could be due to the inclusion of ethnocentrism or the changing context surrounding the 2016 presidential election. Yet, the relationship between LRE and support for each policy proposal remains substantively large. For instance, across the range of LRE found among White Americans today (from 1 to 5 on the LRE scale), the probability of supporting the deportation of all undocumented immigrants increases from about 16 percent to just over 70 percent. A similar effect size is shown between LRE and increasing border patrols. The probability of supporting DACA declines from about 70 percent for someone who has the minimum amount of LRE (a 1 on the scale) to about 16 percent for someone with the maximum amount of LRE (a 5 on the scale). The impact of LRE on opposition to increasing the number of work visas available to immigrants is noticeably smaller. White Americans on the low-end of the LRE scale have roughly a 35 percent probability of favoring additional work visas for immigrants, while those at the high-end of the LRE scale

TABLE 4.2 *Logistic regression estimates of immigration policy preferences on LRE, 2016 CCES*

	Grant legal status		Deport illegals		Increase border patrols		DACA		Work visas	
LRE	−1.01*	(0.14)	0.81*	(0.14)	0.64*	(0.15)	−0.59*	(0.17)	−0.48†	(0.27)
Sex	0.11	(0.25)	0.14	(0.24)	−0.15	(0.26)	−0.26	(0.24)	0.04	(0.53)
Age	−0.01	(0.01)	−0.00	(0.01)	−0.02*	(0.01)	0.00	(0.01)	0.04	(0.02)
Education	0.07	(0.08)	−0.08	(0.08)	0.11	(0.09)	0.16*	(0.08)	0.34	(0.20)
Economic optimism	0.52*	(0.17)	−0.45*	(0.16)	0.02	(0.15)	0.26	(0.17)	0.37	(0.32)
Δ Household income	−0.31*	(0.14)	0.30*	(0.13)	−0.02	(0.13)	−0.04	(0.13)	0.01	(0.28)
Unemployed	−0.62	(0.43)	0.44	(0.49)	0.97	(0.55)	−0.21	(0.47)	0.00	(0.00)
Partisanship	0.02	(0.08)	0.13	(0.07)	0.20*	(0.08)	−0.04	(0.08)	0.44*	(0.17)
Ideology	−0.10	(0.11)	0.19	(0.10)	0.12	(0.09)	−0.17	(0.11)	−0.45*	(0.19)
Cultural preference	−0.18	(0.11)	0.17	(0.12)	0.25	(0.13)	−0.24*	(0.12)	−0.05	(0.23)
Ethnocentrism	−0.20	(0.19)	0.42*	(0.18)	0.33	(0.17)	−0.63*	(0.25)	−0.31	(0.44)
Authoritarianism	0.87	(0.61)	−0.60	(0.62)	0.48	(0.83)	0.10	(0.66)	1.36	(1.67)
Constant	16.41	(14.36)	0.59	(15.17)	43.53*	(14.54)	0.77	(15.54)	−86.79	(47.94)
N	669		669		669		669		155	

*$p < 0.05$. †$p < 0.10$. Coefficients represent logit estimates with standard errors in parentheses. White respondents only. The work visas questions were asked to a subset of 200 respondents of the complete sample reducing the statistical power of our hypothesis test. We find no evidence of multicollinearity with the mean variance inflation factor for the model = 1.43.

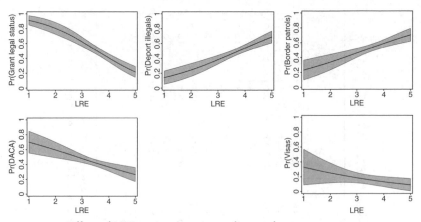

FIGURE 4.4 Effect of LRE on immigration policy preferences, 2016.
Pr = probability

have less than a 10 percent probability of favoring additional work visas for immigrants.[4]

The relationship between LRE and immigration policy preferences appears to be distinct from racial resentment toward African Americans, realistic group conflict, and ethnocentrism. In ten different models, LRE relates to immigration policy preferences even when these other factors are included as potential alternative explanations. How much leverage in explaining immigration policy preferences does LRE have above traditional forms of old-fashioned Latina/o-specific stereotypes? To examine this question, we replaced the measure of ethnocentrism with a measure of negative Latina/o stereotypes – beliefs that Latinos are unintelligent and untrustworthy. The results, summarized in Table 4.3, show that LRE is not simply a replacement for more traditional forms of animus toward Latinos. Instead, LRE shows a relationship to immigration policy preferences in five of the six models even when including a measure of beliefs in negative Latina/o stereotypes. The latter is related to only the grant legal status and deportation policy proposals. Moreover, in each of the models, the relationship between LRE and immigration policy preferences are larger than the relationship between old-fashioned racism and immigration policy preferences. LRE, a belief that Latinos fail to assimilate and adhere to Anglo-American culture, maintains a specific

---

[4] The 2016 CCES asked the work visas questions to a small subsample of respondents, thereby lowering the statistical power of our hypothesis test.

TABLE 4.3 *Logistic regression estimates of immigration policy preferences on Latina/o stereotypes, 2016 CCES*

	Grant legal status		Deport illegals		Increase border patrols		DACA		Work visas	
LRE	-0.99*	(0.14)	0.77*	(0.14)	0.63*	(0.16)	-0.59*	(0.17)	-0.39	(0.28)
Sex	0.13	(0.25)	0.11	(0.25)	-0.20	(0.26)	-0.19	(0.24)	0.00	(0.53)
Age	-0.01	(0.01)	-0.00	(0.01)	-0.02*	(0.01)	-0.00	(0.01)	0.04	(0.02)
Education	0.06	(0.08)	-0.08	(0.08)	0.10	(0.09)	0.18*	(0.08)	0.29	(0.20)
Economic optimism	0.53*	(0.17)	-0.48*	(0.15)	-0.02	(0.15)	0.32*	(0.15)	0.36	(0.30)
Δ Household income	-0.31*	(0.14)	0.28*	(0.13)	-0.03	(0.13)	-0.02	(0.12)	0.12	(0.27)
Unemployed	-0.64	(0.45)	0.47	(0.51)	1.09	(0.62)	-0.35	(0.50)	0.00	(0.00)
Partisanship	0.03	(0.08)	0.11	(0.07)	0.18*	(0.08)	-0.02	(0.07)	0.46*	(0.17)
Ideology	-0.12	(0.11)	0.25*	(0.10)	0.15	(0.09)	-0.22*	(0.11)	-0.48*	(0.19)
Cultural preference	-0.25*	(0.11)	0.27*	(0.12)	0.30*	(0.13)	-0.34*	(0.11)	-0.17	(0.24)
Latina/o stereotypes	0.32*	(0.16)	-0.39*	(0.15)	-0.10	(0.15)	0.14	(0.16)	0.52	(0.29)
Authoritarianism	0.92	(0.61)	-0.61	(0.63)	0.46	(0.85)	0.05	(0.65)	0.61	(1.47)
Constant	15.00	(14.40)	0.93	(15.04)	40.38*	(14.20)	5.35	(15.96)	-85.95	(43.68)
N	668		668		668		668		155	

*$p < 0.05$. Coefficients represent logit estimates with standard errors in parentheses. Data from the 2016 CCES. White respondents only. The work visas questions were asked to a subset of 200 respondents of the complete sample.

relationship to immigration policy preferences that is unique, and more substantively important, than these other forms of racial and ethnic beliefs.

4.2.1 LRE or Immigrant Resentment

We have presented evidence that LRE is related to the immigration policy preferences of White Americans. But we need to be sure that our measure of LRE represents a form of animus toward Latinos rather than all immigrant groups. Like ethnocentrism, immigrant resentment is a form of negativity toward all immigrants rather than specific racial or ethnic groups. Many people who believe that immigrant groups of all races and ethnicities fail to live up to Anglo-American norms and values are likely to harbor resentment toward immigrants in general, which is also related to support for decreasing immigration levels and opposing benefits for immigrants (Schildkraut, 2010, 161–181). Since each question we use to measure LRE references immigrants, despite the subject in each question explicitly referring to "Latinos and Hispanics," it is possible that the findings are merely a reflection of immigrant resentment rather than Latina/o-specific racism-ethnicism. How can we ensure that the result is due to LRE rather than to immigrant resentment?

We rely on a classic approach, the split-ballot survey design, to determine whether the mention of "immigrants" in the LRE questions are the reason we observe a relationship between the LRE scale and people's immigration policy preferences. A split-ballot survey was implemented as part of the 2017 Qualtrics study. The study sampled 2,101 respondents matched to the adult population of the United States. One-half of respondents were asked the LRE questions that included references to immigrants. The other half of the sample were asked a similar set of LRE questions that removed the word "immigrant" from each question. Specifically, respondents in this half of the sample were asked to indicate whether they agree or disagree, and how strongly they did so, with the following statements:

- *Many other ethnic groups have successfully integrated into American culture. Latinos and Hispanics should do the same without any special favors.*

- *Anti-Latino sentiment and racism have created conditions that make it difficult for Latinos and Hispanics to succeed in America.*

. *Latinos and Hispanics would be more welcomed by the rest of us if they would try harder to learn English and adopt US customs like other ethnic groups have done.*

. *Critics of Latinos and the media have overblown the number of crimes committed by Latinos and Hispanics within the United States.*

Since the revised questions do not make any mention of immigrants, we should have little concern that they are measuring immigrant resentment. Instead, these revised questions appear to have even greater face validity than our original measure of LRE since they reference "Latinos and Hispanics" exclusively. However, this does not mean the original questions are invalid indicators of LRE. Indeed, if the original questions show equivalency to these revised questions, and perform similarly in our immigration policy preference models, then we should be satisfied with the validity of the original LRE questions, that is, we should no longer be concerned that the original questions are merely measuring immigrant resentment.

We start by examining the measurement properties of the LRE questions and the revised questions. Cronbach's α indicates that the original LRE scale ($\alpha = 0.64$) is equally as reliable as the revised scale ($\alpha = 0.69$). Moreover, the distribution of responses are statistically equivalent, meaning that the estimated level of LRE in the population does not differ depending on which measure we use. When measured with questions that include the term "immigrant," the estimated degree of LRE in the population (M = 3.28, SD = 0.85) is statistically equivalent to when LRE is measured with questions that exclude the term "immigrant" (M = 3.29, SD = 0.87), $t = -0.26$, $p < 0.79$.

We also assess whether excluding the term "immigrant" reduces or eliminates the relationship between LRE and people's immigration policy preferences. For this analysis, we combine four of the same indicators of people's immigration policy preferences found in the 2014 CCES: should undocumented immigrants be granted legal status, should patrols along the US–Mexican border be increased, should we fine businesses that employ undocumented workers, and should police be allowed to question anyone they suspect of being in the country undocumented? We then regressed respondents' immigration policy preferences on the original and revised LRE scale while including available controls for each respondent's partisanship, ideology, personal financial situation, education, age, and sex.

TABLE 4.4 *Comparing LRE and immigrant resentment on estimates of immigration policy preferences*

	Original items		Revised items	
LRE	0.17*	(0.01)	0.15*	(0.01)
Sex	−0.07*	(0.02)	0.02	(0.02)
Education	−0.01	(0.01)	−0.00	(0.01)
Income	0.01	(0.01)	0.01	(0.00)
Age	0.00	(0.00)	−0.00	(0.00)
Ideology	0.02*	(0.01)	0.04*	(0.01)
Partisanship	0.04*	(0.01)	0.06*	(0.01)
Constant	−0.46*	(0.07)	−0.58*	(0.07)
R^2	0.34		0.34	
N	723		707	

*$p < 0.05$. Coefficients represent ordinary least square estimates with standard errors in parentheses. Data from the 2017 Qualtrics sample. White respondents only.

The results are summarized in Table 4.4. LRE shows a positive and statistically significant relationship with immigration policy preferences. Even when the questions do not contain the term "immigrant," higher values on the LRE scale are associated with support for policies that deter immigrants from coming to the United States. Moreover, an equality of coefficient test shows the substantive effect sizes of the estimates are statistically equivalent, $\chi^2 = 2.02, p < 0.16$. In other words, the LRE scale containing the term "immigrant" appears just as valid as the LRE scale that does not reference immigrants. Moreover, the findings reduce concerns that the term "immigrant" is triggering immigration policy content. The original LRE questions appear equivalent to the revised questions where the potential to prime such policy considerations are largely absent.

The 2017 Qualtrics study also asked respondents if they favored building a wall between the US–Mexican border. The building of a border wall became a hot-button issue during the 2016 presidential election and a policy proposal closely associated with President Donald Trump. Given that support for a border wall might merely reflect support for President Trump, we estimate the role of LRE on support for the border wall separately and include a measure of each respondent's approval of President Trump.

The results are summarized in Table 4.5. Even after controlling for approval for President Trump, both versions of the LRE scale show a positive and statistically significant relationship to building the border

TABLE 4.5 *Estimates of public support for a border wall*

	Original items		Revised items	
LRE	−0.13*	(0.07)	−0.15*	(0.06)
Sex	0.28*	(0.10)	0.21*	(0.10)
Education	−0.04	(0.05)	−0.06	(0.05)
Income	−0.05	(0.03)	−0.02	(0.03)
Age	−0.00	(0.00)	−0.00	(0.00)
Ideology	0.01	(0.04)	−0.01	(0.04)
Partisanship	−0.11	(0.07)	0.23*	(0.07)
Trump approval	0.39*	(0.05)	0.42*	(0.05)
Constant 1	0.41	(0.38)	0.39	(0.37)
Constant 2	1.73*	(0.38)	1.65*	(0.37)
N	718		703	

*$p < 0.05$. Coefficients represent ordinary least square estimates with standard errors in parentheses. Data from the 2017 Qualtrics sample. White respondents only.

wall. An equality of coefficient test demonstrates that the original LRE scale has the same relationship with people's support for the border wall as the revised LRE scale, χ^2 = 0.04, $p < 0.83$. Both question formats appear equally valid.

4.2.2 Context and Contiguity in Immigration Policy Preferences

The importance of context in shaping people's immigration policy preferences has been demonstrated in numerous studies (Branton et al., 2007, 2015; Gravelle, 2016; Hawley, 2011; Hood and Morris, 2000; Newman, 2013; Rocha and Espino, 2009; Rocha et al., 2011). Context has taken on various meanings across these studies, referring to everything from changing demographic patterns to proximity to protest movements. Context can also mean how the survey environment shapes how citizens form and express their policy opinions on the issues of the day. Specifically, citizens might change how they express their policy opinion on an issue when made aware of their preference on a related issue, thereby providing additional insight into the contours and contiguity of an opinion.

For instance, in one of the earliest split-ballot experiments, Hyman and Sheatsley (1950) asked one-half of a sample of Americans a question about a *communist reporter* followed by the same question about an *American reporter*. The questions read,

Do you think the United States should let Communist newspaper reporters from other countries come in here and send back to their papers the news as they see it?

Do you think a Communist country like Russia should let American newspaper reporters come in and send back to America the news as they see it?

The remaining half of the sample were asked the same questions in reverse order. Hyman and Sheatsley (1950) report a significant question ordering effect with respondents more likely to allow a communist reporter into the United States after answering the *American reporter* question and less likely to support an American reporter in a communist country after answering the *communist reporter* question.

The study demonstrated that when made aware of their desire to either suppress a communist reporter from reporting the news in the United States, or allowing an American reporter to report the news in a communist country, people were likely to change their opinion on the second question. It appears that norms of reciprocity, and perhaps fairness, exerted pressure on respondents to provide consistent opinions, even if they might have preferred to allow a US reporter to report the news in a communist country, while opposing a communist reporter from reporting the news within the United States.

Do Americans express a similar degree of contiguity in their immigration policy preferences? The postelection wave of the 2014 CCES contained a split-ballot experiment similar to that of Hyman and Sheatsley (1950). Respondents were asked about free migration – the idea that people should be able to migrate to whatever country they desire. The questions read,

. *How easy do you think it should be for citizens of the United States to live and work in other countries?*

. *How easy do you think it should be for citizens of Mexico and Central America to live and work in the United States?*

Response options were "very easy," "somewhat easy," "somewhat hard," and "very hard."

One-half of the sample were randomly assigned to receive the *US citizen* question, followed by the *Mexico/Central America citizen* question. The other half of the sample were randomly assigned to receive the *Mexico/Central America citizen* question, followed by the *US citizen* question. If support or opposition to free migration is due to political principles or core values, then we would expect contiguity in responses – people should support free migration regardless of the ordering of the questions since the principle or value would be applied equally across each case. This would be the case, for instance, among people who oppose immigration due to nationalistic or related tendencies as well as people who support immigration due to globalist or related values. If opposition to free migration is due, at least in part, to LRE, then we would expect some change in responses due to the ordering of the question. A person high in LRE does not necessarily oppose free migration, but instead opposes the free migration of Latinos. Therefore, they might support free migration for US citizens (and perhaps other White Europeans), but oppose free migration in the specific case of citizens from Mexico or Central America. Thus, we would observe a change in free migration support among these individuals when asked about the United States prior to being asked about someone from a Latina/o country.

An analysis of variance is used to estimate whether the mean responses to each question differ depending on the ordering of the questions. Respondents were more likely to say it should be easier for a US citizen to live and work abroad when they were initially asked the *US citizen* question (M = 2.34, SE = 0.04) than when they were first asked the *Mexico/Central America citizen* question (M = 2.51, SE = 0.04), $F_{1,658} = 8.01$, $p < 0.00$. Most people were supportive of allowing US citizens to live and work abroad, but being initially asked about free migration for citizens of Mexico or Central America led respondents to say it should be harder for US citizens to live and work abroad. Respondents were also more likely to say it should be easier for a citizen of Mexico/Central America to live and work in the United States when they were initially asked the *US citizen* question (M = 2.48, SE = 0.04) than when they were first asked the *Mexico/Central America citizen* question (M = 2.55, SE = 0.04). However, the difference does not reach traditional levels of statistical significance, $F_{1,657} = 1.18$, $p < 0.27$.

We observe much more stability in opinions toward free migration than in similar question ordering studies, but what explains the differences that we do observe? In order to explain the question ordering effect, we created a measure of respondent contiguity by taking the absolute value of the difference between the *US citizen* and *Mexico/Central America citizen* questions. Thus, we have a variable that measures the degree of within-individual change across the two questions, with lower values indicating less change. We model this opinion contiguity using a set of variables that should relate to greater cognitive consistency and

TABLE 4.6 *Estimates of contiguity in opinions toward free migration*

	Contiguity	
Treatment	−0.02	(0.23)
LRE	0.10*	(0.04)
Treatment × LRE	0.01	(0.06)
Age	0.04	(0.02)
Education	0.02	(0.02)
Political sophistication	−0.23*	(0.12)
Partisan strength	0.03	(0.03)
Constant	−0.1709	(0.21)
R^2	0.03	
N	627	

*$p < 0.05$. Coefficients represent ordinary least squares estimates with standard errors in parentheses. Data from the 2014 CCES. White respondents only.

opinion stability: political sophistication, partisan strength, education, and age (Alvarez and Brehm, 2002; Ramirez, 2015). We also include an interaction between LRE and a treatment variable indicating whether the respondent received the *US citizen* question first (treatment = 0) or the *Mexico/Central America citizen* question first (treatment = 1).

Table 4.6 summarizes the results of an ordinary least squares regression of the contiguity variable on the interaction. The interaction coefficient is positive, but statistically insignificant. This indicates that LRE had no effect on contiguity among respondents who received the *Mexico/Central America citizen* question first. The LRE coefficient, however, is positive and statistically significant. This means that among respondents who received the *US citizen* question first, increases in LRE correlates with greater discrepancies between responses to the two questions. In other words, respondents who harbor greater LRE were more likely to offer an inconsistent response when asked about free migration for a US citizen prior to being asked about free migration for a citizen of Mexico or Central America – a response that indicates that they support free migration, but not for someone from Mexico or Central America.

4.3 CONCLUSION

Imagine a person who believes Latinos are not assimilating as fast as previous immigrant groups have done, will not give up their culture and language, and are prone to criminal behavior. This person fails to understand the history of institutional discrimination that contributes to the current situation facing Latinos and instead views Latinos as unwilling to embrace the American dream. Such an individual would be angry that current immigration policies are not enforced. They would be anxious about the future of the country in the face of a growing, mostly Latina/o, immigrant population. And they would mostly blame Latinos, rather than political leaders or society-at-large, for these problems. This person would likely subscribe to the more common racial stereotypes regarding Latinos, and other racial groups, given that a strong adherence to norms of equality are a usual precondition to inhibiting such beliefs (Devine, 1989). Yet such a person clearly harbors animus toward Latinos that is distinct from the negativity they feel toward other racial and ethnic groups. The end result of this LRE would be a person who most likely directs these beliefs and feelings at supporting policies that negatively impact Latinos and push Latinos out of the country – a person who supports policies that restrict immigration. We find evidence of not one person who fits this description, but many White Americans whose opposition to immigration is related to LRE.

The political, social, and moral importance of this relationship is clear. White Americans who subscribe to this Latina/o-specific racist-ethnicist viewpoint often favor policies that result in the inhumane treatment of other men, women, and children. The result is policies where families are separated, due process rights are violated, and immigrants are imprisoned in facilities that violate conventional standards of prisoner care (Enns and Ramirez, 2018; Slack et al., 2015). Moreover, migrants engage in escalated risk-taking behavior to avoid these inhumane outcomes, leading to an exponential increase in migrant deaths. Future attempts to reform immigration will have to consider that immigration policy preferences are associated with deeply held beliefs about Latinos that (1) are engrained in the historical memory of the nation and (2) are being amplified in today's mass media environment.

We should highlight that not everyone who favors tougher enforcement of the US borders and the deportation of undocumented immigrants harbors racism-ethnicism toward Latinos. We have instead uncovered *general tendencies* among people who harbor LRE to favor restrictive immigration policies – tendencies that are both strong and far reaching. But the analysis also illustrated the role that other factors play in shaping people's desire for tougher restrictions on immigration: cultural preferences, economic optimism, and more traditional forms of racial and ethnic animosity. These factors were less consistent, and less impactful, in their association with Whites' immigration policy preferences, but we cannot rule out their contribution.

Moreover, the analysis demonstrates that LRE is not merely another indicator of more traditional and well-known forms of racism or ethnicism. For instance, despite a strong correlation between racial resentment toward African Americans and LRE, it is the latter that shapes people's immigration policy preferences. LRE also was shown to relate to people's immigration policy preferences even after controlling for ethnocentrism and old-fashioned Latina/o-specific stereotypes. We take this as further evidence that LRE is distinct from these concepts and that this analysis advances our understanding of the role of race and ethnicity in shaping how White Americans think about immigration policy.

Also of importance is the inconsistent role that partisanship and ideology play in guiding people's immigration policy choices. These factors were not impactful in any of the 2014 models, but were found to be associated with both support for work visas and increasing border patrols in the 2016 data. However, the evidence suggests that partisan and ideological cleavages on these issues are not completely aligned for most citizens. For instance, Republicans were shown to favor more work visas consistent with the parties historical pro-business position, while conservatives were more opposed to work visas consistent with the anti-immigrant rhetoric coming mostly from opinion leaders on the right of the political spectrum.

One caveat to these findings is that the research here is mostly observational, resulting in correlational rather than causal relationships. Yet, experimental studies have corroborated our analysis by identifying several causal relationships between specific dimensions related to LRE and public opinion toward immigration (Hartman et al., 2014; Haynes et al., 2016; Hopkins et al., 2014; Ostfeld, 2017). This research extends this latter work by showing how the broader concept of LRE relates to public opinion regarding various immigration policy proposals. Although the identification of precise causal relationships are important, the need to specify narrow dimensions of the LRE concept likely attenuates the more significant role that the broader concept plays in shaping people's immigration policy preferences. By taking an observational approach, we have the ability to show how the broader concept relates to the public's immigration policy preferences and gain a better sense of the substantive impact of LRE.

Overall, there appears to be enough evidence to establish the political importance of LRE. However, examining its connection to immigration policy preferences is somewhat of an easy test. Latinos are clearly defined as a group that should suffer from restrictive immigration policies and much of the anti-immigration rhetoric is specifically discussed in terms of the language of LRE. Thus, it is not surprising that we find such a strong and consistent relationship between immigration policy opinions and LRE. In order to further establish the political importance of LRE, we turn to several supposedly race-neutral policy issues: crime control and voting rights.

5

Attitudes about Punishment and Policing

The United States incarcerates a higher percentage of its citizens than any other nation in the world (Enns, 2016). More than 2.2 million Americans are currently behind bars in the United States (Kaeble and Cowhig, 2018). Slightly more than 1.5 million of these prisoners are incarcerated in state and federal prisons, with another 741,000 of these inmates in the custody of local law enforcement agencies.[1] One in every thirty-eight adults aged 18 or older is under some form of correctional supervision (e.g., parole, house arrest). And the United States remains the only democratic nation in the West that continues to use the death penalty as a form of punishment.

Even more astonishing is not the scale of America's prison population, but the color of that population. Although racial disparities in imprisonment and executions have been a historical constant (Carrigan and Webb, 2003; Curtin, 2000; Delgado, 2009; Wood, 2011), the impact of the country's turn toward "tough on crime" policies has exacerbated the degree of racial inequality in the criminal justice system. Whereas 1 in 17 (1:17) White men will be imprisoned during their lifetime, that figure is 1:3 for African Americans and 1:6 for Latinos. Similarly, only 1:111 White women will be imprisoned during their lifetime. That figure is 1:18 for African American women and 1:45 for Latina women (Bonczar, 2003).

This growth in the US carceral state, along with its racial and ethnic disparities, emerged from decades of "penal populism" (Bottoms, 1995; Pratt, 2007; Roberts et al., 2002; Warr, 1995). Whites became increasingly

---

[1] Kaeble and Cowhig, 2018.

favorable toward punitive approaches to crime in response to the civil rights movement (Barkan, 1985; Flamm, 2005; Mauer, 1999). Public officials opposed to racial equality were successful in merging the fight for civil rights with criminal behavior. As concerns about race became infused with beliefs about crime, public support for punitive policies increased (Peffley and Hurwitz, 2002; Peffley et al., 1997; Ramirez, 2013; Ransford, 1972; Skogan, 1995; Tonry, 1995). In an era of equal rights, punitive solutions to crime became the primary means by which Whites opposed to racial equality could keep minority populations subordinate – a form of social control (Garland, 2001).

The question we take up here is: to what extent does Latina/o racism-ethnicism (LRE) influence the opinions of White Americans in regards to criminal justice policy. Although it is clear that antipathy toward other racial and ethnic out-groups, particularly African Americans, relates to support for punitive crime policies, scholars have yet to establish a linkage between any form of racial animus toward Latinos and support for tough-on-crime policies. We focus on LRE given the recent growth in the US Latina/o population and rising fears of expanding Latina/o political power. If the fight for immigrant equality is the new civil rights movement (Johnson, 2012; Johnson and Hing, 2007), then beliefs about Latinos might be connected to citizens' beliefs about punishment as a means of crime and, by extension, social control. If criminal justice policy is a form of social control, then Whites who hold animus toward Latinos, specifically in its most prominent form of LRE, should be more supportive of punitive solutions to crime.

Understanding the racial and ethnic sources of public opinion toward this issue is important, given the compelling amount of evidence that public opinion in the domain of crime is influential in shaping policy. Nicholson-Crotty et al. (2009) find that public demand for more punitive policies is associated with increases in punitive behaviors across a range of political actors – for example, congressional spending on punishment, criminal prosecutions by federal attorneys, and incarceration rates (also see Enns, 2014, 2016). Similarly, increases/decreases in the public's willingness to execute its citizens corresponds to increases/decreases in death penalty sentencing (Baumgartner et al., 2008). State legislators have also been found to pay close attention to state-level opinions regarding punishment when formulating criminal sentencing guidelines (Brace and Hall, 1997). Even the move to privatize state prisons has been found to be closely related to the attitudes of the state citizenry (Burkhardt, 2017; Kim and Price, 2012; Nicholson-Crotty, 2004). Thus, any influence of

LRE on public support for tough-on-crime policies should concern any-one interested in minimizing the current racial disparities in the criminal justice system.

5.1 LATINOS AND THE RACE-CODING OF CRIME

Crime is widely viewed as a "race-coded" issue that activates White Americans' negative views toward racial and ethnic minorities even when no explicit mention of race is provided (Hurwitz and Peffley, 2005; Mendelberg, 2001; Peffley and Hurwitz, 2002; Valentino, 1999). A race-coded issue is a policy problem that, for some citizens, has an implicit, but well-understood, racial dimension (Himelstein, 1983, 156). For instance, welfare is "race-coded" because, despite being a program intended to benefit all Americans, many Americans assume the typical welfare recipient is African American and that welfare policies disproportionately benefit African Americans (Gilens, 1996a, 1996b, 2000; Peffley and Hurwitz, 1998; Peffley et al., 1997). Hence, the very word "welfare" activates racial beliefs that are applied to judgments about the policy. Race has also made its way into other supposedly race-neutral policies, such as urban redevelopment (Macek, 2006), education (Lipman, 2011; Renzulli and Evans, 2005), and health care (Henderson and Hillygus, 2011; Tesler, 2012a).

For decades, it was asserted that support for punitive approaches to crime (e.g., incarceration, mandatory minimums, truth in sentencing, capital punishment) were rooted in concern over crime victimization and conservative ideology (Langworthy and Whitehead, 1986; Scheingold, 1992; Wilson, 1975). Nonpunitive approaches to crime were opposed, it was argued, because citizens feared crime and strongly believed in the ethic of individual responsibility where criminal offenders needed to be held accountable for their crimes. Liberal policies were seen as "coddling" criminals, perpetuating criminal behavior (Beckett and Sasson, 2004; Warr, 2000). Empirical studies took up these claims, showing mixed support among various measures of perceptions of crime (e.g., crime victimization, fear of crime, crime concern) and favorable beliefs toward punishment as a means to control crime (Marion, 1994; Sims and Johnston, 2004; Thomas and Cage, 1976; Thomas and Foster, 1975; Tyler and Weber, 1982; Warr et al., 1983). Similarly, conservative ideology showed only a modest relationship with support for punitive criminal justice policies (Sims and Johnston, 2004; Soss et al., 2003).

Instead, scholars have found that beliefs about race are an important determinant of people's support for tough-on-crime policies. Although support for punishment is pretextually a race-neutral position, race permeates discussions of crime and public thinking about the issue. White Americans who hold negative stereotypes of African Americans, for instance, are more likely to support increases in criminal justice spending, the death penalty, and more severe criminal sentencing (Barkan and Cohn, 2005; Hurwitz and Peffley, 1997; Peffley and Hurwitz, 2002; Peffley et al., 1997). Moreover, supposedly race-neutral phrases such as "inner-city" or "crime" can lead some people to automatically imagine criminals as African Americans, triggering greater support for punitive approaches to crime control (Gilliam and Iyengar, 2000; Hurwitz and Peffley, 2005; Mendelberg, 2001; Valentino, 1999).

5.1.1 The "Browning" of Crime News

One reason for the "race-coding" of crime is the frequent portrayal of racial minorities in the mass media and popular entertainment as violent perpetrators of crime (Dixon and Linz, 2000b; Gomes and Williams, 1990). Historically, African Americans were overrepresented in crime stories and often portrayed as more menacing and violent than White criminal suspects (Entman and Rojecki, 2000; Gilliam et al., 1996; Mauer, 2006). These stories helped shape who citizens envision when they think of crime and how they believe the government should respond to criminal behavior. Peffley et al. (1996) find that exposure to an African American suspect in a television news story lead White Americans to view the suspect as guiltier, more deserving of punishment, and more likely to commit future violence in comparison to a White suspect. Gilliam and Iyengar (2000) also found that exposure to news stories about crime with an African American suspect increased support for punishment as a means to deal with crime.

We suspect that in recent years, crime has been "race-coded" around Latinos. Media coverage of crime has shifted, not necessarily away from African Americans, but incorporating a Latina/o criminality narrative into its reporting. Although Latina/o criminality has historical roots (De Genova, 2002, 2004), the contemporary media environment makes frequent use of the "crime script" when reporting on Latinos and Latina/o immigration (Branton and Dunaway, 2008; Branton et al., 2011; Dixon and Linz, 2000b). The illegality of Latina/o immigrants is a popular narrative in contemporary news stories regarding immigration

(Haynes et al., 2016; Perez, 2016; Suro, 2008). Farris and Mohamed (2018) examine images within news articles about immigration reported in *Newsweek, Time,* and *US News & World Report* and find that Latina/o immigrants are overreported in articles about illegal status as well as crime and criminality. Latinos are also more frequently depicted as engaged in criminal activities such as drug trafficking, human smuggling, kidnapping, trespassing, or being arrested (Branton and Dunaway, 2008, 2009a, 2009b).

Latinos are also prevalent in media reporting related to crime. Research by the National Association of Hispanic Journalists found that of the 115 news stories sampled in their study that focused on Latinos, 27 percent of them featured a Latina/o linked to crime or illegal activity (Abrajano and Singh, 2009). Studies of local television crime coverage in Los Angeles and Orlando have found that Latinos are more likely to be represented as perpetrators than as victims of crime (Dixon and Azocar, 2006; Dixon and Linz, 2000b). Subervi and Sinta (2015) examine all network news stories featuring Latinos on ABC, NBC, CBS, and CNN between 2008 and 2014. They found that Latinos are most frequently featured in stories about immigration and crime followed by electoral politics. Latinos were featured in very few human interest stories. Instead, one in four stories featuring Latinos on CNN was about crime. This says very little about how Latinos compare to African Americans or other racial groups in crime news. However, it is likely that when White Americans do hear about Latinos, it is often within the context of crime.

If Latinos are often featured as crime suspects in the news – as drug smugglers, kidnappers, and murderers – the association between crime and the Latina/o community should be present among White Americans. However, Latinos do not simply need to be featured as criminals for White Americans to link Latina/o race-ethnicity to crime. Stories detailing crime in Latina/o neighborhoods and interactions between the Latina/o community and law enforcement all help reinforce the connection between Latinos and the Latina/o threat narrative (Chavez, 2013). This "browning" of crime news, along with the criminality of Latina/o immigrants, is likely to increase the accessibility and importance of LRE when people think about crime and punishment. When racial and ethnic groups are associated with particular issues (e.g., crime), it can cause individuals to shift their evaluations of the issue away from specific policy merits and toward their opinion of the group (Abrajano and Singh, 2009; Nelson and Kinder, 1996). Much like people who harbor resentment toward African Americans, we expect those with antipathy toward Latinos to be more supportive of punitive criminal justice policies, given that such policies are intended to disproportionately impact the Latina/o community.

5.1.2 How We Examine Crime News?

In order to further verify the claim that media coverage often portrays Latinos as criminals, we examine a sample of crime stories within major US newspapers. The focus on crime stories expands previous efforts that analyze the criminalization of Latinos in immigration news. We chose newspapers since they reflect both national and local crime. This helps ensure we capture important regional variation in how crime news is covered. Newspapers are also more likely than television news to include in-depth stories about crime issues affecting national and local communities since newspapers are less constrained by space. In addition, newspapers often contain clear descriptions of the race or ethnicity of criminal suspects and neighborhoods. Major newspapers also mirror their print coverage online, thereby giving us a glimpse into one of the most common sources of information available to the public.

We identified a sample of crime stories by searching ProQuest's Lexis-Nexis Academic Universe for newspaper entries with the main subject heading of "crime," "sex crimes," "serial crime," "violent crime," and "murder." We searched for all stories with these subject headings between September 30, 2015 and September 30, 2016 – approximately one year prior to the public opinion data we use to measure public attitudes toward crime policies (described later). The resulting articles were narrowed down by focusing on stories about crime within the United States from a range of papers that represent the unique cultural, economic, and racial makeup of American cities. In particular, we made sure to balance out newspapers from cities with large Latina/o populations with newspapers from cities with large African American and White populations. The newspapers sampled are the *Arizona Republic*, *Atlanta Journal-Constitution*, *Austin American Statesmen*, *Boston Globe*, *Chicago Tribune*, *Denver Post*, *Des Moines Register*, *Los Angeles Times*, the *New York Times*, *Philadelphia Inquirer*, *South Florida Sun-Sentinel*, *St. Louis Post-Dispatch*, and the *Washington Post*. We limited our search to articles, lead stories, editorials, and letters to the editor. This resulted in 5,798 crime stories. We then randomly selected 1,200 stories from this pool to analyze.

Trained coders analyzed each entry, providing a count at the article level. First, we examined the number of articles that made an association between each race-ethnicity and crime. This includes, albeit is not limited to, stories that focus on a single criminal suspect, a suspect's criminal hearing, or criminal sentencing. It also includes stories about gang activity, drug abuse, and community crime conditions. The following indicators of race-ethnicity were used to assess an association between race-ethnicity and crime: (1) images of suspect shown, (2) artist's sketch shown, (3) photo shown, (4) race of suspect, neighborhood, or gang stated, and (5) specific mentions of race as a description of a neighborhood, crime problem, or gang. For instance, a story entitled "Latin Kings' Business of Violence Is a Hit" in the *Chicago Tribune* and "Violence in St. Louis Traced to Cheap Mexican Heroin" in the *New York Times* directly associated criminal behavior with Latina/o race-ethnicity.

When these more apparent indicators of race-ethnicity were not available, race-ethnicity was inferred based on characteristics of the story. This included (1) comparing surnames of criminal suspects (or family members) to a list of the 100 most popular Latina/o surnames and (2) a mention relating the suspect to a racial-ethnic community (e.g., member of a Black church).[2] Finally, names of criminal suspects were checked with available mugshots, which provided both visual and specific identification of race-ethnicity. In several cases, articles connected crime to both Latina/o and African American communities. In such instances, we counted the article as pertaining to Latinos and African Americans.[3]

How Does the News Media Report Crime?

We report the data in the aggregate since we have no expectations regarding the temporal dynamics of news coverage on crime within the year. Figure 5.1 shows the racialized coverage of crime news relative to the number of arrests reported by the Department of Justice.[4] As expected, African Americans still remain the racial group most often connected to crime in the news. However, Latinos are associated with crime at a

[2] No comparable list of surnames is available that is uniquely African American or White. Therefore, the racial comparisons are somewhat limited. However, this does not limit our primary goal of examining the frequency of crime stories featuring Latinos.

[3] To test for consistency among coders, we sampled 10 percent of the stories and had them coded independently by two separate coders. We then computed Cohen's kappa to measure intercoder reliability (Lacy et al., 2015). Cohen's kappa statistic ranged from 0.88 to 0.93, indicating a high degree of consistency among coders (Stemler, 2001).

[4] Table 21, Uniform Crime Report. (2016) "Crime in the United States." US Department of Justice. https://ucr.fbi.gov/crime-in-the-u.s/2016/crime-in-the-u.s.-2016.

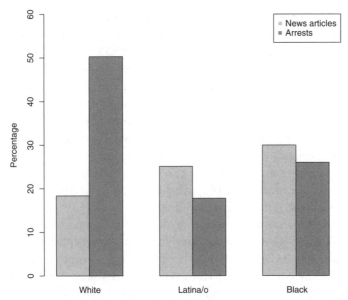

FIGURE 5.1 The racial makeup of crime news versus arrests

frequency greater than Whites (and, by estimation, other racial-ethnic groups). A chi-squared statistic shows that these differences are statistically different rather than observed via sampling error, $\chi^2 = 47.79$, $p < 0.01$.

Next, we utilize national arrest rates as a rough indicator of the over- or under-representation of each racial-ethnic group in crime news stories. It is important to recognize that arrest rates are imperfect indicators of criminal activity committed by each racial-ethnic group (e.g., arrests are a function of law enforcement efforts, profiling, and nature of the crime). Moreover, news stories provide more coverage of single incidences of crime because they tend to cover crime at various stages of the criminal justice system (e.g., investigative, arrest, trial, and conviction).

With these limitations in mind, the comparison of arrest rates to crime news provides a glimpse into the potential overrepresentation of crime news focusing on Latinos and African Americans relative to their reported percentage of arrests in the population. The percentage of crime stories associated with African Americans (31 percent) is 4 percent greater than the African American arrest rate (27 percent). Likewise, the percentage of crime stories associated with Latinos (25 percent) is 7 percent greater than the Latina/o arrest rate (18 percent). Surprisingly, these data suggest that Latinos, not African Americans, are most overrepresented in crime news stories for the time period of analysis. Whites, on the other hand, are significantly underrepresented in crime news coverage – at least in comparison to reported arrest rates. Thus, we find some initial evidence of an environment that we suspect fosters a connection between racial attitudes and policy preferences in the domain of crime.

The focus on race in crime news omits a second potentially influential source of the media on shaping beliefs about Latinos: stories focusing on Latin American countries. Although our analysis limited stories to those reporting on events within the United States, we suspect that the news media are more likely to portray events in Latin American countries as more violent, gang ridden, and drug-infested than stories about other countries. An automated search of the stories in our sample is consistent with this notion. Latin American countries are mentioned 151 times, African countries are mentioned 57 times, and European countries are mentioned a mere 54 times. Thus, even in stories about crime within the United States, Latin American countries appear more likely to be represented, at a rate three times more than are African or European countries.[5]

In order to examine this a bit further, we examine how many times stories are reporting about crime abroad. We reran our search, focusing on the same subject search terms in English-language newspapers during the same time frame described previously. We then limited our search to the *Indianapolis Star*. We chose this outlet to avoid newspapers with an overly international focus (e.g., the *New York Times*) and to minimize newspapers that cater to non-White populations (e.g., coverage of Latin America might be greater in cities with larger Latina/o populations). We then counted the country location of these crime stories. This resulted in 388 crime stories – mostly within the United States. Figure 5.2 shows the frequency of stories focusing on crime in other parts of the world. Crime in Latin American countries appeared more frequently than do stories about crime in Europe, the Middle East, Asia, and Africa. A chi-squared statistic shows that these differences are statistically different rather than observed via sampling error, $\chi^2 = 17.33, p < 0.01$.

Following the same methodology in the more internationally focused *New York Times* shows an even larger bias. In stories detailing crime abroad within the *New York Times*, 32 percent were focused in Latin

5 Although there are Black Hispanics from Latin American countries, it is unlikely that most White Americans imagine Blacks when reading about Latin American countries (e.g., Columbia, Honduras, or Puerto Rico).

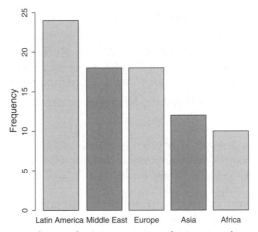

FIGURE 5.2 *Indianapolis Star* reporting of crime in other countries

American counties, while only 6 percent were about European countries and fewer than 3 percent were stories about African countries. Thus, when White Americans read the news, they are likely to encounter information that leads them to perceive that countries with larger Latina/o populations are more crime-ridden than are other nations. Of course, none of this shows a connection between the news and the public's support for tough-on-crime policies. However, it does demonstrate that the information environment that other scholars have deemed necessary for such a linkage is present and with a focus on Latinos.

5.1.3 Does Crime News Activate LRE?

We rely on an experiment to test whether crime news has the ability to activate LRE when people evaluate criminal justice policies. Experimental subjects were recruited from an online distance-learning undergraduate course at Arizona State University. Respondents are, therefore, not representative of the US population. However, the advantage of an experimental design is that we can ensure that exposure to the crime news story, rather than extraneous factors in the environment, is responsible for the activation of LRE when people make judgments about crime control policies. We designed an experiment so that the only difference between groups of readers concerned the race of the criminal suspect. Since all other aspects of the story were identical, we can attribute any differences in how LRE relates to support for punitive policies to the racial cues provided in the news story.

The experiment had subjects complete a survey that included measures of LRE. Midway through the survey, subjects were asked to rate the
importance of various news stories (e.g., the breakup of Pete Davidson
and Ariana Grande, a jobs report). Subjects were also randomly exposed
to the following crime news story where we manipulated the race of the
criminal suspect as either White, Hispanic, or not described at all. The
story read,

> Richmond police arrested a 21-year old (Hispanic/White/race not mentioned)
> male on a warrant Thursday morning charging him with first-degree rob-
> bery, first-degree burglary, second-degree assault and second-degree criminal
> mischief.
>
> According to the warrant, on September 17, the criminal suspect, a known
> gang member from Rice Court, Richmond, entered a home without permission
> and began kicking and punching the victim's bedroom door. According to two
> eyewitnesses, he allegedly entered the bedroom and began striking the victim's legs
> with a broken metal broom handle. He then got on top of the victim, the warrant
> states, and put his hands around the victim's neck, choking the victim. The victim
> was unable to breathe and passed out. The suspect was taken to the Madison
> County Detention Center, where he remained Thursday afternoon, according to
> online jail records.

Afterward, subjects were asked to recall various aspects of the story
(e.g., the gender and age of the suspect, the gender of the victim) as well as
the race of the suspect and whether the suspect was a US citizen. Subjects
were then asked their views regarding several crime control policies.[6]

In an era of heated anti-immigration rhetoric, do Whites assume criminal suspects are Latina/o when the race of the suspect is not mentioned?
We find that 6 percent of respondents falsely recalled that the suspect
was a Latina/o when the news story did not mention the race of the
suspect. Although this percentage is notably small, this is greater than
the 3.6 percent of respondents who falsely recalled the suspect as African
American when the news story did not mention the race of the suspect.
Thus, we have some initial evidence that African Americans are no longer
the only racial group associated with criminal behavior. Instead, Latinos
are just as likely as African Americans to be recalled as the criminal
suspect.[7]

---

[6] As a manipulation check, respondents in all conditions were asked to recall the race of the
suspect. All subjects reading about a White or Hispanic offender were able to correctly
identify the race of the suspect.

[7] Recall is measured with a forced choice question rather than an open-ended response.
This could potentially underestimate the effect.

What is important for our purposes, however, is who falsely recalled the suspect as Latina/o. We estimated a series of logistic regressions to predict who recalled the suspect as Latina/o when the story did not mention the race of the suspect. The results show that those harboring higher levels of LRE were more likely to falsely recall the criminal suspect as a Latina/o when the race of the suspect was not mentioned in the story ($\beta_{ml} = 0.97, \text{SE} = 0.43, p < 0.02$). The predicted probability of recalling the suspect as Latina/o increases from 0.01 when LRE is at its lowest value (1) to 0.26 when LRE is at its highest value (5). We also find that ethnocentrism is not associated with recalling the suspect as Latina/o ($\beta_{ml} = 0.01, \text{SE} = 0.01, p < 0.45$). It is not merely disliking out-groups that leads to falsely inferring the criminal suspect is a Latina/o, but a Latina/o-specific animus that explains why some Whites assume the criminal suspect is Latina/o.

In addition, we find that 9 percent of respondents falsely inferred that the criminal suspect was an illegal immigrant when the race of the criminal suspect was identified as Hispanic, despite the citizenship of the suspect not being mentioned in the story. A nonparametric rank-sum test shows that subjects who read about a Hispanic suspect were more likely to state that the suspect was an illegal immigrant relative to respondents who read about a White suspect or a story where the race of the suspect was not identified, $Z_{1,174} = -2.31, p < 0.02$.

Table 5.1 shows the estimates of a logistic regression of falsely recalling the criminal suspect as an illegal immigrant. The results show that LRE does not have a direct effect on falsely recalling the suspect as an illegal immigrant (model 1). Instead, it is only when the criminal suspect is described as Hispanic that LRE relates to recalling the suspect as an

TABLE 5.1 *Estimating recall of a criminal suspect as an illegal immigrant*

	Model 1		Model 2	
Treatment	1.47	(1.08)	−2.60	(1.85)
LRE	−0.50	(0.76)	−2.11*	(0.70)
Treatment × LRE	–	–	1.86*	(0.64)
Ethnocentrism	0.01	(0.01)	0.01	(0.01)
Partisanship	−0.24	(0.59)	−0.17	(0.54)
Ideology	0.56	(0.70)	0.47	(0.61)
Intercept	−3.94*	(1.07)	−0.40	(1.14)
N	89		82	

*$p < 0.05$. Coefficients are logistic regression estimates with robust standard errors in parentheses.
Source: Data from 2018 student sample.

TABLE 5.2 *Crime news and demand for punitive policies*

	Sentencing		Enforcement	
Treatment	-1.70^*	(0.84)	-2.13	(0.94)
LRE	-0.52^*	(0.24)	-0.27^*	(0.23)
Treatment × LRE	0.54^*	(0.30)	0.47	(0.31)
Feeling toward African Americans	0.01	(0.01)	-0.01	(0.01)
Partisanship	-0.05	(0.14)	-0.09	(0.16)
Ideology	0.38^*	(0.17)	0.38^*	(0.19)
Intercept	4.36^*	(1.09)	3.05^*	(1.17)
R^2	0.23		0.37	
N	82		82	

$^*p < 0.10$. Coefficients are logistic regression estimates with robust standard errors in parentheses.
Source: Data from 2018 student sample.

illegal immigrant – as indicated by the interaction between the Hispanic treatment and LRE variable in model 2.

Turning toward support for punitive crime control policies, we examine public support for increasing the number of law enforcement officers as well as increasing criminal sentencing for violent offenders.[8] We regressed support for each policy on both a variable indicating if the subject read about a Hispanic suspect and LRE. We also included controls for other factors shown to be related to support for punitive policies including partisanship, ideology, and feelings toward African Americans.

The results are shown in Table 5.2. Although we do not find a direct effect of the Hispanic treatment on increasing or decreasing support for either punitive policy, we do find that reading about a Hispanic criminal suspect activates the use of LRE in how subjects evaluated criminal sentencing and increasing law enforcement funding. The coefficient on the interaction between the Hispanic treatment and LRE is positive, indicating that among subjects reading about a Hispanic suspect, LRE increases support for tougher sentencing. This is shown in Figure 5.3. Among respondents low in LRE, support for increasing sentencing is similar after reading about a White or Hispanic criminal suspect. Among those high in LRE, support for criminal sentencing decreases after reading

[8] Respondents were asked, "How much do you support or oppose each of the following policy proposals? (1) Increase the number of police on the street by 10 percent. (2) Increase prison sentences for violent crimes."

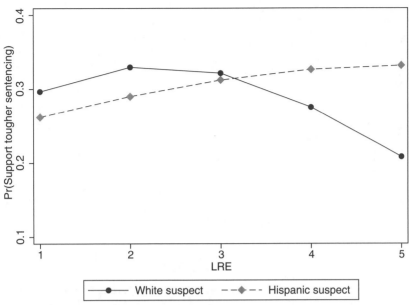

FIGURE 5.3 Race of offender, LRE, and support for criminal sentencing.
Pr = probability

about a White suspect and increases after reading about a Hispanic suspect.

The interaction is positive, but statistically insignificant in the law enforcement model. This is evident in Figure 5.4. Support for increasing the number of law enforcement officers is higher among those low in LRE reading about a White suspect than those reading about a Hispanic suspect. Among those high in LRE, the race of the suspect has little impact on support for increasing law enforcement personnel – although support for this increase does exhibit a statistically insignificant increase among those reading about the Hispanic suspect as LRE increases.

Overall, we have some initial evidence of the "browning" of crime news. People harboring LRE are more likely than people who do not harbor LRE to assume a criminal is Latina/o and infer that a Latina/o suspect is an illegal immigrant. Moreover, crime news that focuses on Latina/o suspects activates LRE, which increases support for punitive crime control policies. Yet does LRE have a similar effect on support for punitive policies outside of an experimental context using a small sample of college students?

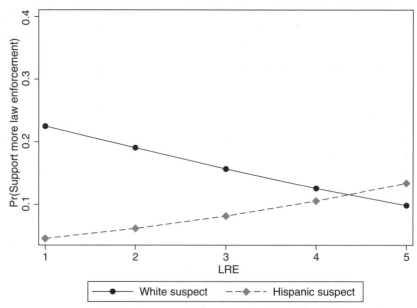

FIGURE 5.4 Race of offender, LRE, and support for law enforcement spending.
Pr = probability

5.2 UNDERSTANDING PUBLIC SUPPORT FOR PUNISHMENT

In order to assess whether LRE is related to public support for tough-on-crime policies outside of the experimental context, we examine the 2016 CCES. The 2016 CCES asked respondents their views on several policies that had recently been discussed among policy circles regarding criminal justice reform and crime control. Specifically, respondents were asked, "Do you support or oppose each of the following proposal?"

. *Increase prison sentences for felons who have already committed two or more serious or violent crimes.*

. *Eliminate mandatory minimum sentences for nonviolent drug offenders.*

. *Increase the number of police on the street by 10 percent, even if it means fewer funds for other public services.*

Responses to item one form the *sentencing* variable, responses to item two form the *minimums* variable, and responses to item three form the *law enforcement* variable. Support for items one and three indicate a preference for punishment, while opposition to item two represents a preference for punishment. All items are recoded where higher values indicate support for more-punitive policies.

We estimate support for each of these policies as a probit model using maximum likelihood estimation.[9] In addition to LRE, we include controls for factors shown in previous studies to influence support for punitive criminal justice policies. We include a measure of negative stereotypes toward non-White out-groups described in the previous chapter. We supplement this measure with an indicator of support for President Obama. We include this latter variable as a means to further control for negative feelings about African Americans given the reasonable assumption that respondents harboring deep-seated resentment toward African Americans are more likely to dislike an African American president.[10] The model also contains a measure indicating if the respondent has "been a victim of a crime" in the past four years. We include controls for attitudes toward the police, partisanship, ideology, sex, education, age, religious preferences, and authoritarianism.

Table 5.3 shows the probit estimates. LRE shows a positive and statistically significant relationship with favoring punishment as a means to control crime across all three models. The predicted probability of supporting increasing prison sentences for existing felons increases from 81 percent for a respondent who harbors the least resentment toward Latinos to 94 percent for a respondent who harbors the highest degree of resentment toward Latinos, holding the rest of the variables at their mean. The predicted probability of supporting an increase in the number of police on the street changes from 37 percent for a respondent who harbors the least resentment toward Latinos to 64 percent for a respondent who harbors the highest degree of resentment toward Latinos, holding the rest of the variables at their mean. Finally, the predicted probability of opposing eliminating mandatory minimums for nonviolent drug offenders increases from 20 percent for a respondent who harbors the least resentment toward Latinos to 40 percent for a respondent who harbors the highest degree of resentment toward Latinos, holding the rest of the variables at their mean. These estimates can be observed more clearly in Figure 5.5.[11]

---

[9] We do not find that these three issues form a single reliable scale. Therefore, we estimate them individually.

[10] The results are similar when we purge Obama's approval from national economic conditions, partisanship, ideology, and unemployment.

[11] We found no evidence that partisanship or political ideology moderates the relationship between LRE and support for punishment among these three policy areas.

TABLE 5.3 *Probit estimates of criminal justice policy preferences*

	Sentencing		Enforcement		Minimums	
LRE	0.17*	(0.08)	0.17*	(0.08)	0.14*	(0.07)
Old-fashioned racial stereotypes	−0.00	(0.08)	0.12	(0.08)	0.23*	(0.07)
Obama approval	−0.13	(0.08)	0.11	(0.07)	−0.05	(0.07)
Authoritarianism	1.32*	(0.44)	0.69*	(0.33)	1.51*	(0.33)
Attitude toward police	0.26*	(0.10)	0.35*	(0.08)	0.03	(0.08)
Partisanship	−0.10	(0.13)	−0.06	(0.11)	−0.04	(0.11)
Ideology	0.10	(0.09)	0.06	(0.08)	0.34*	(0.08)
Sex	0.56*	(0.13)	−0.05	(0.12)	0.28*	(0.12)
Education	−0.16*	(0.05)	−0.00	(0.05)	−0.02	(0.04)
Age	−0.00	(0.00)	−0.01*	(0.00)	−0.00	(0.00)
Born again	0.22	(0.16)	−0.20	(0.14)	0.46*	(0.13)
Crime victim	−0.02	(0.26)	0.07	(0.23)	−0.22	(0.32)
Constant	4.54	(8.45)	25.56*	(7.72)	3.20	(7.32)
N	881		883		882	

*$p < 0.05$. Coefficients are probit estimates with standard errors in parentheses. Data from 2016 CCES. White respondents only.

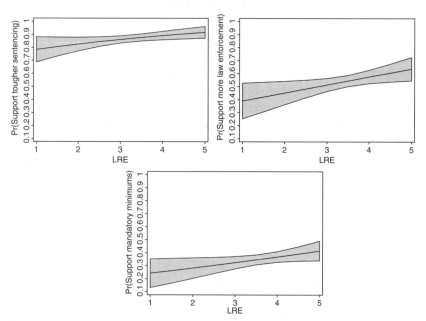

FIGURE 5.5 Predicted probability of supporting punitive policies across levels of LRE. Pr = probability

We reestimated support for punitive policies, including an interaction term between Latino racism-ethnicism and the change in the county-level Latina/o population, to test whether the connection between LRE is partly due to an increase in the number of Latinos in the United States, that is, are punitive policies viewed as a means to control a growing Latina/o population. None of the interactions were statistically significant, indicating that it is LRE, rather than objective changes in Latina/o populations, that correlate with support for punitive policies. Of course, Latinos may threaten Whites in ways beyond rapid changes in the population that affect the relationship between LRE and support for tough-on-crime policies. Yet these results are consistent with those reported in our analysis of immigration policy preferences and suggest that realistic group conflict plays a little role in support for policies that adversely impact Latina/o communities.

5.3 WHITE OPPOSITION TO POLICE BODY CAMERAS

We expand the analysis of public support for punishment by examining the role of race and LRE in shaping public opinion regarding policies forcing police officers to wear body cameras. The desire for police officers to wear body cameras has gained support among traditional advocates of criminal justice reform, that is, citizens concerned about racial injustice and police brutality. The increased visibility of extrajudicial killings of citizens by police officers, for example, Michael Brown and Freddie Gray, has also increased calls for the use of body cameras. Body cameras have been seen as a potential deterrent to police officers engaging in the excessive use of force and extrajudicial killings by offering both transparency when citizens file grievances against police officers and increasing the odds that police officers are held accountable for their actions.

The desire for police officers to wear body cameras has also gained support among policy-makers who believe that body cameras can enhance public trust in the police and improve police-community relations. Police body cameras can become a means for citizens to understand the complexity of situations and dangers that police officers face in the line of duty. Camera footage can also be used to provide evidence to both the courts and the public regarding why the use of force is sometimes necessary. Advocates of body cameras also argue that citizens may become less hostile with police officers if they are aware that their behavior is being filmed. A reduction in citizen hostility in the presence of police body cameras would ultimately increase the safety of police officers. Policy-makers also hope that documenting the daily actions of police officers will reduce the number of false claims filed against the police.

Despite these arguments, there is some opposition to the use of body cameras. First, equipping a law enforcement agency with body cameras comes at a high cost – usually in the range of millions of dollars that could be used elsewhere. This includes financing for equipment, but also training, maintenance, and support personnel. Second, police unions and officers have opposed body cameras under the guise of protecting personal privacy. Police officers fear that body cameras could lead citizens to identify and attack police officers, causing police officers to shy away from doing their job.

We suspect that beliefs about race might also play a role in how the public thinks about police body cameras. First, the call for police body cameras comes amid concerns of racial disparities in officer-involved killings of civilians. For instance, the deaths of unarmed civilians like Jose Raul Cruz in Dallas, Texas and Michal Brown in Ferguson, Missouri have directly resulted in calls for more transparency and accountability of police officers – often in the form of police body cameras. Although the use of force and police killings happen to people of all races and ethnicities, there are clear racial disparities in police killings. For instance, despite comprising 62 percent of the US population, White non-Hispanics comprised 43 percent of unarmed citizens killed by police in 2016. In contrast, African Americans who comprise 12 percent of the US population made up 37 percent of unarmed citizens killed by police in 2016. Latinos, who comprise 16 percent of the population, made up 18 percent of unarmed citizens killed by police in 2016.

We suspect that people who harbor animus toward minorities would be less likely to care about these racial disparities given that police are using their authority toward a disliked out-group. Therefore, people who harbor animus toward minorities should be less likely to support body cameras (and reforms) that attempt to address these problems. In other words, Whites who hold animus toward minorities oppose policies that they perceive to benefit racial minorities.

There is some support for this argument in the existing literature. Whites, relative to racial and ethnic minorities, tend to express more positive views of the police (Decker, 1981; Peffley and Hurwitz, 2010; Wu et al., 2015), while also showing stronger support for the use of force by police (Halim and Stiles, 2001; Thompson and Lee, 2004). Moreover, citizens harboring racial resentment toward minority groups are more likely to approve of the use of force by police officers (Carter and Corra, 2016; Carter and Jenks, 2016). However, existing research has not examined the role that animus toward Latinos has in shaping public support for criminal justice reforms and the question of body cameras. Although the most visible instances of police killings and brutality involve African Americans, and African Americans have been at the forefront of the criminal justice reform movement, priming White Americans to think about how these policies might affect Latinos should provide the condition necessary for the integration of LRE into their thinking. Subsequently, we suspect that LRE will be related to opposition to police body cameras, particularly when Whites are primed to think that body cameras will benefit Latinos.

5.3.1 The Police Body Camera Experiment

The police body camera experiment was designed to test the role that LRE plays in White opposition toward police body cameras when confronted with a situation where a Latina/o citizen is likely to benefit from the increased transparency. We created a unique survey experiment, embedded in the postelection wave of the 2016 CCES, where respondents heard about a recent incident involving the use of force by a police officer where the race of the civilian target is randomized across respondents. Respondents read the following scenario,

There was a recent incident reported in the news in which a police officer was accused of beating a [White/Hispanic] motorist who had been stopped for a traffic violation with his baton. The police officer denies any wrongdoing.

Respondents were then asked the following question, "Do you think police officers should use body-worn cameras?" A sliding scale allowed respondents to choose any point between 0 and 100, where 0 indicated "no, police officers should not have to use body-worn cameras" and 100 indicated "yes, police officers should use body-worn cameras."

Overall, the results are consistent with existing public opinion surveys regarding Americans' support for police body cameras (Sousa et al., 2015). We find that Americans overwhelmingly support the use of body cameras, with 94 percent of our sample providing a response indicating approval of their use (a response above 50 on the scale). However, we also find a great deal of variation in opinions toward body cameras (M = 82, SD = 21). We do not find evidence that the race of the suspect in our scenario altered people's support for body cameras. An analysis of variance shows there is no statistical difference in support for police body cameras between respondents who heard about a White motorist (M = 82.21, SE = 1.21) and respondents who heard about a Hispanic motorist (M = 81.85, SE = 1.17), $F_{df=616} = 0.05$, $p < 0.83$. This result is expected given that there is little reason why those who do not harbor animus toward Latinos would alter their support for body cameras in the face of a Latina/o motorist. Instead, we must examine the difference between those who harbor animus toward Latinos and those who do not.

We believe that it is respondents who harbor animus toward Latinos, in the form of LRE, that are likely to oppose body cameras when such a policy would benefit Latinos. In this instance, body cameras would benefit the Latina/o motorist. In other words, we expect to find a heterogeneous treatment effect where the treatment is moderated by LRE.

Given that support for body cameras ranges on a 0 to 100 scale, we regressed the support variable on the treatment (0 = White motorist, 1 = Latina/o motorist) and the LRE variable, testing our expectation with an interaction between the two variables. The results, shown in Table 5.4, confirms our suspicion.

First, the coefficient on the LRE variable represents the effect of LRE when the treatment variable is zero (i.e., among respondents hearing about a White motorist). The coefficient is positive, but is statistically insignificant. This suggests that LRE had no effect on support for body cameras among respondents hearing about a White motorist.

Second, the coefficient on the treatment variable indicates the relationship between hearing about a Latina/o motorist, relative to a White motorist, among respondents that do not harbor any racism-ethnicism toward Latinos (i.e., when the LRE variable is zero). The coefficient is

TABLE 5.4 *Regression estimates of LRE and Latina/o treatment on support for police body cameras*

	Body cameras		Body cameras	
LRE	2.64	(1.51)	–	–
Treatment (Hispanic = 1)	12.28*	(6.14)	−0.33	(1.74)
LRE × treatment	−3.55*	(1.66)	–	–
Old-fashioned racial stereotypes	–	–	−0.73	(1.44)
Old-fashioned racial stereotypes × treatment	–	–	−0.36	(2.05)
R^2	0.18	–	0.17	–
N	679	–	679	–

*$p < 0.05$. Coefficients are regression estimates with standard errors in parentheses. Data from 2016 CCES. White respondents only. Control variables not shown.

positive and statistically significant, indicating that respondents who do not harbor racism-ethnicism toward Latinos are more likely to support body cameras when the motorist is Latina/o. This suggests that they might view body cameras as a means to reduce racial injustices in the criminal justice system – exactly what we would expect from racially conscious citizens.

Third, the coefficient on the interaction term represents the effect of LRE among respondents hearing about the Latina/o motorist. Among respondents primed to think that body cameras might help a Latina/o, LRE decreases support for body cameras. The coefficient is negative and is statistically significant. Among respondents haboring LRE, endorsement of police body cameras declines when hearing about a Latina/o suspect. Respondents with the highest levels of LRE show the least support for police body cameras when hearing about a Latina/o suspect.

Finally, we reestimated the model, replacing the interaction between the treatment and LRE with an interaction between the treatment and old-fashioned racial stereotypes toward non-Latina/o groups. It is possible that it is not Latinos specifically that shape opposition to body cameras in this instance, but instead a dislike toward non-White minority groups. The results fail to show that old-fashioned racial stereotypes toward other minority groups have a direct effect on support for police body cameras or an effect on police body cameras when the motorist is Latina/o. Thus, the results are consistent with the argument that when facing a Latina/o motorist, it is LRE (dislike of Latinos) that increases opposition for body cameras.

The policy body camera experiment also provides some insight into how LRE relates to various arguments used to support or oppose policy body cameras. After being asked their degree of support for body cameras, respondents were asked, "Will the use of body-worn cameras cause the following to improve or worsen?" Respondents then rated the following items as either improving, worsening, or experiencing no change at all.

- *Police–community relations and public trust.*
- *Public safety.*
- *Officer safety.*
- *The conduct of members of the public when interacting with officers.*
- *The conduct of officers when interacting with members of the public.*

We had no expectations regarding how LRE would shape beliefs in these arguments and suspect their support or opposition is mostly a post hoc justification for their more general belief toward body cameras.

We estimated each variable using an ordered logistic regression using the same specification as described for the models of support for punitive policies except including a variable indicating the treatment condition each respondent received in the body camera experiment.

The results are shown in Table 5.5. The relationship between each potential argument in favor of body cameras and LRE is inconsistent. Among respondents hearing about a White motorist, LRE relates only to believing that body cameras will decrease public safety. It shows no association with any of the other beliefs. However, among respondents hearing about a Latina/o motorist, LRE is related to believing that body cameras will worsen, rather than improve, officer conduct. Thus, when primed that body cameras might benefit Latinos, LRE is related to rejecting the most common argument in favor of body cameras – that they would provide a check on officer conduct. Respondents with more-favorable attitudes toward police officers, and conservatives, are also found to be more likely to reject this argument.

5.4 CONCLUSION

Crime control policies should not be about race and ethnicity. Criminal behavior does not discriminate. White, African Americans, Latinos, Asians, and people of all racial, ethnic, and social groups engage in criminal behavior. The American legal system is supposedly built on the idea, engraved on the US Supreme Court building, that all citizens are "equal … under the law." But many Americans do not see equal justice and treatment by the US criminal justice system (Peffley and Hurwitz, 2010; Ramirez, 2014, 2015; Weitzer and Tuch, 1999; Wu, 2014).

Instead, criminal justice policy in America is "race coded" – a set of policies often implicitly, although now recognized as explicitly, racially driven. Racial and ethnic minorities are discriminated against at almost every stage of the criminal justice system (Alexander, 2010; Tonry, 1995; Walker et al., 1996). And these discriminatory policies are supported foremost by White Americans harboring racial and ethnic animus toward racial minorities. Prior to the studies in this chapter, we knew this was the case regarding African Americans. Whites harboring old-fashioned prejudices and modern forms of racial resentment toward African Americans have been shown repeatedly to be more favorable toward tough-on-crime policies (Barkan and Cohn, 2005; Hurwitz and Peffley, 1997; Peffley and Hurwitz, 2002; Peffley et al., 1997).

This study is the first to demonstrate that similar animus toward Latinos is also related to public support for several punitive policies

TABLE 5.5 *LRE and belief in arguments favoring police body cameras*

	Public trust		Public safety		Officer safety		Public conduct		Officer conduct	
LRE	0.18	(0.20)	−0.46*	(0.18)	−0.23	(0.17)	0.05	(0.19)	0.29	(0.24)
Treatment (Latina/o = 1)	1.16	(0.91)	−0.14	(0.85)	−0.31	(0.76)	0.87	(0.75)	2.40*	(1.06)
LRE × treatment	−0.30	(0.24)	0.02	(0.22)	0.09	(0.20)	−0.21	(0.20)	−0.59*	(0.27)
Ethnocentrism	0.22	(0.17)	0.01	(0.13)	−0.15	(0.15)	−0.02	(0.16)	0.41*	(0.19)
Obama approval	0.17	(0.14)	0.01	(0.15)	0.10	(0.14)	0.06	(0.12)	0.14	(0.14)
Authoritarianism	−1.37*	(0.60)	−0.59	(0.57)	0.05	(0.60)	0.60	(0.58)	−0.81	(0.71)
Attitudes toward police	0.09	(0.16)	−0.42*	(0.16)	0.07	(0.14)	−0.07	(0.14)	−0.62*	(0.19)
Partisanship	0.17*	(0.08)	0.07	(0.09)	0.21*	(0.09)	0.00	(0.08)	0.21*	(0.10)
Ideology	−0.15	(0.09)	−0.18*	(0.09)	−0.17	(0.09)	0.02	(0.09)	−0.30*	(0.11)
Sex	−0.36	(0.24)	0.19	(0.22)	0.45*	(0.22)	0.11	(0.20)	−0.11	(0.26)
Education	−0.15	(0.08)	−0.19*	(0.08)	−0.09	(0.08)	−0.06	(0.08)	−0.10	(0.10)
Age	−0.01	(0.01)	−0.02*	(0.01)	−0.02*	(0.01)	−0.00	(0.01)	−0.02*	(0.01)
Born again	0.12	(0.28)	−0.20	(0.27)	0.24	(0.25)	−0.04	(0.26)	−0.06	(0.34)
Crime victim	0.99	(0.67)	0.35	(0.54)	0.08	(0.51)	0.50	(0.44)	0.30	(0.52)
Threshold 1	−31.59	(17.64)	−43.88*	(16.73)	−50.93*	(15.33)	−10.53	(15.30)	−50.72*	(19.96)
Threshold 2	−29.95	(17.70)	−41.49*	(16.69)	−48.67*	(15.29)	−8.51	(15.32)	−48.65*	(19.98)
N	676		673		675		678		677	

*$p < 0.05$. Coefficients are ordered logit estimates with standard errors in parentheses. Data from 2016 CCES. White respondents only.

debated as potential reforms. Although the results here show only a correlation between LRE and support for punitive policies, the relationship is consistent across all three policy areas. Moreover, it is consistent despite controlling for some of the most prominent alternative reasons that people support tough-on-crime policies. This includes old-fashioned racial stereotypes, suggesting that LRE is not merely a substitute for antipathy toward other out-groups including African Americans. LRE also relates to support for punitive policies after controlling for people's more primordial desire for punishment – as indicated by the authoritarianism scale that measures preferences toward child rearing. Neither is support for punishment simply a rational response to crime victimization, beliefs toward the police, or partisan inclinations. The latter had an inconsistent relationship with support for punitive policies, possibly implying that the era of partisan disagreement on crime control policies is over. Indeed, recent efforts to reform the criminal justice system have come from both the left and the right (Dagan and Teles, 2014) – perhaps for different reasons, but nonetheless criminal justice reform is less of a partisan issue than in the past. Instead, our analysis suggests that those harboring racism-ethnicism toward Latinos are some of the last holdovers of an era of demanding more punitive policies. Thus, we are able to rule out many plausible alternative explanations for why LRE might relate to preferences regarding tough-on-crime policies.

We did not find evidence that changes in the local Latina/o population increased the relationship between LRE and support for punitive policies. Instead, merely harboring racism-ethnicism is all that is required to make the connection. This speaks to the power of the social construction of policy problems since the connection is made without the necessary condition of there being a real change in the status quo of the population. Our earlier analysis showed a strong connection to the belief in the Latina/o crime narrative and the LRE scale. Indeed, that belief forms an integral component of the scale, although the measure used in these analyses do not contain that specific indicator in order to avoid an observational equivalency between our independent and dependent variables (and the measure was not included in the 2016 CCES version of the LRE scale). Thus, we suspect that the crime narrative associated with the racialization of Latinos means that those who harbor LRE view Latinos as a group engaged in crime and therefore likely to be punished by tough-on-crime policies, which is consistent with the idea of crime policies as a form of social control.

6

Why Whites Favor Restrictive Voting Laws

In addition to winning the Electoral College in a landslide, I won the popular vote if you deduct the millions of people who voted illegally.
                    President Donald Trump on Twitter, November 27, 2016

Allegations of voter fraud have been a consistent theme of Donald Trump's communications since before his election. In October 2016, he tweeted multiple times that the election was going to be stolen from him through voter fraud. On November 27, 2016, after the election, he tweeted,

Serious fraud in Virginia, New Hampshire, and California so why isn't the media reporting on this? Serious bias big problem!

The next day he tweeted at two reporters, "You have no sufficient evidence that Donald Trump did not suffer from voter fraud, shame! Bad Reporter." and "There is NO QUESTION THAT #voterfraud did take place, and in favor of #CorruptHillary !" Early in his administration, he created a commission to examine the prevalence of voter fraud in America.

While his tweets hit the highlights of President Trump's claims, they do not necessarily provide much in the way of the nature of this fraud. Scholars and experts disagree with the empirical claims about the amount of voter fraud, but there is a clear consensus that voter fraud is normatively bad and that the country has an interest in making sure elections are fair and accurate. It could be that President Trump has been motivated by this general concern of electoral security. This has been the dominant frame in coverage of voter identification laws (Conover and Miller, 2018).

His rhetoric, however, makes it clear that this is not the only cause of his concerns about voter fraud. To be clear, President Trump has addressed a variety of types of fraud. He has claimed, with no evidence, that millions of voters cast multiple ballots. The consistent theme throughout his communications is not only that voter fraud is widespread, but that it has a partisan slant. He contends that he was hurt in the 2016 election and Hillary Clinton was helped. He believes that voter fraud is dangerous, not only because it challenges the fairness of our elections but because it creates a challenge to the legitimacy of his presidency. Additionally, part of President Trump's arguments about immigration is explicitly about the electoral implications for Republicans. Democrats, he argues, support permissive immigration policies because the large number of Latina/o, particularly Mexican, immigrants will eventually be Democratic voters. In September 2016, Trump said

I think this will be the last election that the Republicans have a chance of winning because you're going to have people flowing across the border, you're going to have illegal immigrants coming in and they're going to be legalized and they're going to be able to vote and once that all happens you can forget it. You're not going to have one Republican vote. And it's already a hard number. Already the path is much more difficult for the Republicans. You just have to look at the maps.[1]

Trump is not the first Republican to make these strategic claims. Much of the 2008 controversy over the Association of Community Organizations for Reform Now (ACORN) was due to allegations that they were engaging in widespread voter fraud. John McCain claimed that ACORN "is on the verge of maybe perpetrating one of the greatest frauds in voter history in this country, maybe destroying the fabric of democracy."[2] Sometimes, Republicans have even been remarkably blunt about the strategic choices. Laws requiring photo identification when voting are held up as tools to help prevent voter fraud and to help Republican electoral fortunes. William Wan of the *Washington Post* quotes North Carolina Republican consultant Carter Wrenn making the point very clearly: "Of course it's political. Why else would you do it? Look, if African Americans voted overwhelmingly Republican, they would have kept early voting right where it was. It wasn't about

---

[1] www.washingtonpost.com/news/the-fix/wp/2016/09/11/the-gops-hispanic-problem-will-grow-whether-or-not-trumps-citizenship-warning-becomes-reality/?utm_term=.

[2] Friedman, Brad. "John McCain: "One of the Greatest Frauds in Voter History."" *HuffPost*, November 16, 2008, available at www.huffpost.com/entry/john-mccain-one-of-the-gr_b_135460.

discriminating against African Americans. They just ended up in the middle of it because they vote Democrat."[3]

Wrenn's quote provides an alternative explanation for attitudes about voter identification laws, there is a second motivation: attitudes about race and ethnicity. While President Trump may suggest that immigration is bad strategically for Republicans in some instances, his rhetoric is frequently much more hostile toward Latinos in general. Even if Republicans claim that their motivations are based on electoral strategy, the racial and ethnic overtones could easily send signals to voters about how Latina/o racism-ethnicism (LRE) connects to attitudes about voter fraud and policies designed to prevent fraud. In this chapter, we explore the sources of voters' attitudes about voter fraud and laws to prevent fraud, comparing how the strategic implications of fraud and LRE contribute to these opinions.

We demonstrate that LRE shapes Whites' attitudes about policies that are less clearly connected to Latinos, specifically support for voter identification laws and ballot access. In particular, we are focusing on this policy area because while the policy has implications for Latinos, the dominant frames in the discussions are often about other aspects of the policies. The dominant frame for voter identification laws has clearly been preventing voter fraud (Conover and Miller, 2018). Finding a strong effect of LRE on attitudes about voter identification helps illustrate the pervasiveness of LRE in Whites' attitudes about American politics. Moreover, as noted, there is a clear alternate explanation for how and why Whites might respond to the implications of voter identification laws for Latinos. Instead of being motivated by beliefs about failed Latina/o assimilation and violation of Anglo-American norms, Whites, particularly Republican Whites, might be motivated by beliefs about the partisan leanings of Latinos instead of LRE. Testing whether LRE or this realistic group conflict is responsible for Whites' support of voter identification laws helps us to understand the potential limits of LRE in shaping policy choices in a domain where the racial and ethnic implications might be less clear.

6.1 THE CONTROVERSY OVER VOTER IDENTIFICATION LAWS

Access to the ballot is one of the foundational tenets of American democracy, but the systematic restrictions on enfranchisement is widely

---

[3] www.washingtonpost.com/politics/courts_law/inside-the-republican-creation-of-the-north-carolina-voting-bill-dubbed-the-monster-law/2016/09/01/79162398-6adf-11e6-8225-fbb8a6fc65bc_story.html.

seen as a stain on our history. Constitutional amendments that have expanded the vote are widely seen as corrective steps in American history. The 15th Amendment's guarantee of the right to vote regardless of race, the 19th Amendment's guarantee of the right to vote regardless of sex, the 24th Amendments abolishment of poll taxes, and the 26th Amendments lowering of the voting age to 18 now seem to most citizens like obvious improvements to the US voting system. Each of these advancements in protections of the franchise were, at the time, controversial and the debate over restrictions of the vote continues in contemporary politics. Instead of debating specific restrictions on a class of citizens, contemporary debates tend to either focus on the disenfranchisement of those who are undeserving because they have been convicted of crimes, or on providing safeguards on the electoral process by attempting to prevent voter fraud. The role of voter identification requirements, in particular, has become a central concern in the debate over access to the polls.

The expansion and retraction of voting rights runs throughout American history. As more and more tools for disenfranchising voters have been removed, efforts to limit voter access have evolved. In 1950, South Carolina became the first state to request that voters provide some form of identification when they went to the polls to vote. This initial law did not require a photo identification, merely some document with the voter's name on it. For twenty years, South Carolina remained the only state with this request on the books, until Hawaii adopted similar legislation in 1970. By the end of 1980, only five states had passed legislation that required identification to be able to vote.

In the next twenty years, voter ID laws began to diffuse across the country, but did so with little controversy or much partisan divide. By 2000, another nine states had adopted some form of voter identification law, but there was little systematic pattern in which states adopted these laws. The laws were passed, seemingly due to the idiosyncratic experiences of the states. The legislatures that passed the bills had both Republican and Democratic majorities. Voter identification laws were seen as one of many different electoral reforms that were being experimented with by various states.

This changed with the 2000 presidential election. The chaos that ensued during the controversial counting of ballots in Florida focused on how we administer and regulate our elections. Moreover, the clear partisan divide over how the votes in Florida were counted started to cleave the parties further. In 2002, the Republican Congress passed, and President George W. Bush signed, the Help America Vote Act (HAVA).

HAVA was intended to limit the possibility of a repeat of the 2000 Florida fiasco. The law created funding for states to improve their electoral systems by increasing the accessibly of voting places and systems, computerizing and updating the registration rolls, requiring provisional ballots for those suspected of being ineligible, funding the purchase of voting machines, and setting out requirements for all voting systems. The law also, however, created a new identification requirement. All voters who registered and had not previously voted in a federal election were required to provide photo identification.

Federal efforts regarding voter ID laws continued. In addition to passing HAVA, the federal government established the Commission on Federal Election Reform, otherwise known as the Carter–Baker Commission. In 2004, the Carter–Baker Commission was charged with addressing the lack of faith many Americans had in our electoral systems as a result of the 2000 election. Among the many recommendations from the commission was a call for voters to be required to provide photo identification before voting. The commission explicitly noted, "[t]here is no evidence of fraud in US elections or of multiple voting, but both occur, and it could affect the outcome of a close election. The electoral system cannot inspire public confidence if no safeguards exist to deter or detect fraud or to confirm the identity of voters."[4] Noting that the disparate requirements of acceptable ID could create impediments to voting, the commission called for the creation of "REAL ID" cards for voting.

During this time, the states continued to propose, pass, and implement different voter ID requirements. By 2005, twenty-four states had passed some form of a voter ID law. These laws differed in two dimensions. First, they are considered to be "strict" or "non-strict." Non-strict laws instruct election officials to request an identification from the voter. In 2004, Arizona passed Proposition 2000, which created the first strict ID law, *requiring* voters to provide some form of identification. The second key dimension is whether the identification must include a photograph. In 2005, Georgia and Indiana became the first states to enact strict photo identification laws. After this point, more states took up the issue. By mid-2018, thirty-three states had some form of voter ID law.

Early (prior to 2000) adoption of voter ID laws were haphazard and not related to the partisanship of state government, but that has

4 *Building Confidence in U.S. Elections: Report of the Commission on Federal Election Reform.* September 2005. Washington, DC: Center for Democracy and Election Management, American University, 18. www.eac.gov/assets/1/6/Exhibit%20M.PDF.

fundamentally changed. In their analysis of state policy adoption of photo identification laws, Rocha and Matsubayashi (2014) find that if a state has unified Republican control, it is sixteen times more likely to adopt a photo ID law than if the Democrats control any part of state government. The relationship with the racial and ethnic composition of the state is more complicated. While there is no main effect from the diversity of the state, in times of Republican control, the higher the percentage of African Americans and Latinos, the higher the probability of the state adopting a photo identification law. After the Supreme Court limited the application of the Voting Rights Act in *Shelby County v. Holder*, several states with large minority populations immediately enacted new voter identification laws. Alabama, in fact, had previously passed the law, but waited for implementation until the *Shelby County* decision. Texas announced their decision to immediately implement their voter identification law within two hours of the release of the *Shelby County* decision.

Other literature on state voter identification policy reaffirms the link with race and ethnicity. Banks and Hicks (2016) find a strong link between the percentage of non-Whites in the state and the likelihood that a restrictive voter ID bill will be introduced in the legislature, although it is a weaker link to the probability of passing the legislation. In their analysis of individual legislator votes, Hicks et al. (2015) find a similar pattern to Rocha and Matsubayashi (2014): Democratic legislators are less likely to vote in favor of voter identification laws when they have more African-American voters in their district. Republican legislators show the opposite pattern. Where there are more African Americans in the Republican legislator's district, he or she is more likely to support strict voter identification laws.

This connection to the Voting Rights Act illustrates the perceived link between voter identification laws and its possible differential effects on African Americans and Latinos. While many states allow for a set of identifications, the modal piece of identification used by voters is their drivers licenses. There are substantial differences in the likelihood of being a licensed driver by race and ethnicity. As a result, these identification laws have a disproportionate impact on Latina/o and African-American communities. The previously mentioned Texas law, for instance, had been struck down in federal court for discrimination. In *Veasy v. Perry*, the court held that "SB 14 creates an unconstitutional burden on the right to vote, has an impermissible discriminatory effect against Hispanic and African American [i.e., they comprise a disproportionate share of the more than 600,000 registered voters and one million eligible voters who lack the requisite photo ID], and was imposed with an unconstitutional discriminatory purpose."

While the courts have held that the laws have a discriminatory impact, there are two other clear reasons for elites to support voter identification laws aside from racial or ethnic animus. First, it is plausible that the disagreement over the priority of fundamental values results in the simple disagreement between the parties. Debate over voter identification requirements result from the trade-off between preventing voting fraud, either through ineligible voters casting ballots or eligible voters voting more than once, and access to the polls for eligible voters. The stricter the rules for identification, the more difficult it is to commit fraud, but the more likely it is that some voters who would otherwise be eligible and willing to vote would be disenfranchised. Neither party openly advocates for either fraud or for denying the vote to eligible citizens. The preference for the strength of voter identification laws could simply be a differential weighting of the two competing concerns. This is normal politics. Some policy creates trade-offs over fundamental principles and the parties chose opposite sides.

The second possible explanation for the divide between the parties is more strategic and crassly political. Voter ID laws are not believed to be electorally neutral. Some citizens could be disproportionately burdened by the requirements. If the modal identification used by voters is a drivers license, then voters who do not have one, or at least a license with a current address, may face a higher hurdle than those who do. There is some evidence that seniors, young adults (particularly college students), African Americans, and Latinos are disproportionately likely to either not have a drivers license at all or to not have one with their current address. It should not be surprising that the party that tends to get a larger share of these voters, the Democrats, are the party who resist these laws. The expectation is that their supporters will be disproportionately affected by these requirements, costing them voters. Thus, support and opposition to voter ID laws, at the elite level at least, may simply be the manifestation of political conflict.

The evidence for the disproportionate impact of voter ID laws on, particularly, minority voters is mixed (see, for instance, the debate between Hajnal et al. (2017) and Grimmer et al. (2018)). While the logic of the argument that certain voters may be dissuaded or prevented from voting is persuasive, the empirical evidence is less clear. Part of the inconclusive evidence is, potentially, the reaction of the parties and others to the laws. If turnout among a group of voters is expected to be minimized, political actors who rely on that support may redouble their efforts to get these groups to vote. Regardless of the actual partisan effect of these laws, however, if legislators believe that these laws will advantage one party, they are likely to support or oppose them based on this strategic consideration.

6.2 MASS POLARIZATION OR RACE?

A partisan divide over voter ID laws among elites is undeniable. The same degree of polarization, however, does not appear to occur among the masses (Daprile, 2015). Voter ID laws are popular and all polling on the topic show that mass levels are less polarized. While partisanship predicts support or opposition to voter ID laws, there is a sizable amount of support for the laws, even among Democrats. This should not be surprising. For most voters, being asked to provide a photo identification for voting is nothing different from providing an ID for getting on a plane or cashing a check. A Brennan Center poll in 2006 found that 89 percent of respondents have some form of government identification (Wilson and Brewer, 2016). For these citizens, the idea that people should have to prove their identity to vote might seem quite intuitive.

The popularity of these laws, then, should not be too surprising. The pro arguments are relatively easy (Carmines and Stimson, 1980). People have to show identification for many things. Giving the concerns about electoral security, this seems like a relatively simple step that, for most voters, will not create much of a burden. The con arguments are more complicated. These are, essentially, appeals to equality and the applications of abstract rights. The large literature on tolerance (see, for instance, Marcus et al., 1995) reliably demonstrate that Americans are bad at making these connections on their own. Moreover, the potential discriminatory effects of voter ID laws require voters to actually care about discrimination. If he or she does not mind if others are hindered, or if he or she actively wants specific others to be deterred from voting, then the discriminatory effects will not persuade him or her to oppose the law.

Additionally, the political elites in favor of voter identification have won the "framing war." The framing of the debate about voter ID laws is potentially quite powerful (Atkeson et al., 2014) and the voter fraud frame is likely to be the more powerful one (Conover and Miller, 2018). The result is that, despite the low levels of reported voter fraud, voters tend to automatically view voter identification as a question of fraud prevention and need to be primed to think of it in other terms.

Much of the evidence on the determinants of voter identification laws shows that attitudes might be quite weak and not well formed. Take the example of Minnesota's proposed constitutional amendment to require voters to show photo identification when voting. As Wilson and Brewer (2016) document, polling about the amendment before the campaign began showed that it was quite popular, with around 80 percent of Minnesotans supporting the amendment. As late as June 2012, five months before the campaign, polling still showed the amendment as popular, with 58 percent indicating they would vote for it. As the election neared, there were concerted efforts by organizations that opposed the amendment to articulate to voters the difficulties this proposal would create. The campaign to oppose the amendment persuaded voters that the amendment would create burdens for elderly, college-aged voters, African Americans, and Latinos. On election day, Minnesota became the first state to vote against a photo identification constitutional amendment or initiative. The lesson from this campaign is that while the voter identification laws are popular, providing information about the potential implications of the laws can reduce their support.

Beyond these observations from a single campaign, there is more systematic evidence about why some voters are more supportive of voter identification laws than others. Wilson and Brewer (2016) were the first to document the general patterns behind support for or opposition to voter ID laws. Not surprisingly, they find a strong connection between the perceptions of voter fraud and the need for voter identification laws. They also find that political predispositions, particularly partisanship and ideology, play a key role. Democrats and liberals are more likely to oppose these laws than are Republicans and conservatives. They also find a strong link to attitudes about African Americans. Voters who harbor higher levels of racial resentment toward African Americans are more supportive of voter identification laws. Finally, they also demonstrate that informing voters that these laws may keep eligible voters from being able to cast a ballot does decrease support for the laws.

Banks and Hicks (2016) show that fear and racial attitudes interact such that when Whites who hold more racist attitudes are made to feel fearful (as opposed to relaxed or angry), they become more supportive of voter identification laws. Similarly, Valentino and Neuner (2017) demonstrate that the possible disenfranchising effects of voter identification, particularly for African Americans, can produce anger at the law, resulting in higher levels of participation among the groups most likely to be disenfranchised. More recent work systematically shows that there are clear racial and ethnocentric bases of public support for voter identification laws (Udani and Kimball, 2018).

The racialization of voter identification might be a relatively recent occurrence. Appleby and Federico (2017) argue that the election of Barack Obama pushed racially conservative Whites to be less likely to perceive the elections as conducted fairly. This was particularly true for Republicans and conservatives. Prior to 2008, however, there was no discernible link between racial resentment and perceptions of electoral fairness. Given the realities of the 2016 election and the politics of the Trump administration, it is unlikely that these effects have dissipated since the last presidential election.

Unfortunately, most work on the racialization of voter identification attitudes focuses exclusively on the ways in which attitudes about African Americans predict attitudes about voter identification laws. While the link between the two is robust and undeniable, it is somewhat surprising that there has been little attention to how Whites attitudes about Latinos matters (but see Udani and Kimball, 2019). First, the potential disenfranchising effects of these laws are greater for Latinos than for African Americans. For a variety of social and economic reasons, the strict voter identification requirement is likely to have a larger effect on Latino voters than African Americans (Hajnal et al., 2017).

Second, the dominant frame in support of voter identification laws is to prevent fraud, particularly preventing ineligible voters from casting ballots. While the racial disparities in crime and felon disenfranchisement laws do result in African Americans being disproportionately likely to be ineligible voters, this is not the fraud that most elites focus on. Instead, much of the fraud debate focuses on immigrants who are barred from voting casting ballots. This is sometimes merely code language. At other times it is quite explicit, as when Tucker Carlson, defending President Trump after his Helsinki press conference with Vladimir Putin said on Fox News' *The Five*, "I think of course [Russia is] trying to interfere in our affairs. They have for a long time. Many countries do, some more successfully than Russia. Like Mexico, which is routinely interfering in our elections by packing our electorate."

As noted earlier, President Trump has consistently made claims about undocumented and fraudulent voting. He has claimed that Democrats are supportive of expansive immigration policies because these policies will eventually result in more Democratic voters as the Latina/o immigrants become citizens (or as undocumented immigrants illegally cast ballots). His and other Republicans recent emphasis on voter fraud has focused much more on the supposed fraud perpetuated by immigrants, particularly Latina/o immigrants. The ACORN scandal of 2008 may have framed the debate over fraud as being tied to African-American organizations, but the frame appears to have shifted over the past several years to focus on ineligible Latina/o voters.

Given this newfound focus on Latinos, we suspect that beliefs about Latinos might have a role in how Whites think about voting identification laws and voting rights. Given the evidence presented in previous chapters, we should expect that Whites who are higher in LRE should be more likely to support voter identification laws. It is likely not the case that all Whites approve of voter identification laws simply to restrict Latina/o voting, but only those who harbor LRE that prefer to do so – and most likely only in cases when the Latina/o frame is accessible. Moreover, these beliefs are probably not the only consideration of importance in shaping attitudes toward voting rights. People are also inundated with concerns over realistic group conflict and partisan strategies. Thus, we must devise a means to tease out how LRE contributes to support for restrictions on voting rights beyond these other factors.

6.3 LRE AND VOTER IDENTIFICATION LAWS

To compare the effect of beliefs about LRE and the partisan group conflict on attitudes about voter identification, we rely on a survey experiment. Survey experiments combine the general approach of survey research – drawing a representative sample of respondents and presenting them with a series of questions – but add a randomized experiment into the body of the survey. In randomly assigning respondents to one of many conditions, the expectation is that this experimental randomization will allow the researcher to have the ability to make stronger causal statements. If there are differences between the experimental conditions and the conditions are randomly assigned, then the only explanation for the differences should be the differences in the conditions.

Our initial study took place in April 2018. The survey was administered via Qualtrics. They solicited a nationwide sample of 1,000 Americans over the age of 18, representative of the US population. The survey had three parts. First, respondents were asked a relatively standard set of social and political questions, including our four-item battery measuring LRE. This section also included standard measures of partisanship, ideology, age, sex, education, and income. The one unique measure is our attempt to operationalize the partisan and strategic implications of the

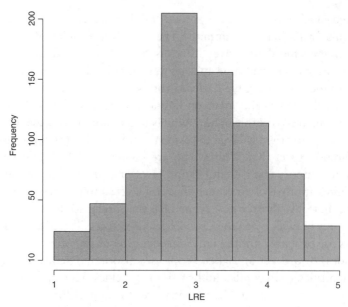

FIGURE 6.1 Distribution of LRE, 2018

voter identification laws. Respondents were presented with a list of groups in America and were asked: "Different groups in America are more or less likely to support each political party. What percentage of each of the following groups do you think vote for the Democratic candidates (as opposed to the Republican candidates)?" The response options for each group was a slider that ranged from 0 ("more likely to vote for Republicans") to 100 ("more likely to vote for Democrats"). Included in this list were Latinos, and seeing Latinos as more likely to vote for the other party serves as our measure of perceptions of realistic (partisan) group conflict.

Figure 6.1 presents the plot of our measure of LRE in the 2018 Qualtrics sample. As we saw with our other samples, the distribution is relatively balanced, with the mean at the midpoint of the scale, but higher levels of animus than commonly reported using measures of Latino stereotypes or feeling thermometers. Figure 6.2 present the histogram of the perceived partisanship of Latinos. The spike in the middle is the midpoint representing respondents who think that Latina/o voting is roughly evenly divided between Democrats and Republicans. This (incorrect) answer is the most frequent response, but the majority of respondents did indicate that Latinos are more likely to vote for

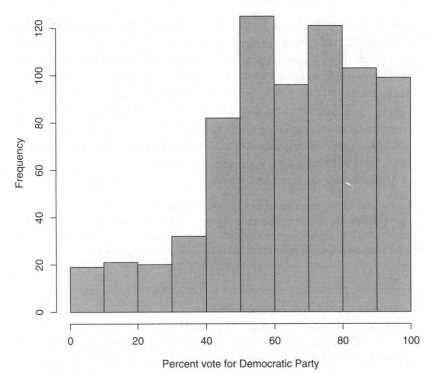

FIGURE 6.2 Perceptions of the percentage of Latinos that vote for the Democratic Party

Democrats than Republicans, with the median response being that 65 percent of Latinos voted for Democrats. Interestingly, the correlation between this measure and our measure of LRE is essentially zero (0.08). Not only do these two things tap different concepts, but the concepts themselves appear to be unrelated.

6.3.1 The Voter Identification Experiment

The experiment was included in the second part of the survey. Respondents were presented with and asked to read an article about voter identification laws. This is where the random assignment occurred. There were three different versions of this article. In all three conditions, respondents read a brief introduction to voter identification laws and a paragraph from an advocate of the laws explaining that they are needed to prevent fraud. In the control condition, the article's final paragraph presented the argument that these laws would create an unnecessary burden for voters who do not own cars. The picture presented at the top of the article was a simple picture of voting booths with no people in it. In the second condition, we changed the final paragraph to argue that the voter identification laws were likely to disenfranchise Latinos and replaced the picture with one featuring "Latino Vote USA," three Latinos, and the phrase "Your Vote is Your Voice" in English and Spanish ("Su Voto Es Su Voz"). In the third condition, we replaced the final paragraph with one arguing that the laws disproportionately disenfranchise African Americans and the photo has several African-American voters at the polls.

After reading the news article, respondents were asked,

As you may know, there have been efforts in some states to require voters to show a photo identification card to vote. Some people say this is needed to prevent people from voting who are not eligible to vote. Other people say such efforts can actually prevent people who are eligible to vote from voting. What do you think – do you support or oppose efforts to require voters to show a photo?

Response options for this question range on a five-point scale from "strongly support" to "strongly oppose."[5]

We have several expectation for what should explain responses to this question. First, the common minority suppression hypothesis would suggest that respondents who receive either the Latina/o or African-American treatments will be more supportive of requiring a photo identification at the polls. Second, the partisan strategy hypothesis predicts that Republicans who perceive Latinos as a monolithic voting block (in support of Democratic Party candidates) will be more likely to support requiring a photo identification prior to voting. Third, the LRE hypothesis expects that those who harbor higher levels of LRE will be more likely to support voter identification laws in the presence of Latina/o voters. This could either take the form of a direct effect if we assume that Latinos are already an accessible belief in how people who harbor LRE think about voting laws or an interaction between LRE and the Latina/o treatment if citizens need additional help linking their racism-ethnicism to the policy. Similarly, to the extent that there is an effect of the partisan conflict due to the partisan nature of Latina/o voting patterns, this should also be stronger among respondents who receive the Latina/o treatment.

Figure 6.3 presents the percent of respondents who gave each response to the question about support for a voter identification law. As is the case

---

[5] A manipulation check asking respondents to confirm which story was read was also used to ensure compliance with the treatment.

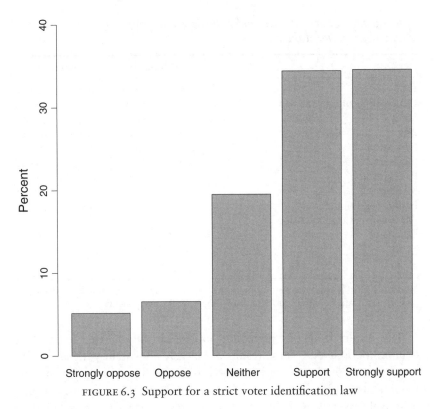

FIGURE 6.3 Support for a strict voter identification law

with essentially all surveys about voter identification laws, the policy was quite popular with respondents. The modal or most frequent response was the highest possible, with 35 percent of respondents indicating that they "strongly support" a law requiring voters to show a photo identification. Only a little more than 11 percent of the respondents expressed any opposition to the law.

Our primary expectation is that the LRE will explain why some respondents support or oppose voter identification laws. Our test of this includes several of the standard predictors of support for voter identification laws. The model includes measures of partisanship (coded so that higher values are more Republican), ideology (higher values are more conservative), sex (male = 1), age in years, education, and income. We also include our measures of realistic (partisan) group conflict, and LRE. This initial specification ignores the experimental component of the survey, but presents a simple observational model of what explains support for voter identification laws. We then turn to the experimental results for comparison.

TABLE 6.1 *Estimates of LRE and realistic group conflict on public support for a voter identification law*

	Model 1		Model 2	
LRE	0.51*	(0.05)	0.51*	(0.05)
Perceived % of Latinos voting Democrat	0.00	(0.00)	0.00	(0.00)
Sex	−0.16*	(0.08)	−0.17*	(0.08)
Age	0.00*	(0.00)	0.01*	(0.00)
Education	−0.08*	(0.04)	−0.08*	(0.04)
Income	0.03	(0.02)	0.03	(0.02)
Partisanship	0.11*	(0.02)	0.11*	(0.02)
Ideology	0.07*	(0.03)	0.07*	(0.03)
Latino condition	–	–	0.18*	(0.08)
African-American condition	–	–	0.10	(0.08)
Constant	1.19*	(0.19)	1.10*	(0.20)
R^2	0.38		0.38	
N	671		671	

*$p < 0.05$. Coefficients represent ordinary least square estimates with standard errors in parentheses. Data from the 2018 Qualtrics sample. White respondents only.

The results from our regression model are summarized in the first column in Table 6.1. These results are largely consistent with the extant literature. Republicans and conservatives are more likely to support voter identification laws, as are older respondents. Education is, as usual, negatively related, with higher-educated respondents more opposed to the voter identification laws. There is no evidence of a link between the perception of Latinos as more Democratic and the respondents' attitude about voter identification laws. In contrast, there is clear evidence that LRE is related to attitudes about voter identification laws. As expected, respondents who express more LRE are much more likely to express support for voter identification laws.

This initial model pools the experimental conditions. The second column in Table 6.1 takes that initial model and adds indicators for being in either the Latina/o or the African-American conditions. These results are quite similar to the first column. The patterns of significance and the substantive effects of the variables do not really change. Which condition the respondent is in does seem to predict their support for voter identification laws. Respondents in the Latina/o condition were more likely to support voter identification laws than respondents in the control condition. We should note that being in the African-American condition did not create a significant difference in support for voter identification laws when compared to either the control or the Latina/o condition. Thus,

TABLE 6.2 *Estimates of partisanship and perception of Latino voting on support for a voter identification law*

	Model	
LRE	0.51*	(0.05)
Perceived % of Latinos voting Democrat	0.00	(0.00)
Perceived % of Latinos voting Democrat × Partisanship	0.00	(0.00)
Sex	−0.17*	(0.08)
Age	0.01*	(0.00)
Education	−0.08*	(0.04)
Income	0.03	(0.02)
Partisanship	0.10*	(0.05)
Ideology	0.07*	(0.03)
Latino condition	0.18*	(0.08)
African-American condition	0.10	(0.08)
Constant	1.10*	(0.31)
R^2	0.38	
N	671	

*$p < 0.05$. Coefficients represent ordinary least square estimates with standard errors in parentheses. Data from the 2018 Qualtrics sample. White respondents only.

there is some suggestive evidence in these data that the debate over voter identification is or has shifted from being about African Americans to being about Latinos.

The results in Table 6.1 may not be a completely fair test of the realistic group conflict measure. It is intuitive that the effect of perceiving Latinos to be more Democrat should depend on the respondents' partisanship. Suppressing the Latina/o vote only has a political benefit to Whites if they think that Latinos are voting for the other party. To test for this effect, we add an interaction between the respondents partisanship and their perception of the percent of Latinos who vote for Democrats. Table 6.2 presents these results. While interactions can sometimes be a little tricky to interpret, in this case the results are clear. There is no link between partisanship and the effect of the perception of Latina/o voting patterns. Respondents' attitudes about voter identification laws appears to be unrelated to the strategic partisan implications of the laws.

An additional possible role for the effect of realistic group conflict is that it has an amplifying effect on LRE. Our test for this is to add an interaction between the measure of LRE and the perceived percentage of Latinos who vote for the Democratic party. The results of this model, presented in Table 6.3 provide no evidence that these two concepts work in tandem. Perceptions of the voting patterns of Latinos still has no effect

TABLE 6.3 *Estimates of Latina/o treatment and realistic group conflict on public support for a voter identification law*

	Model	
LRE	0.38*	(0.14)
Perceived % of Latinos voting Democrat	−0.00	(0.00)
Perceived % of Latinos voting Democrat × LRE	0.00	(0.00)
Sex	−0.18*	(0.08)
Age	0.01*	(0.00)
Education	−0.08*	(0.04)
Income	0.03	(0.02)
Partisanship	0.10*	(0.02)
Ideology	0.07*	(0.03)
Latino condition	0.18*	(0.08)
African-American condition	0.10	(0.08)
Constant	1.54*	(0.48)
R^2	0.38	
N	671	

*$p < 0.05$. Coefficients represent ordinary least square estimates with standard errors in parentheses. Data from the 2018 Qualtrics sample. White respondents only.

on attitudes about voter identification laws and LRE has, essentially, the same relationship at all levels of the perceived voting measure. This relationship holds when examining only Republican respondents.

The final expectation we had about the role of LRE is that the relationship between it and the attitude about voter identification laws should vary across the experimental conditions. In particular, we expected that the relationship would be stronger among the respondents who are randomly assigned to the Latino condition, particularly compared to the control condition. This is hypothesized to be a framing effect. One way to think about framing is that a policy like voter identification has numerous different aspects to it and it can be defined as being "about" these differences aspects. The law could be about fraud, or the burdens it places on different groups in society, or the logistics of enforcement, or the costs of acquiring identification. Information, like that presented in our experimental treatment, helps make different aspects more relevant as the respondent thinks about the policy in that way. If these kinds of framing effects occurred in our experiment, then LRE should have a stronger relationship in the Latino condition.

The test for this is to interact the LRE measure with an indicator of being in the Latino condition. If the framing effects occurred, then this interaction term should be positive and significant. Table 6.4 presents the

TABLE 6.4 *Estimating LRE across treatments on public support for a voter identification law*

	Model	
LRE	0.52*	(0.06)
LRE × Latino condition	0.00	(0.00)
Perceived % of Latinos voting Democrat	0.00	(0.00)
Sex	−0.17*	(0.08)
Age	0.01*	(0.00)
Education	−0.08*	(0.04)
Income	0.03	(0.02)
Partisanship	0.10*	(0.02)
Ideology	0.07*	(0.03)
Latino condition	0.32	(0.29)
African-American condition	0.09	(0.08)
Constant	1.05*	(0.22)
R^2	0.38	
N	671	

*$p < 0.05$. Coefficients represent ordinary least square estimates with standard errors in parentheses. Data from the 2018 Qualtrics sample. White respondents only.

results of this test. There is no evidence that the effect of LRE is any different in the Latina/o condition than it is in the other conditions. If we limit the comparison to just the control condition or just the African-American condition, we get the same null result. Our experimental treatments had no effect on the relationship between LRE and support for voter identification laws. One possible explanation for this finding is that Latinos are already a salient feature of the debate for those harboring LRE, making our treatments unnecessary for these voters.

Overall, these results suggest that LRE plays a strong role in attitudes about voter identification laws. Whites who harbor beliefs that Latinos have not properly assimilated into White-American culture and that Latinos violate norms are much more likely to support these laws. This effect is statistically constant across our conditions and dwarfs the effect of two of the otherwise dominant forces in American politics: partisanship and ideology. Even though the dominant frame around these laws is merely the prevention of voter fraud, this is, apparently for many Whites, tainted by their LRE. Thus, we find partial support for the minority suppression hypothesis and support for the LRE hypothesis.

6.3.2 Estimating Concern about Fraudulent Voting

We have shown a consistent relationship between LRE and support for voter identification laws. However, it remains unclear whether LRE shapes the precursors to people's policy preferences such as their concern about voting fraud. Emotions about voting fraud are an important component to people's policy opinions about voter identification laws (Valentino and Neuner, 2017). The political participation of foreign-born citizens, particularly Latinos, might shape these latter concerns about fraud rather than people's policy preferences toward a voter identification law. This is especially likely, given that support for voter identification laws is widespread, potentially having reached a threshold of support among the public.

In addition, we still need to ensure that people's beliefs in this domain are about Latinos and are not simply a substitute for reservations about out-groups in general. Specifically, we need to observe that concerns about voter fraud occur in the presence of Latinos, but not citizens of other racial or ethnic groups. Of course, the significance of the Latina/o treatment effect (but not the African-American treatment) in the previous study provide some evidence that this is the case, at least in regard to voter identification laws.

In order to provide additional evidence regarding the role of LRE on how White Americans think about voting rights, we conducted a laboratory experiment at a large research university in the Southwest. A total of 296 White undergraduate students were recruited from several political science courses as part of a course requirement. These subjects were told that we were interested in their reactions to commercials and other news programming. Students completed a short survey asking about their personality traits, feelings toward different out-groups, and political preferences including the LRE scale.

Subjects then watched a series of advertisements (i.e., Coca-Cola, Duracell batteries) before being exposed to the treatment. The treatment was a 30-second human interest commercial about a foreign-born US citizen who was expressing his joy to be within the United States, as well as his eagerness to participate in the US political system. All aspects (visual, audio, text) were identical across all conditions with the exception of the stated country of origin of the person of interest in the commercial. The commercial clearly stated (both verbally and in text at the bottom of the screen) that the person of interest had migrated into the United States from either France, Mexico, or Syria prior to becoming a US citizen.[6]

---

[6] The multiracial person in the commercial is identical across treatments, minimizing concerns about physical appearance and skin tones in adding to the treatment. A

After listening to the commercials, respondents were asked how likely they were to use some of the products advertised in the commercials. This provided a distraction from the human interest advertisement. Respondents were then asked to answer some questions about politics. To measure concerns about voting fraud, we asked,

How worried are you about people committing voter fraud? – Fraudulent voting makes you ...

Responses range on a 0- to 100-point sliding scale, from extremely worried (100) to not worried at all (0).

Although we had a range of expectations about the findings across the different country of origin treatments, we focus on those most relevant to the role of Latinos and LRE in shaping concerns about fraudulent voting. First, we expect that exposure to a Mexican American participating in politics will increase concern about voter fraud more so than a French American with White-European ancestry who is participating in politics. It is unclear how exposure to a Syrian American will shape concerns about voter fraud. Subjects might be concerned about all non-Whites participating in US politics or be strictly concerned about Latinos. Second, we expect that LRE will have a direct correlation with concern about voter fraud, even after controlling for feelings toward African Americans and ethnocentrism. The data contain measures of both, allowing us to test whether LRE is simply a substitute for antipathy toward other racial and ethnic groups. Third, we expect that LRE will moderate the Mexican-American participation treatment on concern about voting fraud. Subjects high in LRE should be more sensitive to the Mexican-American treatment, with their Latina/o-specific animus strengthening when primed by that particular treatment.

An analysis of variance (ANOVA) shows that subjects who received the French-American treatment were less concerned about voting fraud (M = 23, SE = 4.7) than were subjects who received the Mexican-American treatment (M = 36, SE = 5.4), $F_{df=94} = 3.33$, $p < 0.07$. In order to determine whether the treatment effect was due to a Latina/o or could be the result of aversion to any minority, we examined the difference between the French-American and Syrian-American conditions.

manipulation check indicates accurate perceptions of the person's country of origin. We pretested the images to determine whether respondents would believe the stated country of origin story and found clear evidence that the person depicted in the story could pass as a originating from all three countries.

TABLE 6.5 *Estimates of student concern about voter fraud*

	Model 1		Model 2	
LRE × Latina/o treatment	–	–	6.21*	(3.09)
LRE	6.71*	(1.80)	5.33*	(2.10)
Treatment (Latina/o treatment)	8.94*	(4.30)	7.89*	(4.41)
Feeling toward African Americans	−0.09	(0.09)	−0.09	(0.09)
Ethnocentrism	9.67*	(3.89)	11.75*	(4.27)
Constant	−10.08	(12.39)	2.25	(12.68)
R^2	0.45		0.42	
N	284		286	

*$p < 0.05$. Coefficients represent ordinary least square estimates with robust standard errors in parentheses. Data from the 2017 student sample. Models control for partisanship, ideology, sex, realistic group conflict, preference for Anglo-American culture, economic optimism, and change in household income.

An ANOVA shows that subjects who received the French-American treatment had no statistically distinguishable difference in concern about voting fraud (M = 23, SE = 4.7) than subjects who received the Syrian-American treatment (M = 30, SE = 4.6), $F_{df=95} = 1.23, p < 0.27$.

Next, we examined the role of LRE on beliefs about voting fraud and sought to determine whether any effect of LRE on beliefs about fraud are merely a substitute for animus toward other racial and ethnic groups. We regressed the concern about voter fraud variable on LRE, a feeling thermometer toward African Americans, ethnocentrism, partisanship, ideology, a measure of realistic group conflict related to if immigrant voting will help the Democratic Party, a preference for Anglo-American culture, and subject demographics.

We summarize the result, in Table 6.5, focusing on the variables related to race and ethnicity. In model 1, we observe that receiving the Latino-voter treatment is related to an 8.9-point increase in concern about voting fraud. This is consistent with the earlier ANOVA estimate. LRE has a direct effect on concern about voting fraud. A 1-point shift in LRE is related to a 6.7-point shift in concern about voting fraud on the 100-point scale. Negative feelings toward African Americans fails to show a statistically significant relationship with concern about voting fraud. Although the desire to implement strict voting requirements has been shown to be related to beliefs about African Americans, racial beliefs toward African Americans do not appear to be related to concerns about voting fraud. Such a concern seems to be related to Latinos and other ethnic groups. The ethnocentrism variable is related to concern about

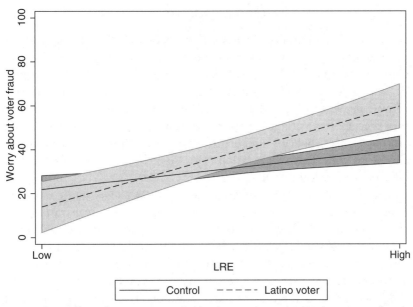

FIGURE 6.4 Effect of exposure to a Latina/o voter on concern about voter fraud across levels of LRE

voting fraud, indicating that people who dislike ethnic out-groups are also more likely to be concerned about fraudulent voting. Perhaps support for stricter voting laws are related to animus toward African Americans (as a means to restrict their vote), but support for stricter voting laws when framed about concerns of fraud (as the case with our previous experiment) makes animus toward Latinos the salient belief. Consistent with the findings here, Udani and Kimball (2018) find that immigrant resentment is a stronger predictor of concerns about the frequency of voter fraud than is resentment toward African Americans.

Model 2 in Table 6.5 reestimates the same model with an interaction between LRE and the Latina/o-treatment variable. We expect that exposure to a Latina/o who is participating in politics might activate LRE and agitate concern about fraudulent voting. The results confirm these expectations. Figure 6.4 provides a visualization of the interaction effect. LRE increases concern about voting fraud for all respondents, but the effect is slightly accentuated for those exposed to a Latina/o participating in politics. We fail to find any similar interactions between LRE and the French-American or Syrian-American treatments. This suggests that LRE is measuring beliefs about Latinos and not a general out-group hostility.

6.4 VOTER REGISTRATION PURGES

So far we have examined the association between LRE and support for voter identification laws as well as concerns about voting fraud. We now turn toward an issue that is perhaps more controversial among the public, but is increasing in its adoption by state governments – the practice of purging voter registration rolls. Voter registration rolls are a necessary precursor to voting. Voting registration rolls are lists of eligible and affirmed voters that are intended to ensure that those who do vote are eligible to vote. Thus, registration rolls are often seen as the first line of defense against voter fraud.[7]

The National Voter Registration Act (NVRA) allows states and local election officials to remove, or purge, citizens from voter registration rolls if the voter moves, dies, becomes mentally incapacitated, is convicted of a felony, or asks to be removed. States and local election officials vary in their process of identifying and removing citizens from registration rolls – a process that has been controversial in recent years.

Most notable is the case of Larry Harmon, a software engineer and US Navy veteran who was purged from the registration rolls in Ohio. Harmon registered and voted in the 2004 and 2008 elections. He did not vote in the 2010 midterm election, which under Ohio law led to a registration confirmation card being mailed to his residency. Harmon failed to receive or return the card. Under Ohio law, failure to return the card *and* abstaining from voting in the next four years results in an automatic purge. Harmon sat out the 2012 president election because he did not find either of the presidential candidates worthy of his vote. He then abstained from voting in the 2014 midterms, which led to his removal from Ohio's voter registration rolls. When Harmon showed up in 2015 to vote against a marijuana initiative, he found he was ineligible to vote after being removed from the registration rolls.

Ohio's process of purging voters from registration rolls was challenged on the basis of violating the NVRA. The case, *Husted v. A. Philip Randolph Institute*, was ultimately decided by the US Supreme Court in a 5-4 split decision in favor of Ohio, allowing similar practices to continue across the country. The decision was championed by those who believe that purging is necessary to prevent voter fraud. However, opponents suggest that such laws are little more than attempts by Republican-

---

7 All states except for North Dakota require citizens to register to vote prior to actually voting.

controlled state governments to make it more difficult for citizens to vote – a policy that many assume will hurt the Democratic Party more than the Republican Party.

In contrast to voter identification laws, we suspect that purging voters from the registration rolls is less popular and more controversial. We also expect that the public should be more supportive of such laws when they target socially marginalized groups such as felons and minorities. The popular image of the persons or groups whose voting rights will be removed by the policy is likely to serve as a powerful symbol or cue that guides people's choices on this issue. This applies to groups with a negative social construction, such as felons. We expect that in this instance a large number of citizens will favor purging felons from registration rolls. However, we also suspect those with animus toward a group will support purging members of that group from the registration rolls. For instance, a person who harbors LRE should be more likely to support registration purges when the person being purged is Latina/o.

6.4.1 The Conjoint Experiment

We test our expectations using a choice-based conjoint experiment of 2,498 White US citizens over the age of 18. Conjoint analysis is common in marketing research and has recently been applied to study various political choices (Hainmueller and Hopkins, 2015; Hainmueller et al., 2014). Conjoint experiments are particularly useful when a scholar is interested in testing the causal effects of differences in multiple dimensions of a choice. In a standard experimental design, such as the ones we have used in previous chapters, the researcher identifies one or two dimensions that he or she theorizes are important in the choice the respondent faces. The researcher then randomly assigns respondents to one of two or more conditions that manipulate those dimensions of the choice.

In our previous experiments, this design served us well. In each case, there is a well-established literature on the predictors of these attitudes and we could move the understanding forward by adding our manipulations and measure of LRE. This is not the situation we find ourselves in with understanding citizens' attitudes about purges of the voter rolls. To the best of our knowledge, there had been no real examination of public opinion on this question when we went into the field. Our motivation, then, is to not only test if Whites' LRE shapes this aspect of opinion on ballot access, but to also provide a more complete picture of what drives attitudes on this relatively new public debate.

To do this, we rely on the strengths of a conjoint analysis. Conjoint analyses have a long history in marketing research. Respondents are presented with repeated choices between two hypothetical profiles that have a list of attributes. The list of attributes are the same for each choice set, but the specific attributes are randomly assigned. For instance, if the respondent's hypothetical choice were to select between two people for some task, one of the attributes could be the sex of the two hypothetical people. For every set of two people the respondent chose from, each of the hypothetical people would be independently randomly assigned to be male or female. But this would be only one of the many attributes included in the list. The conjoint design asks the respondent to make repeated choices where the attributes are each independently randomized.

This design allows the researcher to test the causal effects of each of the randomized attributes and have become a go-to tool for experimental scholars. There are three other important advantages for our particular question. First, because the design offers a list of attributes, it is less obvious which one the researcher is interested in and it gives the respondent "coverage" for using what might be a socially unacceptable motivation like race and ethnicity (Wallander, 2009). Second, they provide an easy way to test for variation in the causal effect due to some observable feature of the subject. In our case, we are hypothesizing that LRE will moderate the effects of several features of the choice and there is a direct way to test this using a conjoint design. Finally, the conjoint design will let us compare the magnitude of the causal effects of multiple dimensions of the choice. Given the lack of existing scholarship on what explains voter's attitudes in this policy area, this allows us to benchmark the effects of the choice attributes and the moderating effect of LRE.

Our study asks respondents to image themselves as an election official who must decide which of two citizens they want to keep on the voter registration rolls and which they believe should be purged. Each respondent was given the following set of instructions:

IMPORTANT INSTRUCTIONS: Voter registration is the requirement that a person otherwise eligible to vote register on an electoral roll before they will be permitted to vote. This study considers a law in Ohio that allows election officials to keep or remove voters from voter registration rolls for a variety of reasons. For the next few minutes, we are going to ask you to act as if you are an election official. We will provide you with several pieces of information about people who might be kept or removed on the voter registration list. For each pair of people, please indicate which of the two people you would personally prefer to KEEP on the voter registration list. This exercise is purely hypothetical. Even if you are not entirely sure, please indicate which of the two people you prefer to KEEP on

Which of these citizens do you prefer to keep registered to vote?

	Person 1	Person 2
Gender	Female	Female
Race/ethnicity	Hispanic	White
Citizenship status	U.S. citizen	U.S. citizen
Past turnout	voted in last election	voted in last election
Valid state identification	has state identification card	has state identification card
Valid address	address confirmed	address not confirmed
Criminal status	Is a convicted felon	No criminal record

FIGURE 6.5 Screenshot of options presented to respondents in the conjoint experiment

the voter registration list. Please type the word "keep" in the box below if you understand these instructions.

After reading these instructions, respondents were presented with the choice of two citizens who are hypothetical voters. Each is a US citizen who is currently on the registration rolls and is being considered for purging. The respondent viewed information about the two citizens that fully randomized the voters' (1) sex (male or female), (2) race-ethnicity (White, African American, or Latino), (3) criminal background (no criminal history or convicted felon), (4) citizenship status (natural-born or foreign-born naturalized citizen), (5) voter history (voted in the last election or not), (6) address confirmed (the citizen's address has been confirmed or not), and (7) state identification (valid state identification or no valid state identification). We measure each respondent's choice across seven randomized matched pairs with the following question, "Which of these citizens do you prefer to keep registered to vote?"

Figure 6.5 shows the image of the profiles of two hypothetical voters as they were displayed to the respondents. While our main interest is the effect of race-ethnicity and citizenship status, the rest of the attributes are either central questions in the debate over ballot access or so obvious as to be noticeable by their absence (gender). Additionally, each of these are attributes that the state government is likely to know, even if the office in charge of maintaining the registration lists may not have access to the particular database.

We asked the respondent to indicate which of the two hypothetical citizens should be kept on the rolls. After making their first choice, the respondent was presented a second pair of hypothetical voters with new randomly generated attributes.[8] Each respondent was asked to make a total of seven choices between randomly generated hypothetical citizens.

While we are interested in the general patterns of effects of these attributes, we will focus mostly on the heterogeneous effects of two of the attributes due to the LRE of the respondents. In particular, we hypothesize that respondents who are high in LRE will be more sensitive to the race/ethnicity of the potential voter and whether or not the hypothetical voter is a natural-born or naturalized citizen. The expected effect of the ethnicity of the respondent should be fairly obvious. Respondents who score high on LRE should be less likely to prioritize the disenfranchise-ment of White or African-American voters over the disenfranchisement of Latino voters. The citizenship hypothesis is predicated on the assumption that for respondents, particularly respondents who score high on LRE, the image of a naturalized citizen is likely to be a Latina/o.[9]

The sample was obtained through the Lucid Fulcrum Exchange. Lucid partners with other companies to recruit a pool of nationally representative subjects for researchers. They work with various partners to ensure data quality and track IPs to prevent respondents from filling out surveys more than once. The Lucid Fulcrum Exchange compares favorability to a host of other possible sources of respondents (Coppock and McClellan, 2019).

Conjoint experiments are complicated, with each respondents making multiple choices and the attributes of the choices varying randomly. It is likely that no two of our respondents experienced the exact same set of hypothetical voters across their seven choices. The estimation of the causal effects of the assigned attributes, however, are relatively straight-forward to estimate because each of the attributes is independently randomized. We report the marginal mean estimates from the conjoint analysis, which represent the mean outcome across all appearances of a

---

[8] The order of the attributes was randomized across respondents, but fixed within respon-dents. The first respondent, for instance, saw citizenship status as the top attribute for each of the choices he or she saw. The second respondent saw gender first for all of the choices. This randomization helps minimize the effect of order of attributes in calculating their causal effect.

[9] We confirm this assumption in a manipulation check.

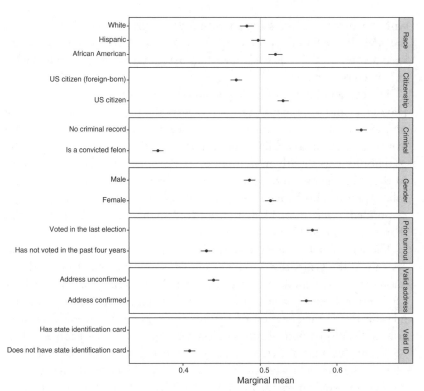

FIGURE 6.6 Marginal mean estimates from conjoint experiment on voter registration purges

particular conjoint attribute, averaging across all other attributes. Since the conjoint forces respondents to make a choice, marginal means average 0.5. Marginal means above 0.5 indicate respondents want to keep voters with that attribute from the registration rolls, while marginal means below 0.5 indicate respondents want to purge voters with that attribute from the registration rolls. For every attribute except race/ethnicity, the hypothetical voter had one of two options of each attribute, so the comparison is straightforward.

We present the marginal means of each of the attributes in Figure 6.6. The largest effects are the difference between a citizen who has a felony conviction and one who does not. The marginal mean of someone with a felony record is 0.37 – significantly lower than the marginal mean of someone without a criminal record, 0.63. Calculating the average marginal component effects (AMCEs) of the conjoint experiment captures the expected change in the probability of the respondent preferring a voter with that attribute versus a voter with the baseline attribute.[10] Examining the AMCE, we find the probability that the respondent would choose to keep a voter on the rolls was more than 0.25 lower if the citizen had been convicted of a felony.

The marginal mean of having a valid state identification card is 0.59. Having a valid state identification increases the probability of being kept on the rolls in our experiment by 0.18. Being a voter and having a confirmed address had smaller effects, but, in both cases, the difference in probability was slightly more than 0.10. Respondents were less sensitive to the race, gender, and whether the citizen was natural-born or naturalized, but each of these effects is statistically significant. Surprisingly, respondents were more likely to keep voters who were African American than a hypothetical White or Hispanic voter.

These results illustrate the general patterns of which hypothetical voters gained the sympathy of our respondents, but not the key hypotheses about how LRE moderates the effect of these attributes. We test how LRE interacts with each attribute, with an expectation that attributes relating to the racialization of Latinos (race of voter, citizenship status, criminality) to be part of the decision-making calculus of people high in LRE. For this analysis, we consider respondents below the mean level of LRE in the sample to be low in their racism-ethnicism toward Latinos and respondents above the mean level of LRE to be high in their racism-ethnicism toward Latinos.[11]

Figure 6.7 presents the marginal mean estimates. Respondents high in LRE are shown in black. Respondents low in LRE are shown in lighter gray. The race of the respondent matters differently for those high in LRE relative to those low in LRE. Respondents who score low on the LRE measure prefer African Americans and Hispanics to be kept on the rolls over Whites. Among high levels of LRE, however, the effects are different. There is no longer a difference between the desire to keep Whites and African Americans. More importantly, these respondents are significantly less likely to keep a Hispanic voter on the registration rolls. In other words, LRE is associated with a flip in the effect of the ethnicity of the hypothetical voter. Those who have low levels want the system to be biased in favor of keeping Latina/o voters on the rolls. Those who are high on this measure seem to want the system to be biased *against* Latina/o voters.

---

[10] We follow the standard practice of clustering the standard errors by respondent.
[11] We find similar effects when we split the data in thirds along the LRE measure.

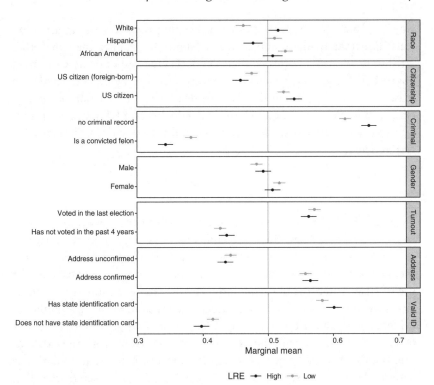

FIGURE 6.7 Moderating effect of LRE on voter registration purges

The moderating effect of LRE is less pronounced for the effect of being presented a hypothetical voter who is a foreign-born citizen instead of a natural-born citizen. Respondents prefer voters who are natural-born citizens, with those high in LRE slightly more likely to purge a foreign-born US citizen than those low in LRE. The slight difference observed in the marginal mean estimate is not statistically significant.

LRE does have a moderating effect on criminal status. All respondents prefer to purge a convicted felon from the voter rolls relative to a voter with no criminal background. However, respondents high in LRE are significantly more likely to want to purge a convicted felon than are respondents low in LRE. Equally important to these results is that LRE does not moderate any of the other attributes – it only moderates those attributes that have been theoretically connected to the racialization of Latinos.

It is important to note the relatively small magnitude of these effects. Our results do suggest that the race and ethnicity of a voter changes the way in which respondents prioritize keeping them on the registration rolls. Fortunately, these effects are substantially smaller than the other attributes we provide (other than gender). Our respondents care more about being a good citizen through voting or not being convicted of a felony than they do about the race, gender, or how the person becomes a citizen. But even with these relatively small effects, LRE plays an important role in shaping how race, ethnicity, and type of citizenship matter to respondents.

6.5 CONCLUSION

Since 2000, the trend in state politics has been the adoption of more restrictive voting rules. Since Republicans took over unified control of over half the states in 2010, we have seen the roll back of early voting, the shrinking of the number of polling places, and an increase in the use of strict voter identification laws. At the elite level, support for these laws have a clear partisans and strategic motivation. Even if the empirical evidence is mixed, Republican state legislators and governors have systematically and efficiently limited access to the ballot, with the expectation that this would be good for Republicans in elections, and numerous commentators suggest that these changes have been consequential. Ken Mayer has gone so far as to claim that Wisconsin's voter identification law is responsible for Trump winning the state in 2016.[12]

If the laws had this strong an effect on elections, one would expect that opinion on them would be quite polarized among Whites, and there is a difference in the mean level of support for these laws between Democrats and Republicans. This difference, however, is nowhere near the magnitude of many other policies.

Voter identification laws have become a salient issue in both state and national politics. On one of the days this chapter was written, President Trump claimed, "You know, if you go out and you want to buy groceries, you need a picture on a card, you need ID." While this is clearly false, it illustrates the increasing role the policy is playing in national discourse. At times, the rhetoric of the debate touches on race and ethnicity. But, in the grocery speech, President Trump did not send any explicit cues about race or ethnicity. The role of LRE in explaining voters' attitudes about voter identification laws, however, does not seem to depend on these cues.

---

[12] www.motherjones.com/politics/2017/10/voter-suppression-wisconsin-election-2016/.

They are an essential piece of them, regardless of what cues or frames they are given.

We think our results illustrate this. The relationship between LRE is clear. The more important result, we think, is the absence of a framing effect in our experiment. We hypothesized that the explicit cues that voter identification laws are "about" Latinos should make LRE a stronger predictor of support for the voter identification laws. It did not. There are a couple of different possibilities for this null effect. First, it could simply be that our manipulations were too weak to have an effect. We do not think this is the case. The design is similar to the other experiments that have focused on the role of attitudes about African Americans (Valentino and Neuner, 2017). In addition to having similar textual cues, our manipulation added an image that included a slogan in Spanish. If a framing effect were possible, this visual cue should have been enough.

The second possible explanation is the one we think is more likely. Framing effects only work if they *change* how respondents think about the issue. The evidence we have presented in this chapter suggests that respondents in the control condition already viewed this as an issue that was about their LRE. Even if we limit our analysis to the control condition, when we did not use a frame about Latinos, LRE is strongly related to attitudes about voter identification; again a stronger relationship than partisanship or ideology. Our experiment possibly failed in framing the issues as being about Latinos because our respondents came into the discussion of the issue already thinking about Latinos. Even when respondents are given no information, this issue is fundamentally one about who is believed to be voting fraudulently.

The implication of this result is that even issues that are ostensibly about something other than the status of Latinas/os in American society are to some extent about race and ethnicity. The absence of the framing effects, then, make a clear statement about the effect of LRE.

7

The Electoral Implications of Latina/o
Racism-Ethnicism

Campaigns and elections are a natural place to continue our investigation of how Latina/o racism-ethnicism (LRE) shapes modern politics. The ways that politicians have discussed Latinos in America during recent campaigns, particularly how they have framed the debate on immigration in a way that reinforces the "racialization" of Latinos as a distinctly non-White alien out-group, makes LRE a potentially important factor shaping contemporary elections. Thus, an examination of the role that LRE plays in the US electoral system has the potential to augment our previous findings: that LRE is an especially powerful belief among White Americans, with important consequences for their political opinions and behaviors.

7.1 RACIAL AND ETHNIC CONFLICT IN US ELECTIONS

Elections are often called "the bedrock of democracy" because of their ability to transfer the will of the people into governing coalitions that ultimately lead to public policy outputs. But elections are foremost contests over power and authority. Candidates align themselves with various groups and compete for the support of the public. Political parties often become the most visible groups competing during US elections, but electoral campaigns frequently become contests between special interest organizations, economic classes, and racial-ethnic groups. The public then decides who should wield power and who should step aside. The prevalence of group competition during electoral campaigns means group-centric thinking often plays a significant role in the decision-making calculus of voters.

Race and ethnic group conflict has been particularly decisive in contemporary electoral campaigns. For much of the twentieth century, US elections were referendums on civil rights legislation and the status of African Americans (Carmines and Stimson, 1989; Dudziak, 2000; Gamble, 1997; Hutchings and Valentino, 2004; Pomper, 1972; Tate, 1994). For example, Strom Thurmond made race a salient feature of the 1948 presidential election. Thurmond campaigned against President Truman's decision to support anti-lynching laws, the elimination of state poll taxes, and an end to racial discrimination in the US Army. Barry Goldwater helped infuse race into the 1964 presidential election by forming a "Southern Strategy" that attempted to court White voters by speaking out against the Civil Rights Act of 1964. Race also surfaced as a key issue in the 1988 presidential election when the campaign of George H. W. Bush ran a series of advertisements featuring an African-American convict, Willie Horton, hoping to implicitly increase the importance of racial attitudes among White voters on election day (Brady, 1996; Mendelberg, 2001). These campaigns often prove effective. Kinder and Sanders (1996, 246–247), for instance, show that the relationship between racial resentment and White Americans' vote choice in the 1988 election nearly doubled after the airing of the Willie Horton advertisement.

Beliefs about race and ethnicity were more recently on display during the 2008 election when Barack Obama became the first African-American major-party candidate for the US presidency. Tesler and Sears (2010) examine an extensive set of polls to show that symbolic racism played a substantial role in how White voters evaluated Barack Obama versus Senator Hillary Clinton in the 2008 Democratic primary election and versus Senator John McCain in the general election. Racist White voters were less likely to vote for Obama more so than their ideological affiliation and policy preferences would have predicted (also see Payne et al., 2010; Schaffner, 2011). They also examined polls in prior election years to show that race-related beliefs mattered more in how people voted in 2008 than they had in previous elections. Tesler (2012b) further shows that both symbolic racism and old-fashioned racial stereotypes became increasingly important in both the 2008 Democratic primary and the 2008 general presidential election, with people expressing racist beliefs of either kind less likely to vote for Obama. Moreover, Obama's presidency infused race into other elections. Tesler (2012b, 119) shows that Whites who believe in old-fashioned racial stereotypes were 35 percent less likely than Whites who do not believe in old-fashioned racial stereotypes to support a Democratic candidate in the 2010 midterm elections.

Overall, the study of race in American elections shows that both race-related issues and minority candidates can increase the salience of beliefs about minority groups when voters go to the polls.[1] Understanding the extent that race permeates elections is important since, as Bell (1978, 15) argues, voting "enables the voters' racial beliefs and fears to be recorded and tabulated in their pure form," leading to "bias discrimination, and prejudice which has marred American democracy from its earliest day." Whereas most of the existing research has focused on how issues related to the struggles of African Americans or African-American candidates shape the voting preferences of Whites (Citrin et al., 1990; Highton, 2004; Kinder and Sanders, 1996; McDermott, 1998; Mendelberg, 2001; Philpot and Walton, 2007; Terkildsen, 1993; Tesler and Sears, 2010), we suggest that in recent elections LRE has become an important factor related to how White Americans vote. The continual increase in the number of Latinos running for elected office in recent elections and the salience of immigration are both likely to make people's existing beliefs about Latinos accessible when they decide who to support during an election. A candidate's race and ethnicity, as well as the position candidates take on immigration, should provide an easy and visible cue that activates group-based reasoning, which has the potential to alter people's voting calculus in a predictable manner.

We test these expectations by examining the relationship between LRE and voting for Latina/o candidates for the US House of Representatives in the 2014 midterm election and the 2016 general election. We then examine how LRE relates to voting for political candidates who campaign on a tough-on-immigration platform during US Senate elections in 2014 and 2016, state gubernatorial elections in 2014, and the 2016 US presidential election.[2]

7.2 SUPPORT FOR LATINA/O CANDIDATES IN US ELECTIONS

We begin by examining White American's support for Latina/o candidates. Although Latinos are still extremely underrepresented in elected positions (Rojas et al., 2016), the last several decades have seen a record

---

[1] Although we focus exclusively on these two mechanisms, a candidate's race or ethnicity and position-taking on race-based issues, we do not intend to imply these are the only means by which race and ethnicity can infuse themselves into an election.

[2] We chose to examine the role of Latina/o candidates during the US House elections because these are the only elections in our data that contain enough Latina/o candidates to ensure a minimal amount of variation needed to systematically test our expectations.

number of Latina/o candidates elected into government offices, ranging from local school boards to the US Senate. We suspect that the presence of a Latina/o candidate on the ballot serves as a cue for White Americans, a cue about the importance of race and ethnicity in the election, which leads voters to integrate group-centric beliefs into their voting calculus

This argument is based on a vast literature detailing the pervasiveness of racial priming in politics. Theories of racial priming have detailed how beliefs about race can be activated when campaigns provide cues or symbols that can be linked to group-centric attitudes (Mendelberg, 1997, 2001; Valentino, 1999; Valentino et al., 2002; White, 2007). A Latina/o candidate on the ballot has the opportunity to provide voters with several cues that might trigger group-centric reasoning. These include a Spanish surname, pale olive to dark brown skin tones, or direct mentions of the candidate's race or national heritage during the campaign. Encountering these cues should activate people's dominant belief about Latina/o group members, which theoretically could be LRE, old-fashioned Latina/o stereotypes, or general ethnocentric hostility toward out-groups. Once these beliefs are activated, they can either be rejected or accepted by voters. For those that accept the depiction of Latinos that is consistent with the Latina/o "racialization" narrative, LRE should become a factor in how they vote. We expect that White Americans who harbor LRE will be less likely to vote or support a Latina/o candidate than someone who harbors less racism-ethnicism toward Latinos.

Why would the activation and acceptance of LRE be associated with White Americans opposing Latina/o candidates? McConnaughy et al. (2010) suggest that the presence of Latina/o candidates during an election raises concerns among Whites about Latina/o political empowerment. Contemporary debates over Latinos in America often center on the growth in the Latina/o population, the expected minority status of Whites, and ultimately a shift in political power away from Whites and into the hands of America's racial minorities. Once the Latina/o cue activates these concerns, these beliefs are likely to trigger whatever negative considerations White Americans hold toward Latinos. For McConnaughy et al. (2010), these considerations reflect old-fashioned racial stereotypes about Latinos. McConnaughy et al. (2010) further suggest that norms of equality and people's desire not to appear racist will ultimately lead voters to reject the use of these stereotypes and replace them with more socially acceptable beliefs about immigration. Consistent with this argument, they find that beliefs about immigration, rather than old-fashioned Latina/o stereotypes, are related to people's opposition to Latina/o candidates.

Given that LRE appears to be an acceptable form of expressing animus toward Latinos, we expect LRE to have a direct influence on how White Americans vote when a Latina/o candidate is on the ballot.[3] Immigration-related concerns might still be relevant to voting for a Latina/o candidate given that Latina/o candidates might be more likely to support more welcoming immigration policies. However, we do not expect people will feel the same need to hide their LRE in their views about immigration as they do with old-fashioned Latina/o stereotypes.

7.2.1 The 2014 and 2016 US House Elections

To test these arguments, we examine the relationship between LRE and vote choice in the 2014 and 2016 elections for the US House of Representatives. Elections to the US House of Representatives have recently seen a record number of Latina/o candidates. The 2014 election cycle saw eleven new Latina/o candidates: Norma Torres (D-CA-35), Raul Garcia (D-CA-23), Luz Robles (D-UT-2), Carlos Curbelo (R-FL-26), Ruben Gallego (D-AZ-7), Peter Aguilar (D-CA-31), Alex Mooney (R-MD-2), Pedro Celis (R-WA-1), Amanda Renteria (D-CA-21), Roxanne Lara (D-NM-2), and Marilinda Garcia (R-NH-2). These eleven newcomers were in addition to the thirty-two existing Latino members of Congress seeking reelection in 2014. Among these candidates, thirty-four were elected to the US House of Representatives serving in the 114th Congress. In contrast, no Latina/o candidate ran for the Senate during the 2014 election.

The 2016 election cycle saw a similar number of Latina/o candidates run for the US House of Representatives: Darren Soto (D-FL-9), Joe Garcia (D-FL-26), Emilio Huerta (D-CA-21), Adriano Espaillat (D-NY-13), Vicente Gonzalez (D-TX-15), Nanette Diaz Barragan (D-CA-44), Lou Correa (D-CA-46), Pete Gallego (D-TX-23), Salud Carbajal (D-CA-24), and Ruben Kihuen (D-NV-4). A total of thirty-nine Latinos were elected to the US House of Representatives to serve in the 115th Congress. In contrast, there were three Latina/o candidates for the US Senate: newcomer

---

[3] We may also find a direct relationship between LRE and vote choice due to the decline in norms of equality and rise in the acceptance of explicit forms of racism. However, neither is central to our argument given that we have shown earlier that LRE is a socially acceptable form of expressing beliefs about Latinos among many White Americans due to its depiction of disapproving of behaviors associated with Latinos rather than its dependence on norms.

Catherine Cortez Masto (D-NV), Loretta Sanchez (D-CA), and Marco Rubio (R-FL). Both Masto and Rubio won their election, with Catherine Cortez Masto becoming the first Latina elected to the US Senate.

To test whether LRE played any role in how White Americans voted in US House elections, we rely on data from the 2014 and 2016 Cooperative Congressional Election Study (CCES). The postelection wave of the CCES asked respondents, "For whom did you vote for US House?" Respondents were then presented with the names of the candidates from their congressional district. We recoded this variable to indicate whether the respondent voted for a Latina/o candidate (1) or a non-Latina/o candidate (0).[4] We restrict the analysis to an examination of voting for candidates nominated by the two major political parties since no third-party Latina/o candidates were identified. We exclude races where Latina/o candidates went head-to-head, but include races where a Latina/o candidate ran against a non-White, non-Latina/o candidate since Latina/o candidates are argued to trigger Latina/o-specific out-group beliefs rather than in-group beliefs favorable toward only Whites. In addition, the vote choice variable does not differentiate between voting for a Latina/o in the Democratic Party versus the Republican Party since those harboring LRE should dislike Latinos based on their race-ethnicity rather than their partisan-related beliefs, that is, the expected effect should be triggered by race and ethnicity rather than any partisan or ideological content.

Given that a large number, although not all, Latina/o candidates run as members of the Democratic Party, it is important that we consider any confounding factors that might also explain why someone would vote for or against a Latina/o candidate – including the partisanship of voters. Voting for a Latina/o or non-Latina/o candidate most likely hinges on beliefs about immigration, racial groups, and factors such as the economy that are often portrayed as being affected by the Latina/o community. Therefore, we model voting for a Latina/o versus non-Latina/o candidate using each respondent's demographic characteristics, partisanship, ideology, optimism about the nation's economy, perceived change in personal household income, and beliefs about immigration.[5]

---

4 An ideal design would oversample respondents in districts with Latina/o candidates. We therefore view these results as suggestive, complementing additional tests in Senate elections and the 2016 presidential election.

5 The 2014 CCES also included a measure of patriotism that we included as a measure of in-group favoritism that could be activated in the presence of a Latina/o candidate. The variable did not show any relationship to voting for a Latina/o candidate.

TABLE 7.1 *Estimates of voting for Latina/o candidates for the US House of Representatives, 2014 and 2016*

	House 2014		House 2016	
LRE	$-6.55^{\dagger}$	(3.58)	3.43	(2.86)
Sex	-0.08	(1.77)	9.41^{*}	(4.52)
Age	-10.55^{*}	(4.71)	-0.66^{*}	(0.29)
Education	-0.38	(1.46)	-23.76^{*}	(10.06)
Economic optimism	-0.73	(2.22)	5.67^{*}	(2.46)
Δ Household income	-1.72	(1.89)	-3.44	(2.22)
Partisanship	-2.53^{*}	(1.24)	-5.94^{*}	(2.91)
Ideology	4.87^{*}	(2.06)	2.93	(1.58)
Immigration policy preferences	-20.79^{*}	(9.65)	1.71	(3.79)
Latina/o stereotypes			-1.63	(1.23)
Constant	18.29	(16.08)	$1,296.09^{*}$	(574.66)
N	599		668	

$^{*}p < 0.05$. $^{\dagger}p < 0.06$. Dependent variable is vote for Latina/o candidate (1) or non-Latina/o candidate (0). Coefficients represent generalized Cauchit estimates with standard errors in parentheses. Data from the 2014 and 2016 CCES. Mean $\mathrm{VIF}_{2014} = 1.53$. Mean $\mathrm{VIF}_{2016} = 1.62$.

Given that the dependent variable is heavily skewed with more respondents voting for non-Latina/o candidates than Latina/o candidates, we estimate respondent vote choice using a Cauchit model. The Cauchit is more appropriate than probit or logit when estimating binary outcomes with more extreme values in either tail since the Cauchit distribution has tails that are larger than the normal and logistic distributions (Koenker and Yoon, 2009; Morgan and Smith, 1992). The results are summarized in Table 7.1. They indicate a negative relationship between LRE and voting for a Latina/o candidate in the 2014 House elections. Moreover, we do not observe any indication that the strong association between partisanship, immigration preferences, and LRE is problematic for our estimates. The variance inflation factor (VIF) fails to uncover any evidence that multicollinearity is attenuating our estimates of model uncertainty.

Given the nonlinear relationship between each independent variable and the vote choice variable, Figure 7.1 shows the predicted probability of voting for a Latina/o candidate in 2014 across levels of LRE and immigration preferences. Overall, the substantive effect sizes are small for each variable because the small number of Latina/o candidates in US House elections means that the probability of anyone voting for a Latina/o candidate is small. Yet we can still get a sense of the relative impact of certain

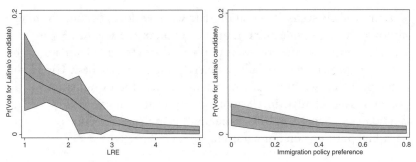

FIGURE 7.1 Predicted probability of voting for a Latina/o candidate in US House elections. Pr = probability

variables in voting for a Latina/o candidate. The predicted probability of voting for a Latina/o candidate across immigration policy preferences is almost flat. This indicates that immigration policy did not have a noticeable influence on voting for a Latina/o candidate in 2014. In contrast, those low in LRE are slightly more likely than those high in LRE to vote for a Latina/o candidate. The decline in the predicted probability of voting for a Latina/o candidate as LRE increases is clear. These results suggest that LRE had a more potent impact on voting for Latina/o House candidates in 2014 than did immigration policy preferences. The election was not just about policies toward immigration, as the anti-immigration rhetoric of the campaigns might suggest. Instead, people are voting more in line with their racism-ethnicism toward Latinos.

The 2016 estimates have the potential to highlight the relative importance of old-fashioned Latina/o stereotypes and LRE on voting for a Latina/o candidate. However, neither LRE or old-fashioned Latina/o stereotypes show a relationship with voting for a Latina/o candidate in 2016. This does not appear to be an issue with the inclusion of the measure of old-fashioned racial stereotypes toward Latinos. Reestimating the 2016 model with the old-fashioned racial stereotype variable removed does not alter the result. It is hard to determine why the relationship between LRE and voting for a Latina/o candidate does not appear in 2016. It could be due to differences in the larger campaign environment or perhaps specific campaigns did not emphasize race and ethnicity enough to prime LRE. It is also possible that race and ethnicity were primed among all respondents in the 2016 election due to the presidential campaign of Donald J. Trump. However, we did not find evidence that LRE is related to voting for all House candidates in 2016.

A more likely scenario is that the data we have does not contain enough information to provide an accurate depiction of the role of LRE in these elections since we did not oversample in districts with Latina/o candidates. We present these results as merely suggestive at best. Given, this latter problem, we now turn to a more systematic examination of the potential role of LRE in US elections by examining voter support for candidates in Senate, gubernatorial, and presidential elections who take hard-line positions on immigration.

7.3 VOTING FOR CANDIDATES WHO SUPPORT IMMIGRATION RESTRICTIONS

We believe that candidates who take a strong position on immigration will likely activate LRE among voters, thereby reshaping how people vote in contemporary elections. Hajnal and Rivera (2014, 774–776) detail several compelling reasons why the immigration debate should link the issue to people's voting preferences. First, the issue is salient (i.e., it has maintained a continual presence in the mass media and in political discourse over the last decade and a half). Even voters who pay little attention to politics are still likely to encounter information about the national debate on immigration. Second, most people are likely to have stable beliefs about immigration. Immigration is what Carmines and Stimson (1989) refer to as an easy issue. The issue is easy for voters to understand because commentators on the issue rely on frames that portray immigration in simple terms (e.g., us versus them) rather than focusing on the technical details of the country's immigration needs (Anderson, 2013; Haynes et al., 2016; Knoll et al., 2011). This relatively simple framing means citizens think about immigration by relying on a set of innate and durable beliefs – typically beliefs related to race and ethnicity (Brader et al., 2008; Kinder and Kam, 2010; Masuoka and Junn, 2013; Schildkraut, 2010). Given that LRE is at the forefront of how people think about Latinos, we expect it to play an important role in voting for tough-on-immigration candidates.

Given that immigration has been a salient and easy-to-understand issue in American elections, we suspect that candidate positions taking on immigration are likely to activate more-enduring and deep-seated group-centric beliefs about race and ethnicity. A tough-on-immigration platform is likely to signal to some voters that the candidate shares not only their preference on immigration, but also their antipathy toward Latinos. Once the Latina/o cue activates these concerns, these beliefs are likely to trigger whatever negative considerations White Americans hold toward Latinos, including LRE. People who harbor racism-ethnicism toward Latinos should be more likely to support a candidate who favors tough-on-immigration policies, given that these policies negatively impact Latina/o communities. A hard-line position on immigration is also likely to signal a general dislike toward Latinos and support for other policies that adversely impact Latina/o communities, for example, voting restrictions or an end to bilingual education. People who do not harbor racism-ethnicism toward Latinos should be less likely to support candidates who favor tough-on-immigration policies, given that their goodwill toward Latinos should lead them to support candidates who support policies that align with their beliefs.

7.3.1 The 2014 and 2016 US Senate Elections

To test these arguments, we start by examining the relationship between LRE and vote choice in the 2014 and 2016 elections for the US Senate. The 2014 midterm elections had thirty-six Senate seats up for grabs, and thirty-four Senate seats were contested in 2016. Immigration and immigration-related concerns were a prominent feature in US Senate races in both of these elections. For instance, the US Senate race in Arkansas became contentious after challenger Tom Cotton (R) ran a series of advertisements that claimed that incumbent Mark Pryor (D) supported giving social security benefits to undocumented immigrants who had forged identity papers. Similarly, David Perdue (R) ran a series of advertisements that claimed that his opponent, Michelle Nunn (D), favored "amnesty" for undocumented immigrants in Georgia's open-seat Senate race. The New Hampshire Senate race saw challenger Scott Brown (R) air attacks on incumbent Jeanne Shaheen (D) by targeting her support for the Development, Relief and Education for Alien Minors (DREAM) Act. Some Democrats also attempted to stake out tough-on-immigration positions to appeal to voters in their state. For instance, Democratic challenger to West Virginia's open Senate seat, Natalie Tennant, told voters during a televised debate, "I do not support amnesty, plain and simple. I believe that it is incumbent upon us to secure our borders before we move forward into any other comprehensive immigration plan."[6] Similarly, Democratic candidate for Mississippi's Senate seat, Travis Childers, attempted to pander to anti-immigration voters in his state by being the first Democrat to sign

---

[6] www.pbs.org/newshour/politics/watch-tonights-west-va-senate-debate.

the Federation for American Immigration Reform anti-amnesty pledge. His Republican opponent did not sign the pledge. Overall, many candidates staked out positions on immigration – either for or against more welcoming policies. We expect that voters who harbor LRE will be more likely to vote for a Senate candidate who favors tougher immigration policies.

Similarly, the candidacy of Donald J. Trump made position-taking on immigration a regular feature of Senate campaigns during the 2016 general election. For instance, incumbent Senator Chuck Grassley (R-IA) introduced a bill during the 2016 election that would block funding for cities and local governments that decline to cooperate with federal immigration enforcement officials. His challenger, Patty Judge (D), was attacked as being soft on immigration when she reported to the *Sioux City Journal* that she did not know how a city had the authority to not cooperate with federal immigration officials. A similar tactic was used by incumbent Senator Pat Toomey (R-PA) who attempted to paint his opponent, Katie McGinty (D), as lax on immigration control by arguing that she supported Philadelphia's policy to limit the city's cooperation with federal immigration enforcement officials. Toomey ran a series of advertisements, most notably one entitled *Endangering Lives*, that highlighted his opposition to such policies and explicitly stated that his opponent supported such policies.

Does LRE increase the likelihood that someone will vote for a candidate who takes a tough-on-immigration position? Respondents in the postelection wave of the 2014 and 2016 CCESs were asked, "For whom did you vote for US Senator?" Respondents were presented with the names of the candidates running in their state. We coded respondents' stated vote choice in the 2014 and 2016 CCESs to reflect whether they voted for a candidate who campaigned on a tough-on-immigration platform (vote choice = 1) or a candidate who either supported more-welcoming immigration policies or did not make immigration a salient part of their campaign (vote choice = 0).[7]

In order to determine the position of Senate candidates on immigration, we assembled a listing of each major-party Senate candidate for both election years and systematically identified candidates who made

---

[7] An ideal measure would contrast each voter's preference on immigration with their perception of where the candidates stand on the issue. Yet, examining the actual statements of candidates on immigration provided somewhat of a more difficult test since it is unclear if all voters receive each candidate's messaging on the issue.

tough-on-immigration policies a focal point of their campaign. For each candidate, we examined (1) their website content and any available official statements regarding immigration, (2) media stories covering the campaign that mentioned "immigration" as an issue, (3) campaign advertisements portraying the candidate as tough-on-immigration, and (4) campaign advertisements portraying the candidate's opponent as soft on immigration (e.g., favoring more-welcoming immigration policies).[8]

We controlled for a range of potential confounding variables, including each respondent's demographic characteristics, partisanship, ideology, optimism about the nation's economy, perceived change in personal household income, and beliefs about immigration.[9] We were also able to control for both old-fashioned Latina/o stereotypes and ethnocentrism when examining vote choice in the 2016 elections. The 2016 CCES also had an advantage in that all of the independent variables were measured in the preelection wave of the survey prior to how people voted on election day.

We estimate each respondent's stated vote choice using a probit model estimated with maximum likelihood. The results are summarized in Table 7.2. Across each model, we observe that LRE has a positive relationship with voting for a Senate candidate who had taken a tough-on-immigration position. For 2016, we estimate two models: one including a measure of old-fashioned Latina/o stereotypes and a second model including the measure of ethnocentrism. Examining the 2016 models, we show that neither old-fashioned racial stereotypes toward Latinos or ethnocentrism appear to be activated by Senate candidates taking tough-on-immigration positions. Instead, it is LRE that is related to how people voted. Moreover, immigration policy preferences are not statistically significant in any of the models, suggesting that taking a hard-line on immigration did not activate policy concerns. Instead, it agitated voters' racist and ethnic-related beliefs toward Latinos.

---

[8] We defined a tough-on-immigration candidate as a person who holds some bundle of the following and related policy positions: deporting all undocumented immigrants, no pathway to citizenship, opposed the DREAM Act, desires tougher border security prior to comprehensive immigration reform, wants to stop federal funding to sanctuary cities, and so on.

[9] We also estimated the models controlling for people's desire to repeal the Affordable Care Act and their preferences toward increasing or decreasing defense spending since both of these issues were prominent during these election years. We do not find strong evidence that either of these factors shaped voting for a tough-on-immigration candidate.

TABLE 7.2 *Estimates of voting for tough-on-immigration candidates for the US Senate, 2014 and 2016*

	Senate 2014		Senate 2016		Senate 2016	
LRE	0.36†	(0.21)	0.26*	(0.12)	0.28*	(0.13)
Sex	−0.12	(0.22)	−0.11	(0.18)	−0.10	(0.19)
Age	0.12†	(0.06)	0.01*	(0.00)	0.01*	(0.00)
Education	0.10	(0.07)	−0.05	(0.06)	−0.02	(0.007)
Economic optimism	−0.01	(0.15)	−0.09	(0.11)	−0.17	(0.12)
Δ Household income	0.01	(0.13)	0.02	(0.08)	0.00	(0.09)
Partisanship	0.31	(0.21)	0.45*	(0.14)	0.44*	(0.16)
Ideology	0.25*	(0.11)	0.25*	(0.11)	0.23†	(0.12)
Immigration policy preference	−0.56	(0.54)	0.01	(0.38)	−0.02	(0.42)
Old-fashioned stereotypes			0.08	(0.12)		
Ethnocentrism					−0.09	(0.12)
Constant	−4.74*	(1.14)	−31.65*	(13.71)	−34.06*	(14.71)
N	273		461		390	

*$p < 0.05$. †$p < 0.10$. Dependent variable is vote for tough-on-immigration US Senate candidate. Coefficients represent probit estimates with standard errors in parentheses. Data from the 2014 and 2016 CCESs. Mean $VIF_{2014} = 1.63$. Mean $VIF_{2016} = 1.61$.

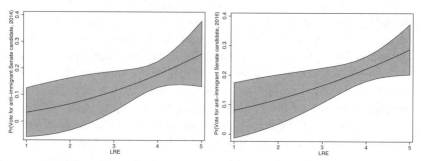

FIGURE 7.2 The relationship between LRE and voting for a tough-on-immigration Senate candidate. Pr = probability

Figure 7.2 displays the predicted probabilities from the 2014 and 2016 estimates of voting across Senate elections. In 2014, a voter who harbored a great deal of LRE (a score of 5 on the scale) was 22 percent more likely to vote for a Senate candidate taking a hard-line on immigration than a comparable voter that does not buy into the "racialization" of Latinos narrative (a score of 1 on the scale). In 2016, voters who harbor a great deal of LRE were 18 percent more likely to vote for a Senate candidate taking a hard-line on immigration than a similar voter without racism-ethnicism toward Latinos. These effects are comparable or greater than the effect partisanship had on voting for tough-on-immigration Senate candidates. In 2014, a Republican would be 12 percent more likely than a Democrat to vote for a Senate candidate taking a tough-on-immigration position. In 2016, a Republican would be 20 percent more likely than a Democrat to vote for a Senate candidate opposing welcoming immigration policies.

7.3.2 Gubernatorial Elections in 2014

LRE appears related to voting for tough-on-immigration candidates in the 2014 and 2016 Senate elections, but we have so far provided no evidence that this relationship extends beyond the Senate. The Senate has not uniquely attempted to tackle the nation's immigration problem, but it is possible that voters equate the issue more so with the Senate than other electoral offices, given the Senate's repeated attempts to pass a bipartisan comprehensive immigration reform bill over the last two decades. Yet, the issue has been prominent during campaigns for state and local public offices since many state and local governments have enacted immigration-related legislation (e.g., SB 1070, municipal noncooperation laws).

We supplement our analysis of the Senate by examining the role of LRE in state gubernatorial elections. In 2014, thirty-six states held gubernatorial elections, with many gubernatorial candidates taking a clear position on the issue of immigration.[10] Therefore, we rely on the 2014 CCES to examine the relationship between LRE and voting for tough-on-immigration gubernatorial candidates. Respondents in the postelection wave of the survey were asked, "For whom did you vote for Governor?" Respondents were presented with the names of the candidates running in their state. We used the same process to categorize gubernatorial candidates into those who supported hardline immigration policies versus those who have supported more-welcoming immigration policies. We then estimate voters' choices in these gubernatorial elections using a probit model. The model controls for factors that might relate to

---

[10] In contrast, just twelve states held gubernatorial elections in the 2016. Given that we did not oversample respondents in these states, there were not enough cases to adequately assess the role of LRE in the 2016 gubernatorial elections.

TABLE 7.3 *Voting for tough-on-immigration gubernatorial candidates, 2014*

	Model 1		Model 2	
LRE	–	–	0.36*	(0.14)
Immigration	0.68†	(0.42)	0.26	(0.35)
Gender	−0.06	(0.17)	−0.06	(0.17)
Age	0.13	(0.06)	0.12*	(0.06)
Education	0.01	(0.07)	0.03	(0.06)
Economic optimism	−0.31*	(0.09)	−0.27*	(0.10)
Δ Household income	0.07	(0.09)	0.09	(0.09)
Partisanship	0.37*	(0.13)	0.36*	(0.13)
Ideology	0.10*	(0.16)	0.06	(0.16)
Constant	−1.41†	(0.82)	−2.77*	(0.75)
N	446		446	

*$p < 0.05$. †$p < 0.10$. Dependent variable is a vote for the more anti-immigrant gubernatorial candidate (1). Coefficients represent probit estimates with standard errors in parentheses. Data from the 2014 CCES.

voting in a gubernatorial election, including respondent demographics, economic optimism, perceived change in household income, partisanship, ideology, and immigration policy preferences.

The results are summarized in Table 7.3. For comparison, we first estimate the model without including LRE to gauge the role of immigration policy preferences on voting for a candidate that takes a tough-on-immigration position. There is a positive relationship, indicating that people who prefer less-welcoming immigration policies are more likely to support candidates who prefer less-welcoming immigration policies. However, once we include LRE, the relationship between immigration policy preferences and vote choice disappears. Instead, those who harbor LRE are more likely to support candidates who are tougher on immigration. A voter who does not harbor LRE (a 1 on the scale) has a 6 percent predicted probability of supporting the candidate who is tough on immigration, while a voter who harbors a great deal of LRE (a 5 on the scale) has a 39 percent predicted probability of supporting the candidate who is tough-on-immigration.

What can we make of these findings? Without controlling for LRE, immigration policy preferences appear to drive candidate support. Yet including LRE makes the relationship disappear, suggesting that immigration policy preferences were nothing more than a thinly veiled expression of LRE.

7.4 THE POLITICS OF RACISM-ETHNICISM IN THE 2016 PRESIDENTIAL ELECTION

The US presidential election held on November 8, 2016, resulted in a surprise victory for real-estate developer and television personality Donald J. Trump. Trump had no prior political experience but managed to defeat sixteen challengers in the Republican primary election before beating former secretary of state, former US senator, and former first lady Hillary R. Clinton in the general election. Despite losing the popular vote by a thin margin, Trump managed to win 29 states with 290 electoral college votes to cement his unconventional path to the presidency.

Many observers of the 2016 presidential election have commented on the origins of Trump's success: his appeal to working-class voters discontent with the economy, attacks on globalization, antiestablishment outsider status, use of social media and ability to maintain visibility in each 24-hour news cycle, and scapegoating a myriad national problems on immigrants, refugees, and religious minorities. However, it was Trump's ability to bestow explicit insults to such as wide-range of groups during the election (e.g., women, the disabled, Jews, Muslims, Asians, African Americans, and Latinos) and continue to maintain his base of support that shattered much of the prevailing wisdom about American political campaigns (Valentino et al., 2018). His attack on Gold Star parents Khizr and Ghazala Khan, for instance, repeated patriarchal stereotypes of the Muslim faith. If his intolerance of Muslims was unclear, he promoted a ban on migrants and refugees from Muslim countries, implying that all Muslims were terrorists. Trump's remark, "Look, I'm a negotiator like you folks; we're negotiators,"[11] to the Republican Jewish Coalition was seen as anti-Semitic. And, for many Americans, his "nasty woman" slight levied at Hillary Clinton during the final presidential debate was a clear symptom of his misogynistic impulses.

Trump spoke to his base of supporters with no filter. He framed the issues and problems facing America in simple "us" versus "them" terms. Free trade became a problem of the United States versus China, Mexico, and its allies in Western Europe. His campaign alluded that the vice-chair of Hillary Clinton's campaign, Huma Abedin, could be a "Saudi spy" or

---

[11] Kelly, Amita. 2015. "Trump to Jewish Republicans: 'I'm A Negotiator Like You Folks'." NPR. December 3, 2015, available at www.npr.org/2015/12/03/458329895/trump-to-jewish-republicans-im-a-negotiator-like-you-folks.

"terrorist agent."[12] Trump often spoke of minority groups in monolithic terms in order to further convey an "us" versus "them" separation: "the Blacks," "the Hispanics," "the Chinese," and "the Muslims." After the death of forty-nine people at the Orlando nightclub Pulse, Trump singled out Muslims as a non-American out-group, saying that they needed to work with Americans instead of against Americans – "They have to work with us. They know what's going on. They know that he was bad."[13]

These constant allusions to dual loyalties became a theme throughout the campaign, leading to the reasonable conclusion that the campaign likely primed ethnocentric beliefs. Various polls throughout the election indicated that more ethnocentric voters were supporting Trump (Edsall, 2016; Kalkan, 2016; McElwee and McDaniel, 2016; Tesler and Sides, 2016). Kalkan (2016) shows that Republicans with the highest levels of ethnocentrism were 15-points more favorable toward Trump than toward other Republican candidates during the primary. Data from the 2016 American National Election Pilot Study showed that ethnocentrism was present among 70 percent of Republicans, with concerns about the status of White Americans strongly correlated with support for Trump (Edsall, 2016; Tesler and Sides, 2016). For these reasons, we should expect voter's broad hostility toward out-groups relative to Whites (i.e., ethnocentrism) to contribute to their support for Donald Trump during the 2016 presidential election.

Yet Trump spent the most time during the campaign attacking Latinos. His denigration of Latinos was both direct and implied in his criticism of immigrants and immigration policy. Trump kickstarted his campaign by remarking that Mexican immigrants are "criminals" and "rapists."[14] He later asserted that federal judge Gonzalo Curiel, who was presiding over a lawsuit against Trump University, was unable to provide a fair trial because "he's a Mexican."[15] When two of his supporters in Boston

---

[12] Terkel, Amanda. "Donald Trump Floats Conspiracy Theory that Huma Abedin Has Terrorist Ties." *HuffPost*, August 29, 2016, available at www.huffpost.com/entry/donald-trump-huma-abedin_n_57c4aaafe4b09cd22d92273c.

[13] Detrow, Scott. "Trump Calls to Ban Immigration from Counties with 'Proven History of Terrorism'." NPR, June 13, 2016, available at www.npr.org/2016/06/13/481910989/trump-expands-immigration-ban-to-countries-with-proven-history-of-terrorism?ft=nprml&f=481910989.

[14] Moreno, Carolina. "9 Outrageous Things Donald Trump Has Said about Latinos." *HuffPost*, August 31, 2015, available at www.huffpost.com/entry/9-outrageous-things-donald-trump-has-said-about-latinos_n_55e483a1e4b0c818f618904b.

[15] Neidig, Harper. "Trump Doubles Down on Judge Attacks: 'He's a Mexican. We're Building a Wall." *The Hill*, June, 03, 2016, available at https://thehill.com/blogs/ballot-box/presidential-races/282172-trump-doubles-down-on-judge-attacks-hes-a-mexican-were.

indicated that they beat a homeless Latino man because "Donald Trump was right – all these illegals need to be deported," Trump responding by saying the "people who are following me are very passionate, they love this country and they want this country to be great again."[16]

This anti-Latina/o rhetoric juxtaposed nicely with the cornerstone of Trump's campaign: his anti-immigrant policies. Trump supported the deportation of undocumented immigrants, an end to "catch and release" policies, an end to birthright citizenship, tougher penalties for migrants caught entering the United States illegally, an increase in visa fees, an end to all Obama administration executive orders related to immigration, tougher border security, and the building of a wall between the United States and Mexico. He also promised to end all funding for sanctuary cities and held these municipalities responsible for "so many needless deaths."[17]

Given his direct attacks on Latinos, and anti-immigration/immigrant rhetoric, we expect the Trump campaign to have primed beliefs specifically related to Latinos. Existing accounts of the election have noted Trump's ability to use explicit racial appeals (Schaffner et al., 2018; Valentino et al., 2018). This would suggest that old-fashioned Latina/o stereotypes would be related to support for Trump since these beliefs are most commonly associated with explicit forms of anti-Latina/o animus. However, if LRE is the more prominent belief that White Americans hold regarding Latinos, then we should expect it to be primed during the election and related to support for Trump.

7.4.1 How Whites Voted in the 2016 Presidential Election

We begin examining the potential role of LRE in voting for Donald Trump by examining two questions from the 2016 CCES. First, we examine a preelection wave question that asked respondents, "Which candidate for President of the United States do you prefer?" Respondents indicating Donald Trump were coded as 1, while respondents indicating voting

[16] Moyer, Justin Wm. "Trump Says Fans Are 'Very Passionate' after Hearing One of Them Allegedly Assaulted Hispanic Man." *Washington Post*, August 20, 2015, available at www.washingtonpost.com/news/morning-mix/wp/2015/08/21/trump-says-fans-are-very-passionate-after-hearing-one-of-them-allegedly-assaulted-hispanic-man/.

[17] Ingraham, Christopher. "Trump Says Sanctuary Cities Are Hotbeds of Crime. Data Say the Opposite." *Washington Post*, January 17, 2017, available at www.washingtonpost .com/news/wonk/wp/2017/01/27/trump-says-sanctuary-cities-are-hotbeds-of-crime-data-say-the-opposite/.

for any other candidate were coded as 0. We chose this coding since we are interested in why people voted for Trump rather than strictly Trump versus Clinton given that all of his opponents were much softer on immigration and many Republicans/conservatives signaled that they would vote for a third-party candidate specifically to protest his racial and ethnocentric tendencies. Unidentified voting preferences were coded as missing data.[18] Second, we examine a postelection wave question that asked respondents, "For whom did you vote for President of the United States?" This variable is also delineated between respondents who indicated that they voted for Trump (1) versus respondents who indicated that they voted for any other candidate (0).

The existing postmortem on the 2016 election shows that the priming of racial and group-centric considerations drove people's support for Trump more so than did economic, trade, and antiestablishment appeals (Inwood, 2018; Major et al., 2016; Mutz, 2018; Schaffner et al., 2018). We rely on this literature to generate a model specification that minimizes confounding factors also related to voting for Trump in the presidential election. These include respondent demographic characteristics (sex, education, age), whether the respondent recently lost his or her job, perceived change in household income, economic optimism, partisanship, perceived ideological distance to the Democratic and Republican parties, and issue preferences on immigration, the Affordable Care Act (ACA), and defense spending. We also control for ethnocentrism and then replace ethnocentrism with old-fashioned stereotypes toward Latinos and Muslims, since Trump specifically targeted these two groups frequently during the election.[19]

The results are summarized in Table 7.4. LRE shows a positive relationship with supporting Trump prior to the election. We also observe that people who felt a loss in their household income, desired tougher immigration policies, and held ethnocentric beliefs were more likely to prefer Trump. Thus, the factors most associated with Trump (economic hardships, immigration, and a preference for Whites over out-groups) factored into his early support. However, none of these beliefs show a

---

[18] We obtain similar results when coding Trump versus Clinton supporters.

[19] Ideally, we would have an indicator of misogynistic beliefs since Trump also targeted women during the campaign (see Schaffner et al., 2018). Such an indicator is not available in the same 2016 CCES data that contains the measure of LRE. Using women's rights issues such as abortion preferences as a proxy did not show a relationship with voting for Trump, suggesting that we might need better indicators to assess the role that such beliefs had on voting in the 2016 election.

TABLE 7.4 *Estimates of candidate support and presidential vote choice, 2016*

	Preelection support		Preelection support		Postelection vote choice		Postelection vote choice	
LRE	0.43*	(0.13)	0.39*	(0.13)	0.34*	(0.13)	0.34*	(0.13)
Sex	-0.06	(0.21)	-0.13	(0.20)	0.20	(0.20)	0.18	(0.20)
Education	0.10	(0.07)	0.09	(0.06)	-0.06	(0.06)	-0.05	(0.06)
Age	-0.01	(0.01)	-0.01	(0.01)	-0.00	(0.01)	-0.00	(0.01)
Unemployed	-0.10	(0.34)	-0.08	(0.31)	-0.51	(0.42)	-0.44	(0.41)
Δ Household income	-0.34*	(0.12)	-0.32*	(0.11)	-0.03	(0.13)	-0.05	(0.13)
Economic optimism	-0.07	(0.11)	-0.09	(0.10)	-0.40*	(0.13)	-0.42*	(0.13)
Partisanship	0.37*	(0.09)	0.34*	(0.10)	0.25*	(0.09)	0.25*	(0.09)
Distance from Democrat	0.16*	(0.07)	0.14*	(0.06)	0.15	(0.08)	0.15	(0.08)
Distance from Republican	0.11	(0.08)	0.07	(0.08)	-0.20*	(0.07)	-0.20*	(0.07)
Immigration	1.12*	(0.35)	1.23*	(0.35)	0.49	(0.38)	0.56	(0.38)
ACA	0.70*	(0.28)	0.63*	(0.28)	0.94*	(0.30)	0.96*	(0.30)
Defense spending	0.10	(0.14)	0.07	(0.14)	0.22	(0.14)	0.22	(0.14)
Ethnocentrism	0.50*	(0.13)	–		0.13	(0.15)	–	
Latina/o stereotypes	–		0.03	(0.16)	–		-0.09	(0.15)
Muslim stereotypes	–		-0.18	(0.14)	–		0.06	(0.14)
Constant	20.66	(15.38)	16.07	(15.52)	7.04	(11.43)	5.95	(11.82)
N	545	–	545	–	480	–	479	–

*$p < 0.05$. Coefficients are probit estimates with standard errors in parentheses. Data from the 2016 CCES. Dependent variable is support for Trump in the pre-election wave and vote for Trump in the post-election wave.

relationship with voting for Trump. Instead, indicating a vote for Trump in the postelection wave of the study is associated with LRE, partisanship, and a desire to repeal the ACA. Ethnocentrism, in addition to old-fashioned racism toward Latinos and Muslims, shows no relationship with voting for Trump. This suggests that it was beliefs about Latinos, rather than general out-group hostility, that ultimately led people to vote for Trump, although we do find that ethnocentrism played a role in his earlier support. Moreover, it is a specific type of animus toward Latinos – one that has been built across time and appears benign to most White Americans – that is associated with the preferences of White voters in the 2016 presidential election. LRE, rather than old-fashioned Latina/o stereotypes, is associated with support for Trump.

Figure 7.3 displays the predicted probabilities from the preelection support model. A voter who harbors no LRE (a score of 1 on the scale) has a 27 percent predicted probability of supporting Trump, while a voter who harbors the highest levels of LRE found in our sample (a 5 on the scale) has a 51 percent predicted probability of supporting Trump. This is comparable in size to the effect of ethnocentrism and partisanship.

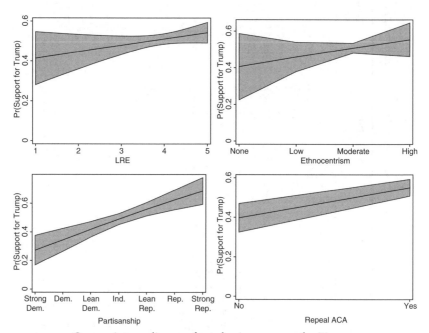

FIGURE 7.3 Comparing predictors of preelection support for Trump.
Pr = probability

Other factors pundits suggest resulted in support for Trump fail to show a sizable impact on his support. For instance, support for repealing the ACA has a 10 percent predicted probability of supporting Trump relative to respondents who oppose repealing the health care bill. It is significant, but not nearly as important as LRE.

Partisanship and Ideology

We find no evidence that LRE had a weaker or stronger relationship with support for Trump among Democrats, Republicans, liberals, and conservatives. None of these interactions showed a unique relationship with LRE on supporting Trump. Although LRE is more widespread among those on the right, it is the ability to use these racial-ethnic considerations to gain votes from moderates and those on the left that make them particularly appealing among mostly right-leaning politicians.

Education

Various election polls showed that the least-educated Americans were some of the strongest supporters of Trump. We find a similar bivariate relationship in the data with those having a higher level of educational attainment less likely to vote Trump (β_{probit} = −0.14, SE = 0.05, p < 0.01). The addition of racial-ethnic considerations such as LRE into the model eliminates the relationship between educational attainment and voting for Trump. Estimating the model with an interaction between education and LRE, however, shows that higher levels of educational attainment can interact with LRE to reduce the impact of LRE on support for Trump (β_{probit} = −0.15, SE = 0.05, p < 0.01). At the same time, we find LRE continues to have a strong relationship with voting for Trump among the least-educated Americans (β_{probit} = 0.78, SE = 0.26, p < 0.01).

Beliefs about African Americans

We have been able to show that LRE played a role in support for Trump in lieu of or in addition to a range of racial and ethnic considerations: beliefs about old-fashioned Latina/o stereotypes, attitudes toward Muslims, and ethnocentrism. However, the 2016 CCES did not contain specific questions measuring potentially racist beliefs toward African Americans. Although we expect a strong correlation between racism toward African Americans and dislike for out-groups measured by ethnocentrism, support for Trump could be shaped by beliefs about African Americans that is not captured by general out-group hostility. Although a direct question regarding beliefs toward African Americans is unavailable, we can reasonable assume that those harboring racism toward African Americans will strongly disapprove of President Obama (Tesler, 2012b; Tesler and Sears, 2010). Reestimating the models including a measure of approval of President Obama continues to show a strong relationship between LRE and voting for Trump (β_{probit} = 0.24, SE = 0.11, p < 0.04), while respondents who approve of President Obama were less inclined to vote for Trump (β_{probit} = −0.87, SE = 0.22, p < 0.01).

7.5 LRE AND THE STRATEGIC CHOICES OF CANDIDATES

So far, we have demonstrated that White Americans' votes are shaped by their levels of LRE and the choices the candidates offer. Voters who have higher levels of LRE reward candidates who take positions that are more hard-line on immigration. In this section we pose the opposite question, asking how candidates respond to the electoral incentives these beliefs toward Latinos create. Are candidates in states where more voters who harbor LRE more likely to take hard-line positions on immigration? If so, this implies that the level of LRE has a reinforcing effect in our elections; candidates take these position in response to the voters and voters reward this position-taking.

There are two possible mechanisms that could produce this effect, but we are unable to effectively delineate between them. First, it could be that candidates are making strategic choices. In a classic Downsian or Key perspective, they can perceive the preferences of the voters and are more likely to take the positions when that is where the voters are. In part, this implies that the key strategic decision is made by the candidates. Voters hold preferences and the candidates give them what they want.

The second process that could generate the pattern we will look for is through the primaries and nominations. Our data examine the position-taking of the general election nominee for each party. To get to that stage, however, he or she had to win the primary election. It could be that candidates make their choices for a position on immigration based on sincere preferences, or because they are trying to curry favor with donors or interest groups and not necessarily for the electoral incentives. Primary voters, then, see the choices they are provided. If there are more voters with high levels of LRE, then the candidates who take these positions in the primary are more likely to succeed. This mechanism provides more agency to voters. They use their policy preferences to make a choice and the result is the set of candidates we observe in November. Obviously, both of these mechanisms can work in concert.[20]

The incentives might differ for candidates of each party. To the extent that the parties have divided on immigration, the candidates are differently constrained in their choices. Because Republican primary voters are more likely to take hard-line positions on immigration, Republican candidates may be more constrained. While our measure of statewide aggregate LRE does not allow us to make distinctions between the attitudes of Republicans and Democrats in a state, it is likely, given the evidence in previous chapters, that the Republicans in the state will have relatively high levels of LRE. This would mean that the primary electorate for Republicans in the state may push Republican candidates to take tough-on-immigration positions, even if the general electorate does not. Similarly, if a Republican candidate is able to resist the pressure of his or her primary voters to take a tougher position on immigration, he or she is likely to resist the general election pressure as well.

Democratic candidates face a different calculation. They might be constrained by their primary voters, but if they are responsive to the general election pressures, they might be more likely to take a hard-line position. While this could alienate some of their base, moving toward the more popular position in the general election could have electoral benefits. The result is that we expect that Democratic candidates will be more likely to respond to the state-level aggregate LRE. We expect, therefore, there to be a positive relationship between the state-level LRE and the probability that the Democratic candidate takes a more conservative position on immigration.

To test this idea, we need to develop a measure of the state-level aggregate LRE. Creating such a measure is more complicated than it might at first appear. The obvious strategy would be to use the survey data we have collected and simply take the average of the respondents in each state. Unfortunately, national surveys are notoriously bad for this. Not only would this result in small samples for essentially all of the states,

---

[20] An equally important question is: How do candidates know if voters harbor LRE? We suspect that candidates cull this information from years of experience in the state or district. Candidates often serve as lower-level officials prior to running for Congress and also work with party strategists, donors, and activists. These experiences allow candidates to see what voters have favored in the past as well as where core loci of support might be in the future. Candidates can also gain access to citizen concerns in town halls, responses to current events, and internal polling.

but there would be several that might be missing entirely. Even if there were a reasonable number for every state, the simple average would be a remarkably inefficient and noisy way to estimate the state level of LRE. Assume, for instance, that there is a relationship between education and a respondent's LRE, where higher-educated voters hold lower levels of these attitudes. That would imply that in states where there are more educated voters, there should be lower levels of LRE.

Thankfully, there are methods for combining both the relationships in the survey data and the auxiliary information about the state-level patterns for these predictors. In particular, we employ multilevel regression with poststratification (MRP)(Park et al., 2004). This is a relatively simple two-step process to get much more accurate estimates of the state-level opinion than simply aggregating to the state mean in a survey. The first stage of the estimation models the individual-level survey responses to the items that make up the LRE measures, as predicted by demographic variables and indicators of the state of residence. Consistent with prior research, we use gender, race, age, education, and the interaction of age and education in the model (Lax and Phillips, 2009a). Each of the variables is coded the same as they are by the census and are included as factor variables. That is, age is not coded as years, but are instead in the basic categories reported by the census. The interaction of age and education creates a category for each combination of age group and education level. The result of the MRP are estimates of the predicted probability that a respondent harbors LRE for every combination of the demographics and states. We can then use these predicted probabilities to estimate state-level LRE in the second step.

The second step is the poststratification. This is the step that actually estimates the state-level measure of LRE. The poststratification takes the estimated predicted probabilities from step one for each combination for the demographic variables and weights these probabilities based on the proportion of each group in each state. The resulting estimate of the state-level opinion is often the best possible measure of state-level opinion when only national surveys are available (Lax and Phillips, 2009a; Park et al., 2004).

The data we use for this is the 2014 CCES described in previous chapters. It is the one national sample that we have that contains all four of the items that make up the LRE measure. In our particular case, this process requires several decisions. First, the multilevel regression is technically a multilevel logistic regression that only works with a dichotomized dependent variable. Therefore, we convert the ordinal measures of the items

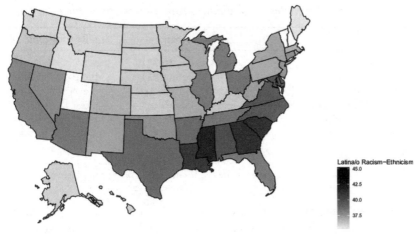

FIGURE 7.4 Statewide estimates of LRE, 2014

that make up LRE into a binary variable, where being in one of the two highest categories is a one and being in the two lowest categories is a zero. Second, we estimate the model for each of the items separately, then take the average for the state for each of the items to create the composite measure. This is the same approach that Lax and Phillips (2009b) use to develop their measure of public opinion toward the LGBT community.

Figure 7.4 presents the map plotting the levels of LRE in each of the states in 2014. Darker states have more people scoring higher on the LRE scale. The map demonstrates several features of the geography of LRE. First, in general, the states of the Confederacy are higher than the rest of the country for most of the items. Second, the states that border Mexico also tend to be higher than others, while the Northwest tends to have the lowest levels of LRE. The states in the Midwest suggest that this is not simply a measure of the conservatism of the state or how Republican it is. Looking at Minnesota, Iowa, Wisconsin, Illinois, Indiana, Michigan, and Ohio (the states that made up the original Big Ten), Indiana is the most traditionally conservative state, but it has the lowest level of aggregate LRE. On the face of it at least, this appears to be a measure distinct from the obvious political confounds.

Our interest is in seeing if these aggregate measures predict the issue stances of the candidates that we observe in the statewide 2014 elections. The main independent variable of interest, statewide LRE, is presented in Figure 7.4. The dependent variable in the analyses to follow is a binary indicator if at least one candidate in the party in the state took a hard-line

TABLE 7.5 *Estimates of candidate position-taking on immigration*

	Democrats		Republicans	
Statewide LRE	0.52*	(0.27)	−0.20	(0.15)
Non-White population	−5.97	(4.94)	0.62	(1.96)
Violent crime rate	0.001	(0.003)	0.004	(0.002)
Statewide personal income	−0.33	(0.32)	−0.07	(0.11)
State immigration laws	0.10	(0.13)	0.08	(0.07)
Constant	−19.33	(9.39)	6.30	(5.28)
N	41		39	

*$p < 0.05$. Coefficients are probit estimates with standard errors in parentheses.

stance on immigration. Because we think that there may be differences in the strategic choices between Democrats and Republicans, we create separate measures for each party. We combine Senate and governor races in each state as a balance between increasing the number of observations (versus estimating separate models for each type of election) and not double-counting states that happen to have two statewide races.

In these models, we control for the percent of the population that is non-White, the violent crime rate in the state, the average personal income in the state, and the state of immigration laws in the state. Given that our analysis is about aggregate behavior, we expect that these factors may also change the politics of the immigration position-taking in the state.

The results in Table 7.5 show our models predicting the probability that a Democrat (column 1) and a Republican (column 2) take a hard-line position on immigration in a state in 2014. The key result is that there is a positive and significant effect of the statewide LRE and the probability of a Democratic candidate's position on immigration. When the state has higher levels of LRE, Democratic candidates are more likely to take positions that would attract these voters. There is no such relationship for Republican candidates. The coefficient in this model is negative and statistically insignificant. It is only the Democratic candidates who respond to these pressures in this way.

7.6 CONCLUSION

The overall consistency of these findings lends strong support to the conclusion that LRE is related to contemporary US elections. In both the 2014 midterm election and 2016 general election, we found some evidence that LRE is related to voting for Latina/o candidates and stronger evidence that LRE is related to voting for nativist candidates in the Senate and state gubernatorial elections. The phenomenon of activating animus toward Latinos either unintentionally through Latina/o candidacy or intentionally via tough-on-immigration rhetoric connected to the Latina/o "racialization" narrative was not limited to the presidential election on 2016. Trump certainly played a significant role in the latter election and we find evidence consistent that his support was bolstered by LRE. But the use of racial appeals has been almost a constant in American electoral campaigns. Whereas African Americans were the focus of American elections for most of US history (and continue to be so), we appear to be witnessing a resurgence in appeals targeting LRE.

The 2016 presidential election, in particular, was a reminder of the prominence of race in American politics. The deep racial divisions between Whites and Latinos that precede the Mexican–American War going back to the colonization of indigenous peoples in the Americas, remains alive and well. These divisions have been held steadfast in the minds of some White Americans in the form of LRE, waiting for entrepreneurial politicians like Donald J. Trump to play on these "racialized" depictions of Latinos. The evidence we present is consistent that these beliefs matter a great deal when primed by political campaigns. Trump might have been seen as the prominent user of appeals to LRE, and his use of such appeals were some of the most explicit, but the targeting of these beliefs among voters existed well before Trump. We provide evidence of this in the 2014 Senate and gubernatorial elections, but we suspect that LRE played a role in earlier elections – at least when issues such as immigration were made salient by the campaign. We also suspect that LRE has played a stronger role in more recent elections than in previous elections. However, since we are the first to attempt to measure this concept, we are left with only clues from recent elections about its pervasiveness.

The results also speak to our argument that LRE is a unique and more common form of animus toward Latinos. Across each of the elections examined here, LRE, rather than old-fashioned racial stereotypes or ethnocentrism, is what consistently related to electoral support. These other forms of animus certainly have their importance, but when examining a political environment that is heavily focused on Latinos, we must look at the ways White Americans feel comfortable expressing animus toward Latinos in order to uncover the greater significance of race-ethnicity in American politics.

Our conclusions are not without their weak spots. We have examined the role of LRE within various elections using observational data ill-suited to make causal inferences. Although we do have some leverage on this issue in that respondents' beliefs were measured in the preelection wave and vote choice was measured in the postelection wave of our studies, we still cannot be certain that the campaigns did not in some way shape LRE. That said, our results are consistent with similar experimental studies examining the role of racial considerations and support for Latina/o candidates (McConnaughy et al., 2010) as well as a large number of studies showing that campaigns predominately work via priming existing attitudes rather than leading voters to change their beliefs or engage in learning (Matthews, 2017; Simon, 2002; Valentino et al., 2002). The findings here are also consistent with observational and experimental studies that find racial-ethnic considerations played a strong role in the 2016 election (Inwood, 2018; Major et al., 2016; Mutz, 2018; Schaffner et al., 2018).

A second shortcoming of this chapter is our inability to contend with the intersectionality of race and gender. Trump specifically ran a campaign that activated racial considerations, but also beliefs about feminism, women, and patriarchy (Schaffner et al., 2018). We would be amiss not to mention the particular effect that beliefs about race and gender had on voting in recent elections (see Philpot and Walton, 2007). Although these past elections have been marked by the rise of Latina candidates, and the first Latina US Senator, Latina women are still vastly underrepresented for reasons we suspect have to do with LRE and beliefs about gender.

These caveats aside, the conclusion that votes reflect LRE is important because why people vote can guide the behavior of elected officials as they attempt to represent their constituencies. Based on these results, Trump may claim to enforce policies that negatively impact Latina/o communities given that this was an important consideration among his supporters. However, the results also seem to suggest that nativist policy preferences are typically unimportant in how people vote once we include LRE. Candidates are not receiving support to enact specific policies, but to govern by racism-ethnicism. In this way, it is not surprising that many institutions have deep racial-ethnic disparities in how they impact society as voters appear to be giving the go-ahead for politicians to enact and maintain discriminatory institutions.

8

Conclusion

White Americans' attitudes about politics are inextricably linked to their views about Latinos. These attitudes are not the central organizing principle of ideology or the key to partisanship, but they are a vital feature in a host of broadly relevant political opinions. In this chapter we tie up the various threads from the earlier chapters to provide the broad view of how Latina/o racism-ethnicism (LRE) influences American politics. The first step in this exercise is to briefly summarize the earlier chapters. The remaining sections of this chapter put these findings in the broader context of contemporary American politics. In particular, we will discuss why LRE seems to play a role in American politics, explore the differences in the policies that are shaped by LRE, examine the policy and political implications of the results, and discuss how the effects of LRE may evolve in the future. Before we delve into these more interesting ideas, we review some of the key findings from each previous chapter.

8.1 WHAT HAVE WE LEARNED?

Whites' beliefs about Latinos are rooted in the ways in which the meaning of Latinos as a racial and ethnic group has been constructed for them. The historical roots of both Latina/o experiences and the ways in which Whites have interpreted these experiences have resulted in a remarkable proportion of Whites holding the belief that Latinos violate basic Anglo-American culture and norms – LRE. The roots of these beliefs can be found in the institutions designed in the early colonial period – consequences of the formal and informal rules that the

Spanish and other European settlers enforced on the early mestizo people. The differences between later generations of mestizo people and White-European settlers were accentuated by nationalistic conflict, especially between England and Spain. The differences in colonial sponsors, the competition over trade routes, the differences in religion all undergirded the competition that led those of White European ancestry to define Latinos as a non-White racial group – a definition that created a path to leading modern-day Latinos to being viewed as unable to assimilate and abide by Anglo-American customs.

As English settlement expanded West, Americans of White-European heritage sought to both exclude and assimilate Latinos. The distinctions between White-European and Latina/o cultures resulted in excuses for new forms of institutional racism and maintenance of White cultural, economic, and political dominance. Whites continued to construct an image of Latinos as immoral, unskilled, unintelligent, and incapable of adhering to "proper" Anglo-American traditions and norms. Institutions of finance, employment, segregation, and crime control all helped to reinforce these beliefs – beliefs that reinforced the justification of discriminatory institutions. Complaints about the lack of assimilation among Latinos have been a persistent narrative in the history of Latinos with little regard for how institutions, informal norms, and LRE contribute to maintaining the differences between Latinos and White Americans. Latinos have been welcomed into various US institutions (primarily economic), but only on the terms of the dominant Anglo-American culture.

Thus, the roots of LRE of today run deep in our cultural history and have regained salience in the past several decades. When Whites today are asked about their beliefs toward Latinos, the same historical themes we have outlined come up spontaneously in conversation. The extant work relying on focus groups of Whites illustrate clearly that these deep-seated themes dominate how some Whites perceive Latinos – even when talking about Latinos outside of the context of politics.

It is this understanding of the history of Whites' beliefs about Latinos and the evidence in the open-ended focus group deliberations that are the foundation for our attempt to measure how racism-ethnicism is held and expressed toward Latinos. We developed and implemented a scale that taps the main dimensions of this concept. Relying on both nationally representative and convenience samples, we demonstrate that the LRE scale maintains several desirable properties of a reliable and valid measurement instrument. The four dimensions of LRE are internally consistent and represent a coherent, single underlying belief. More importantly, the belief we measure is distinct from measures of related concepts such as old-fashioned racist stereotypes of Latinos, racial resentment toward African Americans, partisanship, ideology, moral traditionalism, and ethnocentrism. The analyses in each empirical chapter show that LRE maintains a distinct predictive ability across various political choices beyond these related concepts. Thus, the importance of LRE is not just conceptual, but theoretical.

LRE plays a strong role in explaining the opinion of Whites toward a variety of policy issues. First, it is an essential element of opinions about immigration. Immigration policy in America is tied up with beliefs toward Latinos. The vast majority of discussion about immigration focuses on immigration from Latin America and is inextricably perceived as being about Latinos. Whites who harbor high levels of LRE are much more likely to favor more-restrictive immigration policies, even when controlling for the other main predictors of immigration policy preferences. But there are limits to this pattern. When respondents are asked about immigrants who are explicitly not Latino, the link between LRE and immigration attitudes disappears. It is only when people think that immigration is about Latinos that LRE matters. We reach similar conclusions when we ask about free migration. Whites are more likely to support free migration when asked about US citizens prior to being asked about citizens from countries where the immigrant is likely to be a Latina/o than vice versa – variability we were able to connect to LRE.

Immigration is just the first policy that has a link to the level of LRE among Whites. Given the prominence of the Latino crime narrative and the broader race coding of crime, this is a potentially obvious area to explore. We find that Whites with higher levels of LRE do favor harsher sentences and more police officers on the street. But our results are more subtle than simply connecting these beliefs to opinions about crime policy. LRE changes the ways in which Whites perceive criminals and the criminal justice system. They are more likely to inaccurately recall a suspect as being Latina/o, suggesting the potential for additional biases in the criminal justice system. We also find that LRE changes how Whites think about the accountability of law enforcement officials. Whites who harbor LRE oppose requirements for police officers wearing body cameras, but only when the officer is accused of assaulting a Latina/o. In that case, Whites with higher levels of LRE buck the trend of high-levels of public support for body cameras and even reject the most widely believed argument in their favor – providing citizens with protection from potential abuses in police power.

The third main policy domain we explore, and one that is increasing in political importance, is access to electoral ballots and voting restrictions. We asked voters about a variety of restrictions to ballot access. This is an issue that does not have the same clear linkages to Latinos in public discourse as immigration and crime. Even so, there is a strong connection between a White person's LRE and their attitudes about voting laws – even after we control from ethnocentrism and related forms of animus toward out-groups. The higher a White American's LRE, the stronger his or her support for strict voter identification laws. When the concern about voter identification is framed as having a disproportionate impact on Latina/o voters, the effect is even stronger. We also find an effect in our voter registration rolls experiment. For most citizens, there is a small but significant preference to protect Latinos from being removed from the voter rolls. At the high end of LRE, however, there is a preference for *removing* Latinos from the rolls.

Finally, LRE has electoral implications. LRE is connected to how White Americans have voted in contemporary elections. This connection extends beyond the recent 2016 presidential election and includes both state and federal elections (and we suspect local races where Latina/o candidates or issues have become salient). LRE is associated with Whites being more supportive of candidates who support restrictive immigration policies for both statewide and federal office. Perhaps most importantly, it also led to White voters' support for President Trump, having an effect similar in magnitude to partisanship. Finally, we have evidence that suggests candidates also respond to the amount of LRE within their state-level constituency. Democratic candidates, in particular, are more likely to take more conservative positions on immigration when their constituents have higher levels of LRE.

The obvious overall conclusion from this broad and diverse set of empirical results is that LRE plays a vital role in contemporary American politics.

8.2 LIMITS ON THE ROLE OF LRE

Our argument is that LRE plays an important and overlooked role in American politics, not that it influences public opinion about every issue. Our surveys and experiments are motivated by where our understanding of American politics leads us to expect LRE to have an effect. If Willie Sutton robbed banks because "that's where the money is," we looked at these issues because they have a disproportionate effect on Latino communities. We have not made nearly the same systematic attempt to find examples where LRE does not have an effect.

There are times in the analyses we have presented that show that LRE has a limited or negligible influence on public opinion in some instances. In the final experiment in Chapter 3, LRE has no effect on respondents' attitudes about Irish immigrants, only on immigrants from Mexico. In the body camera experiment in Chapter 5, LRE has no effect on attitudes about requiring body cameras when the motorist is not described as Latino. In these cases, the respondents need the cues of making the issue "about" Latinos for LRE to be a relevant consideration.

Those examples suggest some limits of LRE to explain politics in domains where race and ethnicity are less relevant. Thankfully, the 2016 Cooperative Congressional Election Study (CCES) provided us the opportunity to explore how predictive LRE is of attitudes about other policy domains. Here we examine five other policy attitudes in areas that are highly salient to the public that we do not think LRE will predict White citizen's attitudes: abortion, environmental regulation, gay marriage, education, and health care. These policy attitudes were measured as part of the common content of the CCES. Thankfully, they represent a range of social and economic issues that are at the heart of the dominant left/right divide in American politics. But because they are not explicitly, or even implicitly, framed and discussed as having clear implications for Latinos, we do not expect there to be a relationship with LRE.

As is clear from Table 8.1, LRE does not predict support or opposition to any of these policies. In each case, the standard error of the estimate is as large or larger than the coefficient. Graphing these results to examine the nonlinear relationship between LRE and these policy opinions confirms these assessments. LRE does not add to the power of the standard explanations of these attitudes. Based on these results, there are limits to the influence of LRE. Unless the respondents comprehend the link between the issue or vote choice and their attitudes about Latinos, LRE is simply not a relevant consideration.

8.3 THE BROWNING OF WHITES' ATTITUDES

Scholars of opinion about race and ethnicity will obviously see parallels between our results and the literature on the role of racial resentment in the formation of attitudes toward African Americans. Our measure of LRE has clear intellectual linkages to the measures of racial resentment toward African Americans. Many of the experiments we designed

TABLE 8.1 *Testing the discriminant validity of LRE*

	Abortion		Environment		Gay marriage		Education		Health care	
LRE	0.00	(0.02)	−0.01	(0.03)	0.02	(0.02)	0.02	(0.02)	−0.01	(0.03)
Sex	0.04	(0.04)	0.06	(0.04)	0.03	(0.04)	0.01	(0.04)	−0.06	(0.04)
Age	−0.00	(0.00)	−0.00	(0.00)	0.00*	(0.01)	0.00*	(0.00)	0.00	(0.00)
Education	−0.02*	(0.01)	0.01	(0.01)	−0.01	(0.01)	0.01	(0.01)	0.01	(0.01)
Economic optimism	0.01	(0.02)	0.04	(0.03)	0.04	(0.02)	0.01	(0.02)	0.05	(0.03)
Δ Household income	−0.03	(0.02)	0.01	(0.02)	0.00	(0.02)	−0.00	(0.02)	−0.02	(0.02)
Unemployed	−0.13	(0.09)	0.04	(0.12)	−0.09	(0.10)	0.01	(0.07)	0.08	(0.08)
Partisanship	−0.05*	(0.01)	−0.05*	(0.01)	−0.04*	(0.01)	−0.01	(0.01)	0.01	(0.12)
Ideology	−0.09*	(0.02)	−0.03*	(0.02)	−0.06*	(0.02)	−0.01	(0.02)	−0.00	(0.02)
Cultural preference	−0.26*	(0.05)	−0.05	(0.05)	−0.27*	(0.05)	0.02	(0.04)	0.01	(0.05)
Ethnocentrism	0.04	(0.03)	0.04	(0.03)	−0.06*	(0.02)	−0.03	(0.03)	0.00	(0.03)
Authoritarianism	−0.08	(0.09)	0.04	(0.11)	−0.02	(0.10)	−0.21	(0.11)	−0.28*	(0.12)
Constant	−4.96*	(2.32)	4.96	(2.69)	−5.67*	(2.68)	−6.22*	(2.07)	−3.70	(2.92)
N	668		669		665		668		665	

*$p < 0.05$. Coefficients represent logit estimates with standard errors in parentheses. Data from the 2016 CCES. White respondents only.

were informed by similar work about the role of opinions about African Americans. It is clear from this literature that racial resentment and other implicit and explicit beliefs about African Americans play a foundational role in the structure of attitudes about politics. Such a linkage is the cause of the broad issue evolution and party change in the last sixty years (Carmines and Stimson, 1989) and continues to be a major source of cleavage in American politics.

We are not claiming that LRE has or is going to have a similar effect on American politics. The role of racism focused on African Americans is a central dominant theme in American politics. It was a piece of the design of the constitution, the cause of the Civil War, and continues to be a massively salient issue in American politics. The divide between Republicans and Democrats on the basic question of federal enforcement of civil rights for African Americans remains a central division between the political parties and will remain so for the foreseeable future.

What has changed, however, is Latinos have increased in the population and as a force in American politics. These shifts have likely raised the salience of both issues that disproportionately affect Latinos and beliefs about Latinos. "Hispanic" was not included as a category in the US census until 1970, and the dramatic growth in the Latina/o population has resulted in dramatic shifts in our politics (Barreto and Segura, 2014). These changes have manifest themselves in the party system. Monogan and Doctor (2017), for instance, demonstrate that the alignment between ethnicity and state parties, at least, are fundamentally shaped by recent events. They note that Governor Pete Wilson's support for Prop 187 served as a catalyst for the alignment between Latinos and the Democratic Party in California, which probably preceded the ongoing national trend. The absence of attention to these beliefs in the early literature on racial policy attitudes is understandable, given the timing of both the foundational work in this field and the rising political influence of Latinos.

Over this past half decade, however, Latinos have become socially and politically salient to Whites, and beliefs about Latinos have become politically consequential. Because we do not have data prior to 2014, we cannot provide any clear guidance on when beliefs about Latinos rose to the level of importance it has currently reached. It is plausible that if we had conducted similar studies to the ones in this book in the 1980s that the effects would either have been weaker or nonexistent. But what is clear is that Whites' beliefs about Latinos are now consequential for a host of policy choices. Although we show that the current expression of LRE is not new, we suspect that the connection to such a wide range of political choices is something that has occurred recently – coinciding with both the rise in the Latina/o population and entrepreneurial politicians leveraging the politics of LRE.

While the effects we demonstrate are mostly limited to areas that have implications for Latinos, the broader implication is that this new source of political conflict in the minds of Whites is playing an important role for how they think about politics, one that is likely to continue and grow into the near future. Not only is the divide between Whites and Latinos becoming increasingly salient politically, more and more issues are being described as connecting to this divide. We anticipate that more and more issues in the near future will be "Latina/o-ized" in the minds of Whites, particularly with those who are high in LRE. If political elites can identify a source of leverage and strategic gain by framing an issue in this way, then we should see it used more widely as a tool.

The end result is a "browning" of political opinions. Two of the issues we explore in the book, crime and voter identification, have been identified as have been race-coded by some Whites in America. Those who harbor higher levels of LRE are more likely to favor harsher penalties and more-restrictive voting laws. Our argument is that Whites see these issues as multifaceted and their opinions about several other groups matter when they form these opinions. When, in the minds of White voters, the only important racial divide in America was between Whites and African Americans, their beliefs about African Americans were likely the only relevant beliefs when constructing opinions about crime or voter laws. As American society and politics have shifted, as Latinos play a more prominent role in the minds of Whites, their beliefs about Latinos become a more important predictor alongside those of African Americans.[1] As a result, LRE clearly influences the political choices of Whites in these policy areas.

The elephant in the room for all of this is President Trump. One obvious concern for this work is that our findings are an artifact of Trump's influence on politics. Attitudes about Latinos, one could contend, are important for Whites' more general political attitudes at this moment because of the rhetoric and appeal of President Trump. Once his administration is over and he exits politics, it is possible that the strategic incentives to highlight anti-Latino sentiment in the ways that he has may

---

[1] It is important to note that our results do not find that LRE is simply a replacement for beliefs about other racial groups such as African Americans. Instead, LRE plays an independent role in relation to political choices beyond their beliefs about African Americans or other racial groups.

dissipate and the effects we document may end up being time bound. LRE may recede or the link between it and other political attitudes may weaken.

We are skeptical of this argument. First, while we cannot go back in time as far as we would like, we can go back to before Trump was a presidential candidate. The earliest measurement of LRE is from the 2014 CCES. Trump had been a frequent political commentator and his celebrity did help him receive attention in 2014. But most of his rhetoric was focused on President Obama. His opening campaign event surprised many by its focus on immigration and this was the first time that he publicly called for a full border wall, so the 2014 CCES effectively pre-dates Trump's immigration rhetoric. If we compare the levels of LRE in these data to the comparable data from the 2016 CCES, there is not an appreciable increase. The effect of LRE is also consistent across the studies; the results in the 2016 CCES do not appear to be strong than the effects in the 2014 CCES. It appears that Trump tapped into existing beliefs about Latinos more than he led Whites to hold these beliefs.

Moreover, we have tried to compare the patterns in our results to the timing of Trump's attention on immigration, Latinos, or MS-13. While this provided to be somewhat difficult as he always seemed to be tweeting something critical about Latinos, there did not seem to be any pattern where the strength of the results in our surveys or experiments shifted when Trump had been using anti-Latino rhetoric during the administration of our studies. These external cues from President Trump do not seem to have much of an effect on the patterns we observe.

Additionally, it is not the case that Trump created this anti-Latino rhetoric out of whole cloth. Several of the policies the Trump administration has advocated had support from elected Republicans prior to Trump's election. Our results from the 2014 election show that many statewide Republican candidates had advocated for stricter immigration laws in the 2014 election. These policies were part of the Republican coalition prior to Trump's emergence as a party leader and are likely to continue to be a defining element of the party after he leaves. LRE, then, is likely to continue to play a formative role in American public opinion beyond our deal-maker president.

8.4 THE NATURE OF PUBLIC POLICY OPINIONS

But which opinions does LRE influence? Our brief summary of the results in this book illustrates that LRE has a dramatic influence on public opinion on a range of issues. The set of issues we explored is intentional.

In particular they vary along a few dimensions. First, they have been framed and described as being "about" Latinos to a varying degree. On one end of the spectrum, immigration is thought of almost exclusively as an issue focusing on Latina/o immigration. During the first two years of the Trump administration, immigration not only played an outsized role in political discourse but the vast majority of the attention was on immigration from Mexico and other Latin American countries. The constant discussion of the border wall made this clear. In the final weeks of the 2018 campaign, President Trump's incessant attention was on the caravan of immigrants slowly moving north. Even the ban on travelers from mostly Muslim countries illustrated the dominance of the framing of immigration as connected to Latinos. The language used to discuss the ban was not a ban on immigration, but a ban on "travel." Clearly, the ban touched on a broader set of policies than just immigration, but it is probably not coincidental that it was rarely discussed as being *about* immigration.

Crime is a more complicated issue. As we documented, the "browning" of crime coverage does make the link between criminal justice policy and attitudes about Latinos a relatively easy connection for voters. We trace some of the history of this in Chapter 2 and the more recent media coverage in Chapter 5. President Trump's emphasis on MS-13 reaffirms this connection as well. But in some ways it is more broadly racialized. Much of the literature on attitudes about crime in political science has emphasized the role of race and attitudes about African Americans without considering beliefs about Latinos as either a substitute or additional factor. So it is a middle ground of an issue in our analyses. It has clear connections to Latinos in the minds of voters, but the set of accessible considerations is likely to be broader than for immigration attitudes. The evidence that LRE alters opinions toward criminal justice policies and the complex nature of these relationship indicates that LRE is not just the simple manifestation of attitudes that are perceived as being "about" Latinos.

This is also the importance of the third policy area we explore. Historically, the question of ballot access has been raised in relation to African Americans. However, more recently ballot accessibility is generally framed as a question of voter fraud, not about disenfranchising specific ethnic groups. Some people do target undocumented immigrants as the source of fraud, but this discussion has remained on the fringes rather than pushed en masse by the political elite. Even the small amount of discussion about the exclusionary aspects of voter identification laws do not tend to emphasize the impact on Latina/o voters. But there is still the link between LRE and opinions about ballot access. White citizens seem to be able to make this connection in this issue area even when it is not the dominant focus of discussion.

We should also note that the pattern of results across these issues do seem to follow how strongly an issue has been framed as being about Latinos. The immigration chapter presents the strongest set of results of the three. They are completely consistent across the policy questions we examine and the different ways we approach each question. The crime results are a little more inconsistent across the policy questions we examine, but do not seem to be as substantively strong as in the immigration chapter. Finally, the results in the voter registration chapter are the least consistent. LRE matters in both of the experiments, but the cues sent in the experiments seem to have the least effect on these attitudes. Given the pattern of making these issues about Latinos, we think this should not be surprising.

There is a second possible explanation for the somewhat weaker effects in the voter registration chapter. This is a hard issue. Carmines and Stimson (1980) developed the easy versus hard typology to describe the nature of public opinion on issues. Easy issues are symbolic instead of technical, deal with policy ends instead of means, and have been long on the policy agenda. While voter identification might be symbolic, it is more about means than ends and has been a salient political issue for a much shorter period of time than either immigration or crime. As a result, it is likely that voters have a less well-developed sense of the issue and only weak attitudes. The results may be that there is much more noise in the survey respondents and weaker relationships. Even with these limitations, though, the effect of LRE is still substantial.

We should note that within the policy areas we have tried to vary the specific questions between easier, more symbolic questions and the more difficult technical issues. In the immigration chapter, this is one of the distinctions between the more general measure of immigration policy preferences and the support for more technical policies such as DACA. For the analysis of crime control policy preferences, the first set of results about sentencing and the size of the police force are easier issues, while the issue of police body cameras is more hard. Even in the voter identification chapter, the purging the voter rolls experiment is definitely a harder issue than the more symbolic question about voter identification. In each case, there is evidence that LRE explains attitudes for both easy and hard issues, if the evidence is stronger for the easier issues.

This points to the pervasiveness of LRE in shaping White public opinion. One could imagine that experimental designs that involve more technical or complicated issues might lead respondents to more difficulty for the respondents to construct their opinions, resulting in more noise and weaker effects. This is not what we find. LRE seems to play a strong role in the construction of these opinions regardless of the difficulty of the issue.

8.5 THE REAL IMPLICATIONS

Although our evidence is limited to exploring the role of LRE in relation to a few policy areas, we believe that there are real and consequential implications for American politics. The broader trend we see is the continued endorsement among some Whites to support policies that have a negative impact on Latina/o communities. The support of politicians who also support policies and institutions that explicitly or more covertly discriminate against Latinos has negative and sometimes dire consequences. First, Latinos are more likely to become disaffected with the political system. A 2018 Pew study found that 62 percent of Latinos were dissatisfied "with the way things are going in the country today" – a figure that has increased by 19 percentage points since 2012.[2] This could lead a group that has been historically optimistic and patriotic (de la Garza et al., 1996) to become cynical and untrustworthy of the government – further eroding the legitimacy of governing institutions.

Second, these political choices could further embolden hate groups to act, leading to a return of physical violence against Latinos and even lynchings. The last several years have seen a marked increase in the number of hate crimes against Latinos as recorded by the Federal Bureau of Investigations.[3] The National Crime Victimization Survey reinforces this trend, finding that one in five suspected hate crimes victimized a Latina/o between 2012 and 2016.[4] We expect further waves of direct violence against Latinos if White Americans continue to accept LRE as a socially acceptable belief and endorse public leaders and policies that give further voice to this particular brand of animus.

---

[2] www.pewhispanic.org/2018/10/25/hispanics-have-become-more-dissatisfied-with-direction-of-u-s/.
[3] https://ucr.fbi.gov/hate-crime/2017.
[4] www.bjs.gov/index.cfm?ty=dcdetail&iid=245.

Finally, these political choices directly lead to policies that violate the physical integrity and human rights of Latinos. Immigration policy alone has resulted in the displacement of families, the incarceration of children during important developmental stages of their life, and sexual abuse of migrant children while in US custody. These abuses will surely have a negative effect on the long-term mental health of thousands of migrant families, affecting their ability to gain an education, earn a living, and maintain a physically healthy lifestyle. LRE is also a driver of immigration policies that increase patrols along the border, which lead migrants to engage in riskier behavior in the vast desert along the US–Mexican border. The number of migrants who die crossing the border has been increasing alongside tougher border enforcement – support of which we show is linked to LRE. The dehumanization of these migrants (an extreme extension of the nonassimilation belief) legitimizes these preventable deaths in the minds of some White Americans and we suspect those harboring LRE would hold more antipathy toward these migrant deaths. Many White Americans are either complacent in these deaths, while some actively seek to aid in these deaths by emptying water wells, disposing of humanitarian relief, and engaging in armed patrols of the safer paths through the desert. LRE is, at least indirectly, linked to some of the most blatant human rights violations committed by and endorsed by the United States in the modern era.

8.6 FINAL THOUGHTS

In sum, it is clear that LRE is a powerful force in some of the political choices that White Americans make. The debate over the place of Latinos in American society is not going to disappear. Conservative commentators will continue to make implicit and explicit cues that make accessible beliefs about Latinos as not fitting the broader norms of what they believe it means to be American and their dismay at the perceived lack of assimilation. These specific beliefs that constitute LRE are unlikely to go away.

This is likely to continue to manifest as support by a significant portion of White America for policies that have deleterious implications for Latinos. If support for policies about access to the ballot and treatment by the criminal justice system continues to be eroded by LRE, reform becomes more difficult. Harsher penalties, stricter registration laws, and generally fewer democratic policies will result from public opinion. Conversations about reasonable reforms become difficult when one-side's complaints are rooted in racial animus rather than attacking a genuine problem. Whites' LRE is also likely to prop up the electoral fortunes of candidates committed to these nondemocratic and nonhumanitarian policies. Electoral and political success in overcoming these restrictive policies will require either the diminution of LRE, the breaking of the link between LRE and these policy opinions, or an effort to make the election about other issues.

None of these ideas seem very likely. LRE is grounded in centuries of history and ingrained in White culture. It is not likely to dissipate in the near future. The electoral incentives, at least for the current Republican Party, is to maintain the link between these beliefs and elections. That is how they won in 2016. Hearkening back to the similarity with racial resentment and Whites' beliefs about African Americans, there does not seem to be an effective way forward. The hope must be for a new generation rooted in norms that delegitimizes LRE and the gradual loss in political power of these latter beliefs. The increased political participation of Latinos in 2018 is a potential step along this path. If there are greater electoral costs for politicians who promote and prime LRE, then these beliefs may decline and their political effects may lessen.

Appendix A

Sample Details

The student samples are all convenience samples of White college students participating in either online distance learning courses or in-person classes at Arizona State University. The distance learning samples contain a more representative range of respondents who tend to be older and more widely geographically distributed than the average college student. Each participants' race was screened prior to inclusion in the sample. Students were given extra credit for participation and those wishing to not participate, or those excluded due to their race, were allowed to complete an alternative course assignment for credit. The study shown in Chapter 3 is a sample of distance learning students who completed the study via the Internet between April 14 and 18, 2014. The survey for the crime study in Chapter 5 is also a sample of distance learning students who completed the survey anonymously via the Internet between October 25 and 30, 2018. The voting rights study in Chapter 6 is a sample of college students taking in-person courses who completed the study in the School of Politics and Global Studies experimental laboratory between March 20 and 28, 2017.

The Survey Sampling International (SSI) data is a matched sample representative of the US adult population of White Americans over the age of 18. The sample is produced by matching participants of an opt-in panel to a target sample of registered voters based on age, gender, educational attainment, geographic region, martial status, home ownership, household income, and race/ethnicity. For this sample, each respondent's race/ethnicity was screened prior to inclusion in the sample. Surveys were completely anonymously using SSI's online platform between March 16 and 19, 2015. The sample targeted 350 respondents.

The Cooperative Congressional Election Study (CCES) data is a representative sample of US adults over the age of 18. The CCES is a two-wave election study conducted by YouGov on behalf of a consortium of scholars. YouGov draws a simple random sample from the target population (the US adult population) that is a true population sample. It then matches each respondent in the random sample to members of its opt-in Internet panel of more than 5 million people, using either proximity and entropy matching methods. This creates a sample that closely resembles the US population in terms of demographic characteristics, political preferences, and social behaviors. Once the survey is complete, the final data are statistically weighted to the national profile of all adults aged 18 and over (including people without Internet access). The preelection wave of the 2014 CCES was conducted in October 2014 and the postelection wave of the 2014 CCES was conducted in November 2014. The preelection wave of the 2016 CCES was conducted in October 2016 and the postelection wave of the 2016 CCES was conducted in November 2016. Both samples targeted 1,000 respondents. Drop-off in the postelection wave of the 2014 sample is 12 percent. Drop-off in the postelection wave of the 2016 sample is 19 percent.

The 2017 Qualtrics data is a nationwide survey of US adults over the age of 18. The surveys were completed anonymously using Qualtrics online sampling platform between July 13 and 14, 2017. The sample targeted 1,000 respondents, with an error by the survey firm resulting in a larger sample size of 2,101 respondents.

The 2018 Qualtrics data is from a representative sample of US adult Americans over the age of 18. The survey was completed anonymously using Qualtrics online sampling platform between April 6 and 10, 2018. The sample targeted 1,000 respondents.

Appendix B

Measurement

Old-Fashioned Racial Stereotypes

- How trustworthy are members of each of the following groups? Very untrustworthy, somewhat untrustworthy, neither, somewhat trustworthy, very trustworthy.
- How smart or intelligent are members of each of the following groups? Very intelligent, somewhat intelligent, neither, somewhat intelligent, very unintelligent.
- How hardworking are members of each of the following groups? Very lazy, somewhat lazy, neither, somewhat hardworking, very hardworking.

  [White Americans; Black Americans; Hispanic Americans; Asian Americans; Muslim Americans]

Feelings toward African Americans

- Please indicate how warm or cold you feel toward members of the following groups? A rating of 7 indicates that you feel warm or favorable toward members of the group. A rating of 1 means that you feel unfavorable toward members of the group and don't care much for them.

  [Whites; Blacks; Hispanics/Latinos]

Racial Resentment
Do you agree or disagree with the following statements?

- The Irish, Italians, Jews, and many other minorities overcame prejudice and worked their way up. Blacks should do the same without any special favors.
- Generations of slavery and discrimination have created conditions that make it difficult for Blacks to work their way out of the lower class.

Perceived Percentage of Latinos Voting Democratic
Different groups in America are more or less likely to support each political party. What percentage of each of the following groups do you think vote for the Democratic candidates (as opposed to the Republican candidates)?

[Latinos]

Authoritarianism
Although there are a number of qualities that people feel children should have, every person thinks that some are more important than others. Please indicate which ones you think are more important for a child to have?

- being considerate
- good manners
- respect for elders
- independence
- being well-behaved
- self-reliance
- obedience
- curiosity

Moral Traditionalism
Please indicate if you agree or disagree with each of the following statements?

- We should be more tolerant of people who choose to live according to their own moral standards, even if they are very different from our own.
- The country would have fewer problems if there were more emphasis on traditional family ties.
- The world is always changing and we should adjust our view of moral behavior to those changes.
- The newer lifestyles are contributing to the breakdown of society.

Cultural Preference (2014 Cooperative Congressional Election Study)

- Please choose a point along the scale indicating how much you agree that American culture and values are superior to the culture and values of other countries. (100-point thermometer scale ranges from 100 "absolutely agree" to 0 "absolutely disagree").
- Please choose a point along the scale indicating how important it is to you that the United States be number one in whatever it does. (100-point thermometer scale ranges from 100 "extremely important" to 0 "not at all important").

Cultural Preference (2016 Cooperative Congressional Election Study)
How strongly do you agree or disagree with the following?

- America is a better country than most others.
- The world would be better if more people from other countries were like Americans.

Economic Optimism
Would you say that over the past year the nation's economy has gotten much better, gotten better, stayed about the same, gotten worse, gotten much worse, not sure?

Household Income
Over the past four years, has your household's annual income increased a lot, increased somewhat, stayed about the same, decreased somewhat, or decreased a lot.

Ideology

- (version 1) Do you consider yourself a liberal, a conservative, or something in the middle?
- (version 2) Thinking about politics these days, how would you describe your own political viewpoint? Very liberal, liberal, moderate, conservative, very conservative, not sure.

Partisanship

- (version 1) Do you consider yourself a Democrat, Republican, or Independent?
- (version 2) Generally speaking, do you think of yourself as a Democrat (would you call yourself a strong Democrat or a not very strong Democrat), Republican (would you call yourself a strong Republican or a not very strong Republican), Independent (do you think of yourself as closer to the Democratic or the Republican Party?), Other, Not sure.

Immigration Policy Preferences
What do you think the US government should do about immigration?
Select all that apply.

- Grant legal status to all illegal immigrants who have held jobs and paid taxes for at least three years, and not been convicted of any felony crimes.
- Increase the number of border patrols on the US–Mexican border.
- Allow police to question anyone they think may be in the country illegally.
- Fine US businesses that hire illegal immigrants.
- Grant legal status to people who were brought to the United States illegally as children, but who have graduated from a US high school.
- Increase the number of visas for overseas workers to work in the United States.
- Identify and deport illegal immigrants.

Affordable Care Act (ACA)
Congress considers many issues. If you were in Congress would you vote
FOR or AGAINST each of the following?

- To repeal ACA. Would repeal the ACA of 2009 (also known as Obamacare).

Defense Spending
The federal budget deficit is approximately US$1 trillion this year. If the Congress were to balance the budget, it would have to consider cutting defense spending, cutting domestic spending (such as Medicare and Social Security), or raising taxes to cover the deficit. Please rank the options below from what would you most prefer that Congress do to what you would least prefer they do.

- Cut Defense Spending
- Cut Domestic Spending
- Raise Taxes

Attitude toward Police
Do the police make you feel mostly safe, somewhat safe, somewhat unsafe, mostly unsafe?

Crime Victim
Over the past FOUR YEARS, have you been a victim of a crime?

Obama Approval
Do you approve of the way each of the following is doing their job?

[President Obama]

Political Sophistication

- Which party has a majority of seats in the US House of Representatives?
- Which party has a majority of seats in the US Senate?
- Please indicate whether you've heard of this person and if so which party he or she is affiliated with ... [name US Senator 1].
- Please indicate whether you've heard of this person and if so which party he or she is affiliated with ... [name US Senator 2].
- Please indicate whether you've heard of this person and if so which party he or she is affiliated with ... [name of member of the US House].

Sex

- (version 1) Are you male or female?
- (version 2) Do you consider yourself male, female, or something else?

Education
What is the highest level of education you have completed?

- Did not graduate from high school, high school graduate, some college, but not degree (yet), two-year college degree, four-year college degree, postgraduate degree (MA, MBA, MD, JD, PhD, etc.).

Unemployed
Which of the following best describes your current employment status? Working full-time now, working part-time now, temporarily laid off, unemployed, retired, permanently disabled, taking care of home or family, student, or other. (Respondents that are unemployed or temporarily laid off are coded as unemployed).

Born Again
Would you describe yourself as a "born again" or evangelical Christian, or not?

Bibliography

Abrajano, Marisa, and Singh, Simran. 2009. Examining the Links between Issue Attitudes and News Source: The Case of Latinos and Immigration Reform. *Political Behavior*, 31(1), 1–30.

Alexander, Michelle. 2010. *The New Jim Crow: Mass Incarceration in the Age of Colorblindness*. New York: The New Press.

Alvarez, R. Michael, and Brehm, John. 2002. *Hard Choices, Easy Answers*. Princeton, NJ: Princeton University Press.

Anderson, Bridget. 2013. *Us and Them?: The Dangerous Politics of Immigration Control*. Oxford: Oxford University Press.

Appleby, Jacob, and Federico, Christopher M. 2017. The Racialization of Electoral Fairness in the 2008 and 2012 United States Presidential Elections. *Group Processes & Intergroup Relations*, 21(7), 979–996.

Atkeson, Lonna Rae, Alvarez, R. Michael, Hall, Thad E., and Sinclair, J. Andrew. 2014. Balance Fraud Prevention and Electoral Participation: Attitudes toward Voter Identification. *Social Science Quarterly*, 95(5), 1381–1398.

Ayers, John W., Hofstetter, Richard C., Schnakenberg, Keith, and Kolody, Bohdan. 2009. Is Immigration a Racial Issue? Anglo Attitudes on Immigration Policies in a Border County. *Social Science Quarterly*, 90(3), 593–610.

Balderrama, Francisco E., and Rodriguez, Raymond. 2006. *Decade of Betrayal: Mexican Repatriation in the 1930s*. Albuquerque: University of New Mexico Press.

Banks, Antoine. 2016. Are Group Cues Necessary? How Anger Makes Ethnocentrism among Whites a Stronger Predictor of Racial and Immigration Policy Opinions. *Political Behavior*, 38(3), 635–657.

Banks, Antoine J., and Hicks, Heather M. 2016. Fear and Implicit Racism: Whites' Support for Voter ID Laws. *Political Psychology*, 37(5), 641–658.

Barkan, Steven E. 1985. *Protestors on Trial: Criminal Justice in the Southern Civil Rights and Vietnam Anti-War Movements*. New Brunswick, NJ: Rutgers University Press.

Barkan, Steven E., and Cohn, Steven F. 2005. Why Whites Favor Spending More Money to Fight Crime: The Role of Racial Prejudice. *Social Problems*, 52(2), 300–314.

Barreto, Matt, and Segura, Gary. 2014. *Latino America: How America's Most Dynamic Population Is Poised to Transform the Politics of the Nation*. New York: Public Affairs.

Baumgartner, Frank R., De Boef, Suzanna L., and Boydstun, Amber E. 2008. *The Decline of the Death Penalty and the Discovery of Innocence*. New York: Cambridge University Press.

Beckett, Katherine, and Sasson, Theodore. 2004. *The Politics of Injustice: Crime and Punishment in America*. Thousand Oaks, CA: Sage Publications.

Behnken, Brian D. 2011. *Fighting Their Own Battles: Mexican Americans, African Americans, and the Struggle for Civil Rights in Texas*. Chapel Hill: The University of North Carolina Press.

Bell, Daniel. 1978. The Referendum: Democracy's Barrier to Racial Equality. *Washington Law Review*, 54, 1–29.

Berg, Charles Ramirez. 2002. *Latino Images in Film: Stereotypes, Subversion, and Resistance*. Austin: University of Texas Press.

Bergner, Gwen. 2009. Black Children, White Preferences: *Brown v. Board*, the Doll Tests, and the Politics of Self-Esteem. *American Quarterly*, 61(2), 299–332.

Blair, Irene V., Ma, Jennifer E., and Lenton, Alison P. 2001. Imagining Stereotypes Away: The Moderation of Implicit Stereotypes through Mental Imagery. *Journal of Personality and Social Psychology*, 81(5), 828–841.

Blanchard, Fletcher A., Crandall, Christian S., Brigham, John C., and Vaughn, Leigh Ann. 1994. Condemning and Condoning Racism: A Social Context Approach to Interracial Settings. *Journal of Applied Psychology*, 79(6), 993–997.

Bobo, Lawrence, Kluegel, James R., and Smith, Ryan A. 1997. Laissez-Faire Racism: The Crystallization of a Kinder, Gentler, Antiblack Ideology. Pages 23–25 of: Tuch, Steven A., and Martin, Jack K. (eds.), *Racial Attitudes in the 1990s: Continuity and Change*. Westport, CT: Praeger Publishers.

Bodenhausen, Galen V., Macrae, C. Neil, and Sherman, Jeffery W. 1999. On the Dialectics of Discrimination: Dual Processes in Social Stereotyping. Pages 271–290 of: Chaiken, Shelly, and Trope, Yaacov (eds.), *Dual-Process Theories in Social Psychology*. New York: Guilford.

Bonczar, T. 2003. *Prevalence of Imprisonment in the US Population, 1974–2001*. Washington, DC: Bureau of Justice Statistics.

Bottoms, Anthony. 1995. The Philosophy and Politics of Punishment and Sentencing. Pages 17–49 of: Clarkson, C. M. V., and Morgan, Rodney (eds.), *The Politics of Sentencing Reform*. New York: Oxford University Press.

Brace, Paul R., and Hall, Melinda Gann. 1997. The Interplay of Preferences, Case Facts, Context, and Rules in the Politics of Judicial Choice. *Journal of Politics*, 59(4), 1206–1231.

Brader, Ted, Valentino, Nicholas A., and Suhay, Elizabeth. 2008. What Triggers Public Opposition to Immigration? Anxiety, Group Cues, and Immigration Threat. *American Journal of Political Science*, 52(4), 959–978.

Brady, John. 1996. *Bad Boy: The Life and Politics of Lee Atwater*. Boston, MA: Addison-Wesley.

Branton, Regina, Cassese, Erin C., Jones, Bradford S., and Westerland, Chad. 2011. All along the Watchtower: Acculturation Fear, Anti-Latino Affect, and Immigration. *The Journal of Politics*, 73(3), 664–679.

Branton, Regina, Dillingham, Gavin, Dunaway, Johanna, and Miller, Beth. 2007. Anglo Voting on Nativist Ballot Initiatives: The Partisan Impact of Spatial Proximity to the US–Mexico Border. *Social Science Quarterly*, 88(3), 882–897.

Branton, Regina, and Dunaway, Johanna. 2008. English-and-Spanish-Language Media Coverage of Immigration: A Comparative Analysis. *Social Science Quarterly*, 89(4), 1006–1022.

Branton, Regina, Martinez-Ebers, Valerie, Carey, Tony E., and Matsubayashi, Tetsuya. 2015. Social Protest and Policy Attitudes: The Case of the 2006 Immigrant Rallies. *American Journal of Political Science*, 59(2), 390–402.

Branton, Regina P., and Dunaway, Johanna. 2009a. Slanted Newspaper Coverage of Immigration: The Importance of Economics and Geography. *Policy Studies Journal*, 37(2), 257–273.

Branton, Regina P., and Dunaway, Johanna. 2009b. Spatial Proximity to the US–Mexico Border and Newspaper Coverage of Immigration Issues. *Political Research Quarterly*, 62(2), 289–302.

Brimelow, Peter. 1996. *Alien Nation: Common Sense about America's Immigration Disaster*. Random House: New York.

Buchanan, Patrick. 2006. *State of Emergency: The Third World Invasion and Conquest of America*. New York: St. Martin's Press.

Buriel, Raymond, and Vasquez, Richard. 1982. Stereotypes of Mexican Descent Persons: Attitudes of Three Generations of Mexican Americans and Anglo American Adolescents. *Journal of Cross-Cultural Psychology*, 13(1), 59–70.

Burkhardt, Brett C. 2017. Who Punishes Whom? Bifurcation of Private and Public Responsibilities in Criminal Punishment. *Journal of Crime and Justice*, 40(4), 512–527.

Burns, Peter, and Gimpel, James G. 2000. Economic Insecurity, Prejudicial Stereotypes, and Public Opinion on Immigration. *Political Science Quarterly*, 115(2), 201–225.

Camarillo, Albert. 1975. The Development of the Chicano Working Class in Santa Barbara, California, 1860–1897. In: *National Association for Chicana and Chicano Studies Annual Conference*, vol. Paper 5.

Campbell, Kristina M. 2011. The Road to SB 1070: How Arizona Became Ground Zero for the Immigrant's Rights Movement and the Continuing Struggle for Latino Civil Rights in America. *Harvard Latino Law Review*, 14(1), 1–22.

Capozzola, Christopher. 2008. *Uncle Sam Wants You: World War I and the Making of the Modern American Citizen*. New York: Oxford University Press.

Carmines, Edward G., and Stimson, James A. 1980. The Two Faces of Issue Voting. *American Political Science Review*, 74(1), 78–91.

Carmines, Edward G., and Stimson, James A. 1989. *Issue Evolution*. Princeton, NJ: Princeton University Press.

Carrigan, William D., and Webb, Clive. 2003. The Lynching of Persons of
    Mexican Origin or Descent in the United States, 1848–1928. *Journal of
    Social History*, 37(2), 411–438.
Carter, J. Scott, and Corra, Mamadi. 2016. Racial Resentment and Attitudes
    toward the Use of Force by Police: An Over-Time Trend Analysis. *Socio-
    logical Inquiry*, 86(4), 492–511.
Carter, J. Scott, and Jenks, David A. 2016. In the Shadows of Ferguson: The Role
    of Racial Resentment on White Attitudes towards the Use of Force by Police
    in the United States. *International Journal of Criminal Justice Sciences*, 11(2),
    114–129.
Chanbonpin, Kim D. 2005. How the Border Crossed Us: Filling the Gap
    between Plume v. Seward and the Dispossession of Mexican Landowners
    in California after 1848. *Cleveland State Law Review*, 52(1–2), 297–319.
Chavez, Leo. 2013. *The Latino Threat: Constructing Immigrants, Citizens, and
    the Nation*. Palo Alto, CA: Stanford University Press.
Citrin, Jack, Green, Donald P., Muste, Christopher, and Wong, Cara. 1997. Public
    Opinion toward Immigration Reform: The Role of Economic Motivations.
    Journal of Politics, 59(3), 858–881.
Citrin, Jack, Green, Donald Phillip, and Sears, David O. 1990. White Reactions
    to Black Candidates: When Does Race Matter? *Public Opinion Quarterly*,
    54(1), 74–96.
Clark, Kenneth B., and Clark, Mamie P. 1950. Emotional Factors in Racial
    Identification and Preference in Negro Children. *The Journal of Negro
    Education*, 19(3), 341–350.
Conover, Pamela Johnston, and Miller, Patrick R. 2018. How Republicans Won
    on Voter Identification Laws: The Roles of Strategic Reasoning and Moral
    Conviction. *Social Science Quarterly*, 99(2), 490–511.
Coppock, Alexander, and McClellan, Oliver A. 2019. Validating the Demo-
    graphic, Political, Psychological, and Experimental Results Obtained from
    a New Source of Online Survey Respondents. *Research and Politics*, 6(1),
    1–14.
Crandall, Christian S., Miller, Jason M., and Mark H. White, II. 2018. Changing
    Norms Following the 2016 U.S. Presidential Election: The Trump Effect on
    Prejudice. *Social Psychology and Personality Science*, 9(2), 186–192.
Culver, Leigh. 2004. The Impact of New Immigration Patterns on the Provision
    of Police Services in Midwestern Communities. *Journal of Criminal Justice*,
    32(4), 329–344.
Curtin, Mary Ellen. 2000. *Black Prisoners and Their World, Alabama,
    1865–1900*. Charlottesville: The University Press of Virginia.
Dagan, David, and Teles, Steven M. 2014. Locked In? Conservative Reform and
    the Future of Mass Incarceration. *The Annals of the American Academy of
    Political and Social Science*, 651(1), 266–276.
Daprile, Lucas. 2015. Scott Walker Says Most Americans Support Voter ID Laws,
    Which Make It Easier to Vote. *PolitiFact*, June 29.
Davis, Kingsley, and Senior, Clarence. 1949. Immigration from the Western
    Hemisphere. *The Annals of the American Academy of Political and Social
    Science*, 262(1), 70–81.

De Garine, Igor. 2001. Views about Food Prejudice and Stereotypes. *Social Science Information*, 40(3), 487–507.

De Genova, Nicholas P. 2002. Migrant "Illegality" and Deportability in Everyday Life. *Annual Review of Anthropology*, 31(1), 419–447.

De Genova, Nicholas P. 2004. The Legal Production of Mexican/Migrant "Illegality." *Latino Studies*, 2(2), 160–185.

de la Garza, Rodolfo O., Falcon, Angelo, and Garcia, F. Chris. 1996. Will the Real Americans Please Stand Up: Anglo and Mexican-American Support of Core American Political Values. *American Journal of Political Science*, 40(2), 335–351.

De León, Arnoldo. 2010. *They Called Them Greasers: Anglo Attitudes toward Mexicans in Texas, 1821–1900*. Austin: University of Texas Press.

Decker, Scott H. 1981. Citizen Attitudes toward the Police: A Review of Past Findings and Suggestions for Future Policy. *Journal of Police Science and Administration*, 9(1), 80–87.

Del Castillo, Richard Griswold. 1992. *The Treaty of Guadalupe Hidalgo: A Legacy of Conflict*. Norman: University of Oklahoma Press.

Del Castillo, Richard Griswold. 1998. Manifest Destiny: The Mexican-American War and the Treaty of Guadalupe Hidalgo. *Southwestern Journal of Law and Trade in the Americas*, 5(1), 31–43.

Delgado, Richard. 2009. The Law of the Noose: A History of Latino Lynching. *Harvard Civil Rights-Civil Liberties Law Review*, 44(2), 297–312.

Devine, Patricia G. 1989. Stereotypes and Prejudice: The Automatic and Controlled Components. *Journal of Personality and Social Psychology*, 56(1), 5–18.

Dixon, Travis L., and Azocar, Cristina L. 2006. The Representation of Juvenile Offenders by Race on Los Angeles Area Television News. *Howard Journal of Communications*, 17(2), 143–161.

Dixon, Travis Lemar, and Linz, Daniel. 2000b. Overrepresentation and Underrepresentation of African Americans and Latinos as Lawbreakers on Television News. *Journal of Communication*, 50(2), 131–154.

Dixon, Travis L., and Linz, Daniel. 2000a. Race and the Misrepresentation of Victimization on Local Television News. *Communication Research*, 27(5), 547–573.

Dovidio, John F., Kawakami, Kerry, Johnson, Craig, Johnson, Brenda, and Howard, Adaiah. 1997. On the Nature of Prejudice: Automatic and Controlled Processes. *Journal of Experimental Social Psychology*, 33(5), 510–540.

Duany, Jorge. 1998. Reconstructing Racial Identity: Ethnicity, Color, and Class among Dominicans in the United States and Puerto Rico. *Latin American Perspectives*, 25(3), 147–172.

Duany, Jorge. 2016. Racializing Ethnicity in the Spanish-Speaking Caribbean: A Comparison of Haitians in the Dominican Republic and Dominicans in Puerto Rico. Pages 231–248 of Cobas, Jose A., Duany, Jorge, and Feagin, Joe R. (eds.), *How the United States Racializes Latinos: White Hegemony & its Consequences*. New York: Routledge.

Dudziak, Mary L. 2000. *Cold War Civil Rights: Race and the Image of American Democracy*. Princeton, NJ: Princeton University Press.

Earle, Rebecca. 2012. *The Body of the Conquistador: Food, Race and the Colonial Experience in Spanish America, 1492–1700*. New York: Cambridge University Press.

Edsall, Thomas B. 2016. How Many People Support Trump but Don't Want to Admit It? *The New York Times*, May 11, www.nytimes.com/2016/05/11/opinion/campaign-stops/how-many-people-support-trump-but-dont-want-to-admit-it.html.

Enns, Peter K. 2014. The Public's Increasing Punitiveness and Its Influence on Mass Incarceration in the United States. *American Journal of Political Science*, 58(4), 857–872.

Enns, Peter K. 2016. *Incarceration Nation: How the United States Became the Most Punitive Democracy in the World*. New York: Cambridge University Press.

Enns, Peter K., and Ramirez, Mark D. 2018. Privatizing Punishment: Testing Theories of Public Support for Private Prison and Immigration Detention Facilites. *Criminology*, 56(3), 546–573.

Entman, Robert M., and Rojecki, Andrew. 2000. *The Black Image in the White Mind*. Chicago: University of Chicago Press.

Espenshade, Thomas J., and Calhoun, Charles A. 1993. An Analysis of Public Opinion toward Undocumented Immigration. *Population Research and Policy Review*, 12(3), 189–224.

Farris, Emily M., and Mohamed, Heather Silber. 2018. Picturing Immigration: How the Media Criminalizes Immigrants. *Politics, Groups, and Identities*, 6(4), 814–824.

Feagin, Joe R. 2010. *Racist America: Roots, Current Realities, and Future Reparations*. New York: Routledge.

Feagin, Joe R. 2013. *The White Racial Frame: Centuries of Racial Framing and Counter-Framing*. New York: Routledge.

Feagin, Joe R., and Cobas, Jose A. 2008. Latinos/as and White Racial Frame: The Procrustean Bed of Assimilation. *Sociological Inquiry*, 78(1), 39–53.

Feagin, Joe R., and Dirks, Danielle. 2004. *Who Is White? College Students' Assessments of Key US Racial and Ethnic Groups*. College Station: Department of Sociology, Texas A&M University.

Feagin, Joe R., and Sikes, Melvin P. 1994. *Living with Racism: The Black Middle-Class Experience*. Boston: Beacon Press.

Feldman, Stanley, and Huddy, Leonie. 2005. Racial Resentment and White Opposition to Race-Concious Programs: Principles or Prejudice? *American Journal of Political Science*, 49(1), 168–183.

Fennelly, Katherine. 2008. Prejudice toward Immigrants in the Midwest. Pages 151–178 of: Massey, Douglas S. (ed.), *New Faces in New Places: The Changing Geography of American Immigration*. New York: Russel Sage Foundation.

Fennelly, Katherine, and Orfield, Myron. 2008. Impediments to Integration of Immigrants: A Case Study in the Twin Cities. Pages 200–224 of Singer, Audrey, Hardwick, Susan W., and Brettell, Caroline B. (eds.), *America's*

Twenty-First Century Immigrant Gateways: Immigrant Incorporation in Suburbia. Washington, DC: Brookings Institution Press.

Flamm, Michael W. 2005. *Law and Order: Street Crime, Civil Unrest, and the Crisis of Liberalism in the 1960s*. New York: Columbia University Press.

Foley, Neil. 2014. *Mexicans in the Making of America*. Cambridge, MA: The Belknap Press of Harvard University Press.

Ford, Donna Y. 1994. Nurturing Resilience in Gifted Black Youth. *Roeper Review*, 17(2), 80–85.

Gamble, Barbara S. 1997. Putting Civil Rights to a Popular Vote. *American Journal of Political Science*, 41(1), 245–269.

Garland, David. 2001. *The Culture of Control*. New York: Oxford University Press.

Gawronski, Bertram, Deutsch, Roland, Mbirkou, Sawsan, Seibt, Beate, and Strack, Fritz. 2008. When "Just Say No" Is Not Enough: Affirmation versus Negation Training and the Reduction of Automatic Stereotype Activation. *Journal of Experimental Social Psychology*, 44(2), 370–377.

Gilens, Martin. 1996a. Race and Poverty in America: Public Misperceptions and the American News Media. *Public Opinion Quarterly*, 60(4), 515–541.

Gilens, Martin. 1996b. "Race Coding" and White Opposition to Welfare. *American Political Science Review*, 90(3), 593–604.

Gilens, Martin. 2000. *Why Americans Hate Welfare: Race, Media, and the Politics of Antipoverty Policy*. Chicago: University of Chicago Press.

Gilliam, Franklin D., and Iyengar, Shanto. 2000. Prime Suspects: The Influence of Local Television on the Viewing Public. *American Journal of Political Science*, 44(3), 560–573.

Gilliam, Franklin D., Iyengar, Shanto, Simon, Adam, and Wright, Oliver. 1996. The Violent, Scary World of Local News. *Harvard International Journal of Press/Politics*, 1(3), 6–23.

Gomes, Ralph C., and Williams, Linda Faye. 1990. Race and Crime: The Role of the Media in Perpetuating Racism and Classism in America. *Urban League Review*, 14(1), 57–69.

Gonzalez, Jaime. 2015. I'm White in Barcelona but in Los Angeles I'm Hispanic? *PRI*, October, 28, www.pri.org/stories/2015-10-28/im-white-barcelona-los-angeles-im-hispanic.

Gravelle, Timothy B. 2016. Party Identification, Contact, Contexts, and Public Attitudes toward Illegal Immigration. *Public Opinion Quarterly*, 80(1), 1–25.

Grimmer, Justin, Hersh, Eitan, Meredith, Marc, Mummolo, Jonathan, and Nall, Clayton. 2018. Obstacles to Estimating Voter ID Laws' Effect on Turnout. *Journal of Politics*, 80(3), 1045–1051.

Grosfoguel, Ramón, and Georas, Chloe S. 2000. Coloniality of Power and Racial Dynamics: Notes toward a Reinterpretation of Latino Caribbeans in New York City. *Identities*, 7(1), 85–125.

Guth, James L., Kellstedt, Lyman A., Smidt, Corwin E., and Green, John C. 1993. Theological Perspectives and Environmentalism among Religious Activists. *Journal for the Scientific Study of Religion*, 32(4), 373–382.

Hainmueller, Jens, and Hiscox, Michael J. 2007. Educated Preferences: Explaining Attitudes toward Immigration in Europe. *International Organization*, 61(2), 399–442.

Hainmueller, Jens, and Hiscox, Michael J. 2010. Attitudes toward Highly Skilled and Low-Skilled Immigration: Evidence from a Survey Experiment. *American Political Science Review*, 104(1), 61–84.

Hainmueller, Jens, Hiscox, Michael J., and Margalit, Yotam. 2015. Do Concerns about Labor Market Competition Shape Attitudes toward Immigration. *Journal of International Economics*, 97(1), 193–207.

Hainmueller, Jens, and Hopkins, Daniel J. 2014. Public Attitudes toward Immigrations. *Annual Review of Political Science*, 17(February), 225–249.

Hainmueller, Jens, and Hopkins, Daniel J. 2015. The Hidden American Immigration Consensus: A Conjoint Analysis of Attitudes toward Immigrants. *American Journal of Political Science*, 59(3), 529–548.

Hainmueller, Jens, Hopkins, Daniel J., and Yamamoto, Teppei. 2014. Casual Inference in Conjoint Analysis: Understanding Multidimensional Choices via State Preference Experiments. *Political Analysis*, 22(1), 1–30.

Hajnal, Zoltan, Lajevardi, Nazita, and Nielson, Lindsay. 2017. Voter Identification Laws and the Suppression of Minority Votes. *Journal of Politics*, 79(2), 363–379.

Hajnal, Zoltan, and Rivera, Michael U. 2014. Immigration, Latinos, and White Partisan Politics: The New Democratic Defection. *American Journal of Political Science*, 58(4), 773–789.

Halim, Shaheen, and Stiles, Beverly L. 2001. Differential Support for Police Use of Force, the Death Penalty, and Perceived Harshness of the Courts: Effects of Race, Gender, and Region. *Criminal Justice and Behavior*, 28(1), 3–23.

Hartman, Todd K., Newman, Benjamin J., and Bell, C. Scott. 2014. Decoding Prejudice toward Hispanics: Group Cues and Public Reactions to Threatening Immigrant Behavior. *Political Behavior*, 36(1), 143–163.

Hawley, George. 2011. Political Threat and Immigration: Party Identification, Demographic Context, and Immigration Policy Preference. *Social Science Quarterly*, 92(2), 404–422.

Haynes, Chris, Merolla, Jennifer, and Ramakrishnan, S. Karthick. 2016. *Framing Immigrants: News Coverage, Public Opinion, and Policy*. New York: Russel Sage Foundation.

Henderson, Michael, and Hillygus, D. Sunshine. 2011. The Dynamics of Health Care Opinion, 2008–2010: Partisanship, Self-Interest, and Racial Resentment. *Journal of Health Politics, Policy and Law*, 36(6), 945–960.

Henry, Patrick J., and Sears, David O. 2002. The Symbolic Racism 2000 Scale. *Political Psychology*, 23(2), 253–283.

Hero, Rodney E. 1992. *Latinos and the U.S. Political System*. Philadelphia: Temple University Press.

Hetherington, Marc J., and Weiler, Jonathan D. 2009. *Authoritarianism and Polarization in American Politics*. New York: Cambridge University Press.

Hicks, William D., McKee, Seth C., Sellers, Mitchell D., and Smith, Daniel A. 2015. A Principle or Strategy? Voter Identification Laws and Partisan Competition in the American States. *Political Research Quarterly*, 68(1), 18–33.

Highton, Benjamin. 2004. White Voters and African American Candidates for Congress. *Political Behavior*, 26(1), 1–25.

Himelstein, Jerry. 1983. Rhetorical Continuities in the Politics of Race: The Closed Society Revisited. *Southern Journal of Communication*, 48(2), 153–166.

Hoffman, Abraham. 1974. *Unwanted Mexican Americans in the Great Depression: Repatriation Pressures, 1929–1939*. Tucson: The University of Arizona Press.

Holt, Lanier Frush. 2013. Writing the Wrong: Can Counter-Stereotypes Offset Negative Media Messages about African Americans? *Journalism & Mass Communication Quarterly*, 90(1), 108–125.

Hood, M. V., and Morris, Irwin L. 2000. Brother, Can You Spare a Dime? Racial/Ethnic Context and the Anglo Vote on Proposition 187. *Social Science Quarterly*, 81(1), 194–206.

Hopkins, Daniel J., Tran, Van C., and Fisher, Abigail. 2014. See No Spanish: Language, Local Context, and Attitudes toward Immigration. *Politics, Groups, and Identities*, 2(1), 35–51.

Huddy, Leonie, and Sears, David O. 1995. Opposition to Bilingual Education: Prejudice or the Defense of Realistic Interests? *Social Psychology Quarterly*, 58(2), 133–143.

Hungtington Samuel P. 2005. *Who Are We? The Challenges to America's National Identity*. London: The Free Press.

Hurwitz, Jon, and Peffley, Mark. 1997. Public Perceptions of Race and Crime: The Role of Racial Stereotypes. *American Journal of Political Science*, 41(2), 375–401.

Hurwitz, Jon, and Peffley, Mark. 2005. Playing the Race Card in the Post-Willie Horton Era: The Impact of Racialized Code Words on Support for Punitive Crime Policy. *Public Opinion Quarterly*, 69(1), 99–112.

Hutchings, Vincent L., and Valentino, Nicholas A. 2004. The Centrality of Race in American Politics. *Annual Review of Political Science*, 7, 383–408.

Hyman, Herbert H., and Sheatsley, Paul B. 1950. The Current Status of American Public Opinion. Pages 11–34 of: Payne, J. C. (ed.), *The Teaching of Contemporary Affairs, Twenty-First Yearbook of the National Council of Social Studies*. Washington, DC: National Council of Social Studies.

Inwood, Joshua. 2018. White Supremacy, White Counter-Revolutionary Politics, and the Rise of Donald Trump. *Environment and Planning C: Politics and Space*, 37(4).

Jackson, Linda A. 1995. *Stereotypes, Emotions, Behavior, and Overall Attitudes toward Hispanics by Anglos*. Lansing, MI: Research Report 10, Julian Samora Research Institute, Michigan State University.

Jiménez, Tomás Roberto. 2010. *Replenished Ethnicity: Mexican Americans, Immigration, and Identity*. Berkeley: University of California Press.

Johnson, Kevin R. 2012. Immigration and Civil Rights: Is the New Birmingham the Same as the Old Birmingham? *William & Mary Bill of Rights Journal*, 21(2), 367–398.

Johnson, Kevin R., and Hing, Bill Ong. 2007. The Immigrant Rights Marches of 2006 and the Prospects for a New Civil Rights Movement. *Harvard Civil Rights-Civil Liberties Law Review*, 42(1), 99–138.

Jonas, Kai J., and Sassenberg, Kai. 2006. Knowing How to React: Automatic Response Priming from Social Categories. *Journal of Personality and Social Psychology*, 90(5), 709–721.

Kaeble, Danielle, and Cowhig, Mary. 2018. Correctional Populations in the United States, 2016. *Bureau of Justice Statistics*, U.S. Department of Justice Programs (April).

Kalkan, Kerem Ozan. 2016. What Differentiates Trump Supporters from Other Republicans? Ethnocentrism. *Washington Post*, February, 28, www.washingtonpost.com/news/monkey-cage/wp/2016/02/28/what-differentiates-trump-supporters-from-other-republicans-ethnocentrism/?utm_term=.93def240e99a.

Kalunta-Crumpton, Anita. 2012. *Race, Ethnicity, Crime and Criminal Justice in the Americas*. New York: Palgrave Macmillan.

Karmen, Andrew. 2000. *New York Murder Mystery: The True Story*. New York: New York University Press.

Kim, Younhee, and Price, Byrone E. 2012. Revisiting Prison Privatization: An Examination of the Magnitude of Prison Privatization. *Administration & Society*, 46(3), 255–275.

Kinder, Donald R., and Kam, Cindy D. 2010. *Us Against Them: Ethnocentric Foundations of American Opinion*. Chicago: University of Chicago Press.

Kinder, Donald R., and Sanders, Lynn M. 1996. *Divided by Color*. Chicago: University of Chicago Press.

Kinder, Donald R., and Sears, David O. 1981. Prejudice and Politics: Symbolic Racism Versus Racial Threats to the Good Life. *Journal of Personality and Social Psychology*, 40(3), 414–431.

Knoll, Benjamin R., Redlawsk, David P., and Sanborn, Howard. 2011. Framing Labels and Immigration Policy Attitudes in the Iowa Caucuses: "Trying to Out-Tancredo Tancredo." *Political Behavior*, 33(3), 433–454.

Koenker, Roger, and Yoon, Jungmo. 2009. Parametric Links for Binary Choice Models: A Fisherian-Bayesian Colloquy. *Journal of Econometrics*, 152(2), 120–130.

Lacayo, Celia. 2016. Latinos Need to Stay in Their Place: Differential Segregation in a Multi-Ethnic Suburb. *Societies*, 6(3), 1–18.

Lacy, Stephen, Watson, Brendan R., Riffe, Daniel, and Lovejoy, Jennette. 2015. Issues and Best Practices in Content Analysis. *Journalism & Mass Communication Quarterly*, 92(4), 791–811.

Langworthy, Robert H., and Whitehead, John T. 1986. Liberalism and Fear as Explanations of Punitiveness. *Criminology*, 24(3), 575–591.

Lax, Jeffrey R., and Phillips, Justin H. 2009a. How Should We Estimate Public Opinion in the States? *American Journal of Political Science*, 53(1), 107–121.

Lax, Jeffrey R., and Phillips, Justin H. 2009b. Gay Rights in the States: Public Opinion and Policy Responsiveness. *American Political Science Review*, 103(3), 367–386.

Lee, Matthew T., and Martinez Jr., Ramiro. 2009. Immigration Reduces Crime: An Emerging Scholarly Consensus. Pages 3–16 of: McDonald, William F.

(ed.), *Immigration, Crime, and Justice*. Bingley: Emerald Group Publishing Limited.

Leitner, Helga. 2012. Spaces of Encounters: Immigration, Race, Class, and the Politics of Belonging in Small-Town America. *Annals of the Association of American Geographers*, 102(4), 828–846.

Li, Qiong, and Brewer, Marilynn B. 2004. What Does It Mean to Be an American? Patriotism, Nationalism, and American Identity. *Political Psychology*, 25(5), 727–739.

Lipman, Pauline. 2011. *The New Political Economy of Urban Education: Neoliberalism, Race, and the Right to the City*. New York: Routledge.

Longazel, Jamie. 2013. Subordinating Myth: Latino/a Immigration, Crime, and Exclusion. *Sociology Compass*, 7(2), 87–96.

Macek, Steve. 2006. *Urban Nightmares: The Media, the Right, and the Moral Panic over the City*. Minneapolis: University of Minnesota Press.

Major, Brenda, Blodorn, Alison, and Blascovich, Gregory Major. 2016. The Threat of Increasing Diversity: Why Many White Americans Support Trump in the 2016 Presidential Election. *Group Processes & Intergroup Relations*, 21(6).

Marcus, George E., Sullivan, John L., Theiss-Morse, Elizabeth, and Wood, Sandra L. 1995. *With Malice toward Some*. New York: Cambridge University Press.

Marion, Nancy E. 1994. *A History of Federal Crime Control Initiatives, 1960–1993*. London: Praeger.

Martinez Jr., Ramiro. 2014. *Latino Homicide: Immigration, Violence, and Community*. New York: Routledge.

Masuoka, Natalie, and Junn, Jane. 2013. *The Politics of Belonging: Race, Public Opinion, and Immigration*. Chicago: The University of Chicago Press.

Matthews, J. Scott. 2017. Issue Priming Revisited: Susceptible Voters and Detectable Effects. *British Journal of Political Science*, 49(2), 513–531.

Mauer, Marc. 1999. Why Are Tough on Crime Policies So Popular? *Stanford Law & Policy Review*, 11(1), 9–22.

Mauer, Marc. 2006. *Race to Incarcerate*. New York: The New Press.

McConahay, John B. 1986. Modern Racism, Ambivalence, and the Modern Racism Scale. Pages 91–125 of: Dovidio, John F., and Gaertner, Samuel L. (eds.), *Prejudice, Discrimination, and Racism*. San Diego, CA: Academic Press.

McConnaughy, Corrine M., White, Ismail K., Leal, David L., and Casellas, Jason P. 2010. A Latino on the Ballot: Explaining Coethnic Voting among Latinos and the Response of White Americans. *Journal of Politics*, 72(4), 1199–1211.

McDermott, Monika L. 1998. Race and Gender Cues in Low-Information Elections. *Political Research Quarterly*, 51(4), 895–918.

McElwee, Sean, and McDaniel, Jason. 2016. Anatomy of a Donald Trump Supporter: What Really Motivates This Terrifying Political Movement. *Salon*, May 16, www.salon.com/2016/05/16/anatomy_of_a_donald_trump_supporter_what_really_motivates_this_terrifying_political_movement/.

McKay, R. Reynolds. 1982. The Mexican Repatriation during the Great Depression. *The University of Oklahoma at Norman, PhD dissertation*.

Meeks, Eric V. 2010. *Border Citizens: The Making of Indians, Mexicans, and Anglos in Arizona*. Austin: University of Texas Press.

Meier, Kenneth J. 1994. *The Politics of Sin*. New York: M. E. Sharpe.

Mendelberg, Tali. 1997. Executing Hortons: Racial Crime in the 1988 Presidential Campaign. *Public Opinion Quarterly*, 61(1), 134–157.

Mendelberg, Tali. 2001. *The Race Card*. Princeton, NJ: Princeton University Press.

Millard, Ann V., and Chapa, Jorge. 2004. *Apple Pie and Enchiladas: Latino Newcomers in the Rural Midwest*. Austin: University of Texas Press.

Monogan, James E., and Doctor, Austin C. 2017. Immigration Politics and Partisan Realignment: California, Texas, and the 1994 Election. *State Politics & Policy Quarterly*, 17(1), 3–23.

Moore, Joan, and Pachon, Harry. 1985. *Hispanics in the United States*. Englewood Cliffs, NJ: Prentice-Hall.

Moreno, Kristen N., and Bodenhausen, Galen V. 1999. Resisting Stereotype Change: The Role of Motivation and Attentional Capacity in Defending Social Beliefs. *Group Processes & Intergroup Relations*, 2(1), 5–16.

Morgan, Byron J. T., and Smith, D. M. 1992. A Note on Wadley's Problem with Overdispersion. *Applied Statistics*, 41(2), 349–354.

Muste, Christopher P. 2013. The Dynamics of Immigration Opinion in the United States, 1992–2012. *Public Opinion Quarterly*, 77(1), 398–416.

Musto, David F. 1991. Opium, Cocaine, and Marijuana in American History. *Scientific American*, 265(1), 40–47.

Mutz, Diana C. 2018. Status Threat, Not Economic Hardship, Explains the 2016 Presidential Vote. *Proceedings of the National Academy of Sciences*, 115(19), E4330–E4339.

Nelson, Thomas E., and Kinder, Donald R. 1996. Issue Frames and Group-Centrism in American Public Opinion. *Journal of Politics*, 58(4), 1055–1078.

Newman, Benjamin J. 2013. Acculturating Contexts and Anglo Opposition to Immigration in the United States. *American Journal of Political Science*, 57(2), 374–390.

Nicholson-Crotty, Sean. 2004. The Politics and Administration of Privatization: Contracting Out for Corrections Management in the United States. *Policy Studies Journal*, 32(1), 41–57.

Nicholson-Crotty, Sean, Peterson, David A.M., and Ramirez, Mark D. 2009. Dynamic Representation(s): Federal Criminal Justice Policy and an Alternative Dimension of Policy Mood. *Political Behavior*, 31(4), 629–655.

Novas, Himilce. 2007. *Everything You Need to Know about Latino History*. New York: Plume.

Omi, Michael, and Winant, Howard. 1994. *Racial Formation in the United States*. New York: Routledge.

Omi, Michael, and Winant, Howard. 2007. Racial Formations. Pages 13–22 of: Rothenberg, Paula S. (ed.), *Race, Class, and Gender in the United States*. New York: Worth Publishers.

Ortiz, Ana Teresa, and Briggs, Laura. 2003. The Culture of Poverty, Crack Babies, and Welfare Cheats: The Making of the "Healthy White Baby Crisis." *Social Text*, 21(3), 39–57.

Ostfeld, Mara. 2017. The Backyard Politics of Attitudes toward Immigration. *Political Psychology*, 38(1), 21–37.

Park, David K., Gelman, Andrew, and Bafumi, Joseph. 2004. Bayesian Multi-level Estimation with Poststratification: State-Level Estimates from National Polls. *Political Analysis*, 12(4), 375–385.

Park, Robert E. 1928. Human Migration and the Marginal Man. *American Journal of Sociology*, 33(6), 881–893.

Paxton, Pamela, and Mughan, Anthony. 2006. What's to Fear from Immigrants? Creating an Assimilationist Threat Scale. *Political Psychology*, 27(4), 549–568.

Payne, Keith B., Krosnick, Jon A., Pasek, Josh, Lelkes, Yphtach, Akhtar, Omair, and Tompson, Trevor. 2010. Implicit and Explicit Prejudice in the 2008 American Presidential Election. *Journal of Experimental Social Psychology*, 46(2), 367–374.

Peffley, Mark, and Hurwitz, Jon. 1998. Whites' Stereotypes of Blacks: Sources and Political Consequences. Pages 58–99 of: Hurwitz, Jon, and Peffley, Mark (eds.), *Perception and Prejudice*. New Haven, CT: Yale University Press.

Peffley, Mark, and Hurwitz, Jon. 2002. The Racial Components of "Race-Neutral" Crime Policy Attitudes. *Political Psychology*, 23(1), 59–75.

Peffley, Mark, and Hurwitz, Jon. 2010. *Justice in America: The Separate Realities of Blacks and Whites*. New York: Cambridge University Press.

Peffley, Mark, Hurwitz, Jon, and Sniderman, Paul M. 1997. Racial Stereotypes and Whites' Political Views of Blacks in the Context of Welfare and Crime. *American Journal of Political Science*, 41(1), 30–60.

Peffley, Mark, Shields, Todd, and Williams, Bruce. 1996. The Intersection of Race and Crime in Television News Stories: An Experimental Study. *Political Communication*, 13(3), 309–328.

Perales, Alonso S. 1974. *Are We Good Neighbors?* Austin: University of Texas Press.

Pérez, Efrén O. 2010. Explicit Evidence on the Import of Implicit Attitudes: The IAT and Immigration Policy Judgments. *Political Behavior*, 32(4), 517–545.

Perez, Lisandro. 2016. Racialization among Cubans and Cuban Americans. Pages 134–148 of Cobas, Jose A., Duany, Jorge, and Feagin, Joe R. (eds.), *How the United States Racializes Latinos: White Hegemony & Its Consequences*. New York: Routledge.

Philpot, Tasha S., and Walton, Hanes. 2007. One of Our Own: Black Female Candidates and the Voters Who Support Them. *American Journal of Political Science*, 51(1), 49–62.

Phinney, Jean S. 1989. Stages of Ethnic Identity Development in Minority Group Adolescents. *The Journal of Early Adolescence*, 9(1–2), 34–49.

Piatt, Bill. 1990. *Only English? Law and Language Policy in the United States*. Albuquerque: University of New Mexico Press.

Polsby, Nelson W. 1993. Where Do You Get Your Ideas? *PS: Political Science and Politics*, 26(1), 83–87.

Pomper, Gerald M. 1972. From Confusion to Clarity: Issues and American Voters, 1956–1968. *American Political Science Review*, 66(2), 415–428.

Power, Gerard J., Murphy, Sheila T., and Coover, Gail. 1996. Priming Preju-
    dice: How Stereotypes and Counter-Stereotypes Influence Attribution of
    Responsibility and Credibility among Ingroups and Outgroups. *Human
    Communication Research*, 23(1), 36–58.
Pratt, John. 2007. *Penal Populism*. New York: Routledge.
Purcell, Fernando. 2016. Becoming Dark: The Chilean Experience in California,
    1848–1870. Pages 54–67 of: Cobas, Jose A., Duany, Jorge, and Feagin, Joe R.
    (eds.), *How the United States Racializes Latinos: White Hegemony & Its
    Consequences*. New York: Routledge.
Ramirez, Mark D. 2013. Punitive Sentiment. *Criminology*, 51(2), 329–364.
Ramirez, Mark D. 2014. Competing Pressures and Complex Choices: African
    Americans and the Death Penalty. *Race and Justice*, 4(2), 75–97.
Ramirez, Mark D. 2015. Racial Discrimination, Fear of Crime, and Variability
    in Black's Preferences for Punitive and Preventative Anti-Crime Policies.
    Political Behavior, 37(2), 419–439.
Ransford, H. Edward. 1972. Blue Collar Anger: Reactions to Student and Black
    Protest. *American Sociological Review*, 37(3), 333–346.
Renzulli, Linda A., and Evans, Lorraine. 2005. School Choice, Charter Schools,
    and White Flight. *Social Problems*, 52(3), 398–418.
Roberts, Julian V., Stalans, Loretta J., Indermaur, David, and Hough, Mike. 2002.
    Penal Populism and Public Opinion: Lessons from Five Countries. New
    York: Oxford University Press.
Rocha, Rene R., and Espino, Rodolfo. 2009. Racial Threat, Residential Segrega-
    tion, and the Policy Attitudes of Anglos. *Political Research Quarterly*, 62(3),
    415–426.
Rocha, Rene R., Longoria, Thomas, Wrinkle, Robert D., Knoll, Benjamin R.,
    Polinard, Jerry L., and Wenzel, James. 2011. Ethnic Context and Immigra-
    tion Policy Preferences among Latinos and Anglos. *Social Science Quarterly*,
    92(1), 1–19.
Rocha, Rene R., and Matsubayashi, Tetsuya. 2014. The Politics of Race and Voter
    ID Laws in the States: The Return of Jim Crow? *Political Research Quarterly*,
    67(3), 666–679.
Rodriguez, Clara E. 1997. Keeping it Reel? Films of the 1980s and 1990s. Pages
    180–184 of: Rodriguez, Clara E. (ed.), *Latin Looks: Images of Latinas and
    Latinos in the U.S. Media*. New York: Taylor & Francis.
Rojas, Ronny, Felix, Melvin J., Gomez, Juanje, and Corbella, Nacho. 2016. The
    Latino Struggle to Reach Public Office. *Univision News*, October 13, www
    .univision.com/univision-news/the-latino-struggle-to-reach-public-office.
Román, Ediberto. 2013. *Those Damned Immigrants: America's Hysteria over
    Undocumented Immigration*. New York: New York University Press.
Romero, Mary. 2001. State Violence, and the Social and Legal Construction of
    Latino Criminality: From El Bandido to Gang Member. *Denver University
    Law Review*, 78(4), 1081–1118.
Rothbart, Myron, and John, Oliver P. 1985. Social Categorization and Behavioral
    Episodes: A Cognitive Analysis of the Effects of Intergroup Contact. *Journal
    of Social Issues*, 41(3), 81–104.

Rubio, Angelica. 2011. Undocumented, Not Illegal: Beyond the Rhetoric of Immigration Coverage. *NACLA Report on the Americas*, 44(6), 50–52.

Sampson, Robert J., Morenoff, Jeffrey D., and Raudenbush, Stephen. 2005. Social Anatomy of Racial and Ethnic Disparities in Violence. *American Journal of Public Health*, 95(2), 224–232.

Sanchez, George J. 1997. Face the Nation: Race, Immigration, and the Rise of Nativism in the Late Twentieth Century America. *International Migration Review*, 31(4), 1009–1030.

Schaffner, Brian F. 2011. Racial Salience and the Obama Vote. *Political Psychology*, 32(6), 963–988.

Schaffner, Brian F., MacWilliams, Matthew, and Nteta, Tatishe. 2018. Understanding White Polarization in the 2016 Vote for President: The Sobering Role of Racism and Sexism. *Political Science Quarterly*, 133(1), 9–34.

Scheingold, Stuart. 1992. *The Politics of Street Crime: Criminal Process and Cultural Obsession*. Philadelphia: Temple University Press.

Scheve, Kenneth F., and Slaughter, Matthew J. 2001. Labor Market Competition and Individual Preferences over Immigration. *Review of Economics and Statistics*, 83(1), 133–145.

Schildkraut, Deborah J. 2005. *Press One for English: Language Policy, Public Opinion, and American Identity*. Princeton, NJ: Princeton University Press.

Schildkraut, Deborah J. 2010. *Americanism in the Twenty-First Century: Public Opinion in the Age of Immigration*. New York: Cambridge University Press.

Schuman, Howard, Steeh, Charlotte, Bobo, Lawrence, and Krysan, Maria. 1997. *Racial Attitudes in America*. Cambridge, MA: Harvard University Press.

Sears, David O. 1988. Symbolic Racism. Pages 53–84 of: Katz, Phyllis A., and Taylor, Dalmas A. (eds.), *Eliminating Racism: Profiles in Controversy*. New York: Plenum Press.

Sears, David O., Henry, P. J., and Kosterman, Rick. 2000a. Egalitarian Values and Contemporary Racial Politics. Pages 75–117 of: Sears, David O., Sidanius, Jim, and Bobo, Lawrence (eds.), *Racialized Politics*. Chicago: The University of Chicago Press.

Sears, David O., Sidanius, Jim, and Bobo, Lawrence. 2000b. *Racialized Politics*. Chicago: The University of Chicago Press.

Segovia, Fancine, and Defever, Renatta. 2010. Trends – American Public Opinion on Immigrants and Immigration Policy. *Public Opinion Quarterly*, 74(2), 375–394.

Simon, Adam F. 2002. *The Winning Message: Candidate Behavior, Campaign Discourse, and Democracy*. Cambridge: Cambridge University Press.

Simonett, Helena. 2006. Los Gallos Valientes: Examining Violence in Mexican Popular Music. *Trans: Revista Transcultural de Musica*, 10, 1–19.

Sims, Barbara, and Johnston, Eric. 2004. Examining Public Opinion about Crime and Justice: A Statewide Study. *Criminal Justice Policy Review*, 15(3), 270–293.

Sinclair, Lisa, and Kunda, Ziva. 1999. Reactions to a Black Professional: Motivated Inhibition and Activation of Conflicting Stereotypes. *Journal of Personality and Social Psychology*, 77(5), 885–904.

Skogan, Wesley G. 1995. Crime and Racial Fears of White Americans. *Annals of the American Academy of Political and Social Science*, 539(May), 59–71.

Slack, Jeremy, Martinez, Daniel E., Whiteford, Scott, and Peiffer, Emily. 2015. In Harm's Way: Family Separation, Immigration Enforcement Programs and Security on the US–Mexico Border. *Journal on Migration and Human Security*, 3(2), 109–128.

Sniderman, Paul M., and Carmines, Edward G. 1997. *Reaching beyond Race.* Cambridge, MA: Harvard University Press.

Sniderman, Paul M., Crosby, Gretchen C., and Howell, William G. 2000. The Politics of Race. Pages 236–279 of: Sears, David O., Sidanius, Jim, and Bobo, Lawrence (eds.), *Racialized Politics.* Chicago: The University of Chicago Press.

Sniderman, Paul M., and Piazza, Thomas. 1993. *The Scar of Race.* Cambridge, MA: Harvard University Press.

Sniderman, Paul M., and Tetlock, Philip E. 1986. Symbolic Racism: Problems of Motive Attribution in Political Analysis. *Journal of Social Issues*, 42(2), 129–150.

Sobczak, Michael. 2010. *American Attitudes toward Immigrants and Immigration Policy.* El Paso, TX: LFB Scholary Publishing.

Soss, Joe, Langbein, Laura, and Metelko, Alan R. 2003. Why Do White Americans Support the Death Penalty? *Journal of Politics*, 65(2), 397–421.

Sousa, William H., Miethe, Terance D., and Sakiyama, Mari. 2015. Body Work Cameras on Police: Results from a National Survey of Public Attitudes. *UNLV Center for Crime and Justice Policy*, CCJP 2015-02, 1–8.

Spanierman, Lisa B., Oh, Euna, Poteat, V. Paul, et al. 2008. White University Students' Responses to Societal Racism: A Qualitative Investigation. *The Counseling Psychologist*, 36(6), 839–870.

Stemler, Steven E. 2001. An Overview of Content Analysis. *Practical Assessment, Research & Evaluation*, 7(17), http://PAREonline.net/getvn.asp?v=7&n=17.

Stoddard, Lothrop. 1920. *The Rising Tide of Color against White World-Supremacy.* New York: Scribner.

Strum, Philippa. 2016. How Mexican Immigrants Ended "Separate but Equal" in California. *The Los Angeles Times*, March 2, www.latimes.com/opinion/op-ed/la-oe-0302-strum-mendez-case-20160302-story.html.

Subervi, Federico, and Sinta, Vinicio. 2015. Latinos in TV Network News 2008–2014: Still Mostly Invisible and Problematic. *Communication Workers of American & the Newspaper Guild, Washington, DC*, 1–36.

Suro, Roberto. 2008. The Triumph of No: How the Media Influence the Immigration Debate. Pages 1–47 of Suro, Roberto (ed.), *A Report on the Media and the Immigration Debate.* Washington, DC: Brookings Institution.

Tarman, Christopher, and Sears, David O. 2005. The Conceptualization and Measurement of Symbolic Racism. *Journal of Politics*, 67(3), 731–761.

Tatalovich, Raymond. 1995. *Nativism Reborn? The Official Language Movement in the American States.* Lexington: University of Kentucky Press.

Tate, Katherine. 1994. *From Protest to Politics: The New Black Voters in American Elections.* Cambridge, MA: Harvard University Press.

Terkildsen, Nayda. 1993. When White Voters Evaluate Black Candidates: The Processing Implications of Candidate Skin Color, Prejudice, and Self-Monitoring. *American Journal of Political Science*, 37(4), 1032–1053.

Terraciano, Kevin. 1998. Crime and Culture in Colonial Mexico: The Case of the Mixtec Murder Note. *Ehnohistory*, 45(4), 709–745.

Tesler, Michael. 2012a. The Spillover of Racialization into Health Care: How President Obama Polarized Public Opinion by Racial Attitudes and Race. *American Journal of Political Science*, 56(3), 690–704.

Tesler, Michael. 2012b. The Return of Old-Fashioned Racism to White Americans' Partisan Preferences in the Early Obama Era. *Journal of Politics*, 75(1), 110–123.

Tesler, Michael, and Sears, David O. 2010. *Obama's Race: The 2008 Election and the Dream of a Post-Racial America*. Chicago: University of Chicago Press.

Tesler, Michael, and Sides, John. 2016. How Political Science Helps Explain the Rise of Trump: The Role of White Identity and Grievances. *The Washington Post*, March 3, www.washingtonpost.com/news/monkey-cage/wp/2016/03/03/how-political-science-helps-explain-the-rise-of-trump-the-role-of-white-identity-and-grievances/?utm_term=.f514aae9e93e.

Thomas, Charles, and Cage, Robin. 1976. Correlates of Public Attitudes toward Legal Sanctions. *International Journal of Criminology and Penology*, 4(August), 239–255.

Thomas, Charles, and Foster, Samuel. 1975. A Sociological Perspective on Public Support for Capital Punishment. *American Journal of Orthopsychiatry*, 45(4), 641–657.

Thompson, Brian L., and Lee, James Daniel. 2004. Who Cares If Police Become Violent? Explaining Approval of Police Use of Force Using a National Sample. *Sociological Inquiry*, 74(3), 381–410.

Tingley, Dustin. 2013. Public Finance and Immigration Preferences: A Lost Connection. *Polity*, 45(1), 4–33.

Tonry, Michael. 1995. *Malign Neglect – Race, Crime and Punishment in America*. New York: Oxford University Press.

Tyler, Tom R., and Weber, Renee. 1982. Support for the Death Penalty; Instrumental Response to Crime, or Symbolic Attitude? *Law & Society Review*, 17(1), 21–46.

Udani, Adriano, and Kimball, David C. 2018. Immigrant Resentment and Voter Fraud Beliefs in the US Electorate. *American Politics Research*, 46(3), 402–433.

Udani, Adriano, and Kimball, David C. 2019. What Fraud Looks Like: Typification Theory and Perceptions of Voter Fraud. *Presented at the Annual Meeting of the Southern Political Science Association*.

Valdez, Avelardo, and Halley, Jeffrey A. 1999. Teaching Mexican American Experiences through Film: Private Issues and Public Problems. *Teaching Sociology*, 27(3), 286–295.

Valentino, Nicholas A. 1999. Crime News and the Priming of Racial Attitudes during Evaluations of the President. *Public Opinion Quarterly*, 63(3), 293–320.

Valentino, Nicholas A., Brader, Ted, and Jardina, Ashley E. 2013. Immigration Opposition among US Whites: General Ethnocentrism or Media Priming of Attitudes about Latinos? *Political Psychology*, 34(2), 149–166.

Valentino, Nicholas A., Hutchings, Vincent L., and White, Ismail K. 2002. Cues that Matter: How Political Ads Prime Racial Attitudes during Campaigns. *American Political Science Review*, 96(1), 75–90.

Valentino, Nicholas A., and Neuner, Fabian G. 2017. Why the Sky Didn't Fall: Mobilizing Anger in Reaction to Voter ID Laws. *Political Psychology*, 38(2), 331–350.

Valentino, Nicholas A., Neuner, Fabian G., and Vandenbroek, L. Matthew. 2018. The Changing Norms of Racial Political Rhetoric and the End of Racial Priming. *Journal of Politics*, 80(3), 757–771.

Vallejo, Jody Agius. 2015. How Class Background Affects Mexican Americans' Experiences of Subtle Racism in the White-Collar Workplace. *Latino Studies*, 13(1), 69–87.

Varela, Julio R. 2013. The Troubling Study on U.S. Latinos CNN Didn't Want You to See. *Latino Rebels*, http://www.latinorebels.com/2013/04/11/the-troubling-study-on-u-s-latinos-cnn-didnt-want-you-to-see/.

Vasquez, Jessica M. 2011. *Mexican Americans across Generations*. New York: New York University Press.

Villanueva, Nicholoas. 2017. *The Lynching of Mexicans in the Texas Borderlands*. Albuquerque: University of New Mexico Press.

Waldman, Paul, Ventura, Elbert, Savillo, Robert, Lin, Susan, and Lewis, Greg. 2008. Fear and Loathing in Prime Time: Immigration Myths and Cable News. *Report, Media Matters Action Network*. Washington, DC: Media Matters Action Network.

Walker, Samuel, Spohn, Cassia, and DeLone, Mirian. 1996. *The Color of Justice*. New York: Wadsworth Publishing Company.

Wallander, Lisa. 2009. 25 Years of Factorial Surveys in Sociology: A Review. *Social Science Research*, 38(3), 505–520.

Walsh, Katherine Cramer. 2003. *Talking about Politics: Informal Groups and Social Identity in American Life*. Chicago: University of Chicago Press.

Warr, Mark. 1995. Poll Trends: Public Opinion on Crime and Punishment. *Public Opinion Quarterly*, 59(2), 296–310.

Warr, Mark. 2000. Public Perceptions of and Reactions to Crime. Pages 13–31 of: Sheley, Joseph F. (ed.), *Criminology: A Contemporary Handbook*. Belmont, CA: Wadsworth.

Warr, Mark, Meier, Robert F., and Erickson, Maynard L. 1983. Norms, Theories of Punishment, and Publicly Preferred Penalties for Crimes. *The Sociological Quarterly*, 24(Winter), 75–91.

Weitzer, Ronald, and Tuch, Steven A. 1999. Race, Class, and Perceptions of Discrimination by the Police. *Crime & Delinquency*, 45(4), 494–507.

Welch, Kelly. 2007. Black Criminal Stereotypes and Racial Profiling. *Journal of Contemporary Criminal Justice*, 23(3), 276–288.

Weyant, James M. 2005. Implicit Stereotyping of Hispanics: Development and Validity of a Hispanic Version of the Implicit Association Test. *Hispanic Journal of Behavioral Sciences*, 27(3), 355–363.

White, Ismail K. 2007. When Race Matters and When It Doesn't: Racial Group Differences in Response to Racial Cues. *American Political Science Review*, 101(2), 339–354.

Whitehead, Kevin A. 2009. "Categorizing the Categorizer': The Management of Racial Common Sense in Interaction. *Social Psychology Quarterly*, 72(4), 325–342.

Wilson, David C., and Brewer, Paul R. 2016. Do Frames Emphasizing Harm to Age and Racial-Ethnic Groups Reduce Support for Voter ID Laws? *Social Science Quarterly*, 97(2), 391–406.

Wilson, David C., and Davis, Darren W. 2011. Reexamining Racial Resentment: Conceptualization and Content. *The Annals of the American Academy of Political and Social Science*, 634(1), 117–133.

Wilson, James Q. 1975. *Thinking about Crime*. New York: Basic Books.

Wood, Amy Louise. 2011. *Lynching and Spectacle: Witnessing Racial Violence in America, 1890–1940*. Chapel Hill: University of North Carolina Press.

Wu, Yuning. 2014. Race/Ethnicity and Perceptions of the Police: A Comparison of White, Black, Asian and Hispanic Americans. *Policing and Society*, 24(2), 135–157.

Wu, Yuning, Lake, Rodney, and Cao, Liqun. 2015. Race, Social Bonds, and Juvenile Attitudes toward the Police. *Justice Quarterly*, 32(3), 445–470.

Younes, Maha N., and Killip, Elizabeth A. 2010. Forever Changed: The Transformation of Rural American through Immigration. *Contemporary Rural Social Work*, 2(May), 8–23.

Index

Abedin, Huma, 159
Affordable Care Act (ACA), 60, 155
African Americans, 11, 24, 98
  antipathy, 87
  crime suspects, 89
  criticized, 38
  in crime stories, 89
  drug abuse, 10
  ineligible voters, 120
  racial resentment, 38, 69
  violence, 10
  voter identification, 119, 120
Afro Cubans, 17
alien, 17
Alien Nation (Brimelow), 2
American elections, 146
  Latina/o candidates, support for, 146
American Federation of Labor, 17
American National Election Study (ANES)
  attitudes, 38
  about Hispanic and Latinos in, 39
  pilot study, 160
Americans
  immigration policy, opinion on, 59
  labor unions, 17
Anglo Americans, 13, 27
  cultural values, 67
  culture, 17, 25, 28, 174
  culture and behavior, 33
  language, 25
  legal norms, 21
  norms, 2–5, 35

  norms of civil obedience, 34
  settlers, 13
  society, 2, 15, 17
  traits, 22
  values, 51
  work style, 15
Anglo-Protestant traditions, 15
animus toward minorities, 104
anti-immigration, 21
  hysteria, 57
  policies, 67, 161
  rhetoric, 57, 96
  sentiment, 19, 58, 67
  sentiments, 25
  voters, 153
anti-Latino affect, 4
anti-Latino rhetoric, 181
anti-Latino sentiment, 36, 43
Association of Community Organizations
  for Reform Now (ACORN), 112
authoritarianism, 67, 71, 110

ballot access, 113
Beason–Hammon Alabama Taxpayer and
  Citizen Protection Act, 58
Beck, Glenn, 21
bigotry, 3
Black respondents, 140
black-market traders, 10
body-worn cameras, 103, 105, 106
Border Protection, Antiterrorism, and
  Illegal Immigration Control Act, 58

Trump, Donald, 4, 23, 78, 111, 159, 181
  election campaign, 60
  presidential campaign, 151
  racist belief system, 4

un-American, 17
undocumented immigrants, 21, 58
US Border Patrol, 18
US Citizenship and Immigration Services
    (USCIS), 57
US Coast Guard, 57
US elections
  racial and ethnic conflict, 144
US House elections, 148
US immigration laws, 56
US immigration policy, 56
US Secret Service, 57
US Senate elections, 153
US–Mexican border, 18

voter fraud, 111, 112, 118
  frame, 118
  prevention attempts, 114
voter ID bill, 116
voter ID laws, 114, 115
voter identification, 117
  experiment, 123
voter identification laws, 111, 113, 114,
    119, 125, 126, 129, 142
  controversy over, 113
  Latina/o racism-ethnicity (LRE), 121
  Latinos, 113
voter registration purges, 134

voters
  decision-making calculus, 144
  racist White, 145
voting
  candidates support immigration
    restrictions, 152
  registration, 7
  restrictions, 153
Voting Rights Act, 116

Wan, William, 112
Wheeler, Harry, 18
White Americans
  attitudes about politics, 173
  immigration policy preferences, 62, 65
  about Latinos, 34
  racial attitudes, 28
  views on Latinos, 28
White Animus toward Latinos, 16
White-European immigrants, 2, 17
White Europeans, 12
  settlers, 174
White supremacist ideologies, 3
Whites, 9, 22
  opioid addiction and abuse, 10
Whites' attitudes
  browning of, 177
Wilson, Pete, 179
working-class Democrats, 68
Wrenn, Carter, 112

Zoot Suit Riots of 1943, 6, 20
zoot suits, 20